THE ATOMIC PAPERS:

A Citizen's Guide To Selected
Books And Articles On The Bomb,
The Arms Race, Nuclear Power,
The Peace Movement, And
Related Issues

by
GRANT BURNS

The Scarecrow Press, Inc.
Metuchen, N.J., & London
1984

327.174016
B967

Library of Congress Cataloging in Publication Data

Burns, Grant, 1947–
  The atomic papers.

  Includes indexes.
  1. Atomic weapons and disarmament--Bibliography.
2. Nuclear warfare--Bibliography. 3. Arms race--
Bibliography. 4. Nuclear power--Bibliography.
5. Peace--Bibliography. I. Title.
Z6464.D6B85 1984 [JX1974.7] 016.3271'74   84-1390
ISBN 0-8108-1692-X

● For Andrea and Steven ●

TABLE OF CONTENTS

Introduction   vii

I: Nuclear Bombs: Invention, Effects
       and Some Early Reactions   1

II: Playing the Game: Nuclear Strategies,
       Tactics and Worldviews   25

III: Upping the Ante: The Arms Race   73

IV: All God's Children Got Bombs: Nuclear
       Weapons Proliferation   87

V: Trying to Keep It in Hand: Arms
       Control   103

VI: To Banish the Nuclear Specter: The
       Peace Movement   125

VII: Nuclear Power: The Establishment's
       Case   153

VIII: Radiation Blues: The Anti-Nuclear
       Power Case   179

IX: They Built the Bomb: The Atomic
       Scientists   191

X: They Administered the Bomb: The
       Atomic Energy Commission   201

XI: They Stole the Bomb (Or Did They?):
       The Atomic Spies   205

XII: They Said We Could Hide from the Bomb:
       The Civil Defense Advocates   209

XIII: The Time We Almost Did It: The Cuban
       Missile Crisis   217

XIV: The Bomb and the Cross: Christian Per-
       spectives   221

XV: Children Under the Bomb   225

XVI: Three Mile Island: Political, Health and
       Economic Fallout   229

XVII: An Atomic Miscellany   235

XVIII: The Art of Fission: Novels and Stories
       with Nuclear Themes   259

Subject Index   293

Author Index   299

INTRODUCTION

A specter is haunting the earth. It is the specter of nuclear war. On every hope and ambition falls the shadow of the bomb. The nuclear arsenals of the United States and the Soviet Union contain approximately 50,000 bombs, with well over 10,000 megatons of destructive power on each side. A one-megaton bomb possesses the explosive force of almost 50 Hiroshima bombs; in today's strategic arsenals a one-megaton bomb is a modest weapon.

We are not comforted by the apparently inexorable proliferation of the bomb. During preparation of this essay, Argentina announced its nuclear bomb capability. The Non-Proliferation Treaty has not kept the bomb from falling into, or close to, the hands of India, Pakistan, South Africa, Israel, Brazil, and other countries. In one of the most ironic arguments put forward by some writers on proliferation, we are assured that the more countries that possess the bomb, the less likely it is that anyone will use it. These writers support their arguments with probability calculations and statistical tables.

Statistical tables seldom impress madmen. What would Idi Amin have done with the bomb? The broader the bomb's dissemination, the more likely it is to come into the control of a man, or woman, not only committed to the nuclear worldview, but to a "cause" whose end justifies any means.

Our sense of security receives little encouragement from a Secretary of State who speculates about "demonstration" nuclear shots in Europe; from a Vice President who easily chats with journalists about how we can "win" a nuclear war; from a President who (with no sense of irony) dubs a terrible new missile a "Peacekeeper"; from a Navy which blasphemes when it names a nuclear submarine the "Corpus Christi"; or from the grisly mass burial exercise--

widely interpreted as practice for a "limited" nuclear war--conducted by the U.S. Army in West Germany (see the New York Times, Sept. 28, 1983, p. 4).

Such slovenly disregard for either diplomatic discretion or simple decency often reduces us to despair and head-in-sand attitudes. Despair and willful ignorance, however, do not help the cause of peace. Contrary to the message on Big Brother's Ministry of Truth in 1984, ignorance is not strength. This bibliography will allow the reader to easily identify books and some recent journal and magazine articles on the panoply of nuclear issues, with the assumption that better information enables more effective involvement in the effort to secure real peace, and not the dubious "peace" achieved through nuclear terror.

An unforgettable vision of where we all stand on the nuclear road occurs in John Le Carré's The Spy Who Came in From the Cold (Coward-McCann, 1964). A spy racing along a West German highway jammed with heavy trucks sees a little Fiat pull out in front of his car. The spy stamps on the brake pedal, sounds his horn, flashes his headlights, and misses the Fiat by a fraction of a second. The Fiat is full of laughing children; their father, his face stupid and frightened, holds the steering wheel like a farmer holding a handplow.

The spy speeds on, cursing this little family which got in the way of his sinister business. Soon a ghastly image overtakes him, an image of this innocent family caught "in the hurtling stream of giant lorries ... pounded and smashed, until there was nothing left, nothing but the frenetic whine of klaxons and blue lights flashing; and the bodies of the children, torn, like the murdered refugees on the road across the dunes" (p. 122).

The Fiat, its frightened driver, and the children, pitifully ignorant of their danger, are us, the citizens of West and East, caught in the overwhelming menace of our nuclear-armed governments. We are caught in a predicament which raises the slightest miscalculation or inattentiveness of the superpowers to stakes of mortal consequence for anyone in their way. We are all in their way.

Many believe that a nuclear collision between the superpowers is inevitable. I do not. I believe that the ability to insure that we do not banish the human race, or even a

viii

large part of it, through fission's indifferent graces lies within our moral, scientific, and political powers.

To exercise these powers requires some degree of historical knowledge as well as an awareness of current events. The material referred to by this bibliography should help provide such awareness. I am particularly hopeful that the bibliography will find its way before young people at the high school and college levels. In my work with young adults as a reference librarian I have often found in them a remarkable innocence of historical knowledge. This is a common complaint about the young, but I do not think that we can hold them at fault. Their innocence, a perilous innocence which encourages their manipulation by cynical and inept politicians and public media, arises not from their own slothfulness but from our lax attention to their needs. This laxity has been especially prominent in nuclear matters.

I grew up in the 1950s and 60s, at the height of the Cold War's first coming. I began to worry about the prospects of global war at the age of ten, when the U.S. and China parried on the verge of war over the islands of Quemoy and Matsu. Through all the bomb-related anxiety of the 1950s and early 60s, not one of my teachers made any effort to raise the nuclear issue in the classroom. Not once, not in any form. The only time the question of the bomb came up while I was in high school, a period which encompassed the Berlin Crisis of 1961, the Cuban Missile Crisis of 1962, and the Test Ban Treaty of 1963, was through an English teacher's oblique reference to the optimism of those who would choose to live in the future rather than in the distant past. They were optimists, she said, because they thought there would be a future. I was one of them.

My experience, I am sure, was commonplace. An entire generation of teachers, paralyzed by their own fear, intimidated by Cold War hysteria (if you're against the bomb you're a communist or crazy or both), abdicated their responsibility to introduce their students to an inescapable issue of life-and-death importance.

We can never go back to that era of nuclear repression. This bibliography represents a small part of today's awakening to the true meanings of the bomb. I was happy to learn while researching the bibliography that a definite movement exists to bring nuclear and peace issues into the light of the classroom, from the earliest grades on. (For further information, write Educators for Social Responsibility, 639 Massachusetts Ave., Cambridge, MA 02139.)

We cannot return to the time when the bomb was a subject more taboo in the classroom than human reproduction. Oh, it is understandable that the bomb became a taboo; if there was ever such a thing as a vile, embarrassing secret that adults might wish to keep from children, what else could qualify so well?

I have tried to cover the nuclear book publishing record by citing and annotating the most important works, along with many others published since 1945. Any bibliographer is prey to an obsession to find every last item of importance, from the oldest to the newest. I resisted this obsession, for in the nuclear arena a degree of promptness has a stronger case than plodding, utter comprehensiveness. I have undoubtedly missed some significant books--even now some new books sit on my desk deserving of a notice that they will not receive here--but I think that those included will do a good job of informing the concerned citizen on the issues at hand. Many of the books cited deal specifically and almost exclusively with nuclear weapons and delivery systems; others concern strategic theory, civil defense, the mechanics and history of the bomb, atomic scientists, the arms race, arms control and disarmament from an establishmentarian point of view, the radical anti-nuclear and peace movement (with which I sympathize), and nuclear proliferation.

Many of the fears associated with the bomb are also associated with civilian nuclear power. Next to the U.S.-Soviet face-off, nuclear power is a trivial issue, but because it concerns many and because there is a clear link between nuclear power and nuclear weapons proliferation, I have included items on nuclear power which should allow the layman to come to an informed position on nuclear power's advisability.

While the books treated here cover the post-Hiroshima period, I have drawn only a small selection of periodical articles to the reader's attention, beginning with 1980. I chose that date for several reasons: the quantity of periodical literature on the bomb and related issues is enormous, far beyond comprehensive accommodation in a work within the dimensions I need to observe. The relatively temporary nature of magazine and journal articles also argues in favor of dealing with the most recent work; most of the significant ideas on nuclear affairs reaching periodical print, 1945-1979, will be embodied in the books covered here. The beginning date of 1980 also offers an opportunity to focus on the rapid increase in nuclear publication which coincided with the Presidential victory of Ronald Reagan.

I have deliberately avoided most of the magazines that the average reader or library user would turn to out of habit or convenience. Anyone can look up articles in Time or New Republic or Harper's through the Readers' Guide to Periodical Literature, available in almost every library. I have tried to present a sample of articles from a variety of more technically, professionally, and academically-oriented sources, including a number of foreign publications, in hopes of expanding the reader's recognition of how nuclear issues cut across diverse lines of concern.

I have also included a number of articles from another source too often unknown to most readers--the alternative press. The "alternative press" is perhaps best-defined as the segment of publishing whose editorial stance is dedicated to a basic questioning of the values and assumptions by which our society directs itself, a stance not at all that of the magazines accessible through the Readers' Guide. This publishing sector is especially important for the literature of the antinuclear movement.

Those wishing to pursue the alternative press further will find the easiest route through the Alternative Press Index, published by the Alternative Press Center (P. O. Box 7229, Baltimore, MD 21218). Because of those values and assumptions mentioned above, which also dominate most libraries, few readers will find this index locally at hand, and will probably find the kinds of magazines it covers also hard to come by. There is no excuse for this failure of our libraries (and of most bookstores) to make such publications available, but it is a fact of life in most communities. The reader who wants to see this material in the local library or bookstore should make his or her wishes known!

Other sources the reader may wish to turn to for citations to articles on nuclear topics include Social Sciences Index, Humanities Index, General Science Index and many other "standard" indexes and abstracts available in all but very small libraries. The New York Times and its index are also helpful.

I have for the most part omitted U.S. government

documents from the bibliography, although there are some here of historic importance, including a few of recent publication. For those interested in the federal end of nuclear publishing, the Monthly Catalog of United States Government Publications, found in many libraries, will help identify specific items. The assistance of a patient documents librarian will also prove beneficial.

No item has been denied entry to the bibliography because of its point of view; it is always valuable to recognize both the best and the worst of opposing arguments. I have generally tried to keep the annotations free of excessive opinionating, but I have yielded to my inclinations when confronted with many works whose arguments are not simply wrong, but morally frigid. I cannot pretend to cold objectivity when discussing the work of those who advocate preparing for the massacre of innocent millions, or who accept that massacre as an inevitability that we can do nothing about but try (hope?) to survive.

The real source of our nuclear discomfort is not the bomb itself. In the face of its awesome capacity to destroy everything that we care about, we tend to forget that the bomb stands as the logical end of many centuries of misbegotten values and errant beliefs. It is these values and beliefs which themselves must change if we are ever to greet a future free of the fear of war. Immediate, pragmatic steps toward reducing international tension and reversing the course of the arms race are undeniably our prime objectives of the moment, but as we embark on them we should also attend to the roots of our dilemma. War, like slavery, is an institution, not an inherent attribute of human behavior. The institution of slavery has been universally repudiated, in spite of past claims--often based in religious belief--for its status as an "inherent" and "inevitable" component of our lives. The institution of war waits for us to dismantle it as our ancestors dismantled slavery. The rule of human enterprise has been one of peaceful cooperation for the common good at most times, in most places. There is no reason to believe that this rule cannot come to characterize the whole of our existence together on this small planet. If we succumb to the intellectually lazy belief that war is inevitable, our future will be short and bleak.

Albert Einstein called for a new way of thinking, a new way of seeing the world, as the only way to finally move out of the bomb's shadow, out of the shadow of War itself.

xii

The change in global consciousness Einstein invoked has begun. It is manifested in the millions of Americans and Europeans--and Soviet citizens--who have recognized the threat to the earth posed not only by nuclear bombs, but by the institution of war. It is manifested in contemporary literature and popular films and television programs; it is manifested in many of the books and articles described below.

The question of the era is how quickly may proceed the growth of this consciousness that peace and cooperation are rational, workable alternatives to war as the basis for international relations. If this global consciousness can develop quickly enough, it will render the system of nuclear terror which now enslaves us a curiosity of history, rather than the means of ending history itself.

Among the newest work which I cannot cover in the bibliography proper is Freeman Dyson's series "Reflections (Nuclear Weapons)"; it began in the February 6, 1984 New Yorker and continues in the next three issues. His discussion of nuclear developments, technological channels of the arms race and grounds for hope is freshly-conceived and mildly encouraging. His work follows in the New Yorker's tradition of serious and original attention to the issues by writers like John Hersey and Jonathan Schell.

The one great lesson of nuclear publishing resides in the tone of urgency in the voice of critics of the nuclear world-view. From the movement of the American atomic scientists who opposed the unannounced nuclear bombing of Japan to the many writers who oppose today's grossly exacerbated dedication to nuclear weapons as the linchpin of national security, there has been a tone touched by the desperate sense of time running out. This tone has grown markedly in volume and insistence since 1980, but the basic content of arguments against the bomb, the arms race, and war as a way of life have hardly changed since Dexter Masters published One World or None in 1946 (item 533). Indeed, they have hardly changed since H.G. Wells's prophetic novel of 1914, The World Set Free (item 1125).

There is probably nothing easier than to despair over the failure of world governments to respond to the arguments against war and the bomb made relentlessly since the immolation of Hiroshima and Nagasaki, but we would do well to keep in mind that these arguments' growing strength and determination may yet force a response in the direction of real

xiii

peace and security. The citizens of the world do not need to cooperate in their own annihilation; our refusal to so cooperate may very well prevent that final event of history that even the keepers of the weapons do not desire.

GB
December, 1983

• I •

Nuclear Bombs:
Invention, Effects, and Some Early Reactions

First Atomic Bomb Dropped on Japan;

Missile is Equal to 20,000 Tons of TNT;

Truman Warns Foe of a 'Rain of Ruin'

> --Headline, New York Times,
> August 7, 1945

"We have a different regard

for human life than those monsters do."

> --Ronald Reagan, on Russian
> values, in an interview with
> Robert Scheer (item 223).

1. ALPEROVITZ, Gar. Atomic Diplomacy: Hiroshima and Potsdam; The Use of the Atomic Bomb and the American Confrontation with Soviet Power. Simon & Schuster, 1965. 317 p.

One of the most influential Cold War revisionist examinations of the decision to drop the bomb on Japan; Alperovitz argues, and documents his argument well, that the bomb was clearly intended more as an influence on postwar foreign relations than as a tool to bring Japan's unconditional surrender, and that Truman "radically altered" Franklin D. Roosevelt's policies toward the Soviet Union. A book of fundamental importance in understanding both the origins of the Cold War and the arms race.

2. AMRINE, Michael. The Great Decision: The Secret History of the Atomic Bomb. Putnam's, 1959. 251 p.

Covers the period between Roosevelt's death and the bombing of Japan. Amrine chronicles the decisions leading to the bomb's use, and reveals them as often reached with less than painstaking care.

3. ATOMIC Scientists of Chicago. The Atomic Bomb: Facts and Implications. Atomic Scientists of Chicago, 1946. 62 p.

This brief early book from a concerned group of atomic scientists lays out some very basic assumptions which have yet to be accepted, including among others the belief that "No big secret protects the atomic bomb." We cannot expect any defense against the bomb; "atomic bomb stockpiles increase the probability of war"; "the threat of atomic warfare far outweighs in importance the peacetime benefits of atomic power." These points and others are followed by essays which help illuminate them.

4. AUSUBEL, Nathan, ed. Voices of History, 1945-46: Speeches and Papers of Roosevelt, Truman, Churchill ... and Other Leaders Delivered During 1945. Gramercy Publishing Co., 1946. 810 p.

A handy source for public statements pertaining to the bomb; contains the full texts of Truman's announcement of the bomb's first use, the Attlee-Churchill statement on the bomb, Truman's message to Congress and several others.

5. BADASH, Laurence, et al., eds. Reminiscences of
   Los Alamos, 1943-1945. Reidel, 1980. 188 p.

Behind the scenes at the bomb's chief gestation site, with insights on the domestic situation, tensions between military
and scientists, security problems, etc. A collection of lectures given at the University of California--Santa Barbara in
1975.

6. BAKER, Paul R., ed. The Atomic Bomb: The Great
   Decision. Holt, Rinehart & Winston, 1968. 122 p.

Essays and excerpts from books addressing various bomb-
related topics, including strategic problems at the close of
WW II, diplomacy and the Cold War, moral considerations,
etc. Authors are well-known authorities and government officials; various points of view are represented.

7. BATCHELDER, Robert C. The Irreversible Decision,
   1939-1950. Houghton, 1962. 306 p.

A moral and ethical analysis of the bomb and its use. The
historical treatment covers a lot of familiar ground for those
who have read much in the area. Originated as a doctoral
dissertation.

8. BERTIN, Leonard. Atom Harvest. Secker & Warburg,
   1955. 253 p.

The author's aim is to "tell a little more about the British contribution" to the development of the bomb, along with providing some discussion of atomic energy in the U.K. Chapter
titles like "Energy Spells Prosperity" and "Isotopes--Friends
of Man" suggest the tone and attitude. There is a very good
first-hand account here of an atomic bomb test in "The Second Bang."

9. BRODIE, Bernard, ed. The Absolute Weapon: Atomic
   Power and World Order. Harcourt, Brace, 1946.
   214 p.

Essays by Brodie and others on "The Weapon," "The Political
Consequences," "Implications for Military Policy," etc. Includes one of the early pleas for international control of
atomic energy. A thoughtful attempt at the atomic starting
gate to make sense of the era in both military and civil respects, this book still makes valid points which have not been

adequately recognized by policy makers; the authors' ruminations on deterrence, the lack of perceived security inherent
in what has come to be known as the "balance of terror, "
and the psychology of armaments are quite up-to-date.

10.   BUSH, Vannevar.   Endless Horizons.   Public Affairs
      Press, 1946.   182 p.

Bush, Director of the U.S. Office of Scientific Research and
Development, which oversaw creation of the bomb, calls for
"The Control of Atomic Energy" (p. 101-106) on an international basis, because "it is imperative that people be safe-
guarded against sudden destruction by atomic bombs. "

11.   _____.   Modern Arms and Free Men: A Discussion
      of the Role of Science in Preserving Democracy.
      Simon & Schuster, 1949.   273 p.

An optimistic examination of the elements of war, including
guided missiles and the bomb, with the conclusion that stead-
fastness in freedom and refusal to panic will allow the West
to persevere.

12.   CAVE-BROWN, Anthony and MacDonald, Charles B.,
      eds.   The Secret History of the Atomic Bomb.
      Dial Press, 1977.   582 p.

At this date it is a little hard to determine where the "secret"
lies, since the story has been told in detail in several places.
Inclusion of the long-available "Smyth Report" (see item 79)
doesn't lend much credence to the title, either.   The rest of
the book consists primarily of papers from other official
sources.

13.   CHASE, Stuart.   "E=MC^2"   In his For This We Fought,
      p. 111-123.   Twentieth Century Fund, 1946.

A sensible and plain-spoken call for international control of
atomic power and fissionable materials.   Advocates widespread viewing of photos and films of Hiroshima and Nagasaki damage.   This book also contains a good short essay,
"Atomic Age--Year One, " which surveys the immediate post-
war world and concludes: "The hot breath of World War
III ... seems to come nearer every day.   Did we fight for
this ?"

14.   CHINNOCK, Frank W.   Nagasaki: The Forgotten Bomb.
      World Pub, 1969.   304 p.

Chronological treatment of "Fat Man's" career; an effective portrait of what it means for civilians to be victimized by a nuclear attack. Told in anecdotal style, based on over 2,000 first-hand experiences obtained by written word, voice, or through relatives.

15. CLARK, Ronald W. Birth of the Bomb: Britain's Part. Horizon Press, 1961. 209 p.

A journalistic account of British involvement in the research leading to the bomb. Based on interviews with those concerned, and on study of available documents. Pays attention to the arguments the scientists use, with others and on themselves, to rationalize their work on what they knew would be not merely a more powerful explosive, but a leap to a new plane in the conduct of war.

16. COALE, Ansley J. The Problem of Reducing Vulnerability to Atomic Bombs. Princeton University Press, 1947. 116 p.

Ponders the likely damage inflicted by a nuclear war, and dwells on three possible strategic options: to win nuclear war, to prevent its taking place, and to minimize damage. A pitifully small portion of the book is given to the middle option, thus leaving the reader of 1947 less than optimistic.

17. COMMITTEE for the Compilation of Materials on Damage Caused by Atomic Bombs. Hiroshima and Nagasaki: The Physical, Medical and Social Effects of the Atomic Bombings. Basic Books, 1981. 706 p.

No other written record comes close to matching the thoroughness of this immense account of what happened to these two cities and their people when the bombs fell. Four major parts cover physical aspects of the destruction, injury to the human body, the impact on society and daily life, and the movement toward the abolition of nuclear arms. Many charts, tables and photographs, the last-named frequently unbearable.

18. COTTRELL, Leonard S. and Eberhart, Sylvia. American Opinion on World Affairs in the Atomic Age. Princeton University Press, 1948. 152 p.

An interesting study of Americans' attitudes toward foreign affairs just after the war, with considerable attention to the bomb. "Public Awareness of the Atomic Bomb" and "The

People's Views on International Control of Atomic Energy"
are the two most pertinent nuclear-related portions.

● ● ●

"With restless hands we work feverishly in dark laboratories
to find the means to destroy all at one blow. "

--Gen. Douglas MacArthur,
Item 870, p. xiii

● ● ●

19. DEAN, Gordon E. Report on the Atom: What You
Should Know About the Atomic Energy Program of the
United States. Knopf, 1953. 321 p.

Dean, a former chairman of the Atomic Energy Commission,
writes a general introduction to the U.S. program, with attention to international efforts in atomic development, the
ability of the U.S.S.R. to proceed with its nuclear ambitions
regardless of spies, the nature of deterrence and other issues.

20. DEVOVE, Robert. "What the Atomic Bomb Really Did."
In Science Year Book of 1947, p. 1-11. Edited by
J.D. Ratcliff. Doubleday, 1947.

Reprinted from a 1946 Collier's, this is one of the first ex-
tensively-detailed descriptions of the atomic bomb effects on
Japan to appear in a mass-market magazine. Notable for a
passage in which the author imagines the effects of an atomic
attack on New York City.

21. DIETZ, David. Atomic Energy in the Coming Era.
Dodd, 1945. 184 p.

A journalistic treatment, relying on popular science, of the
bomb's development, with speculation on future military and
civilian applications of atomic power.

22. EATHERLY, Claude. Burning Conscience: The Case
of the Hiroshima Pilot. Monthly Review Press,
1962. 139 p.

One of the peculiar human interest stories of the atomic era.
To all appearances, Major Eatherly did not mind letting people think that he was the pilot of the "Enola Gay" the day it
bombed Hiroshima. He wasn't. Though often held out as an

example of a man who, under the stress of guilt, has re-
nounced violence in favor of pacifism, his motives seem a
little more complicated. This book is an exchange of letters
between Eatherly and Vienna philosopher Gunther Anders. It
doesn't do much to set the record straight.

23. ELIOT, George F., et al. The H Bomb. Didier,
    1950. 175 p.

Includes an introduction by Albert Einstein, who says "It is
impossible to achieve peace as long as every single action is
taken with a possible future conflict in view." A set of articles from journalistic sources like the New York Times's
Hanson Baldwin and the editors of Time to government officials and atomic scientists on the H-bomb's potential and advisability. (Advisable or not, the U.S. detonated the world's
first hydrogen bomb on November 1, 1952. The Soviets followed suit a few months later.)

24. FEIS, Herbert. The Atomic Bomb and the End of
    World War II. Princeton University Press, 1966.
    213 p.

A revised edition of the author's 1961 book with grudging recognition that the bombs were dropped on Japan partly to "impress the Russians."

25. _____. Japan Subdued: The Atomic Bomb and the
    End of the War in the Pacific. Princeton University
    Press, 1961. 199 p.

Feis, who won a Pulitzer Prize for a history of the Potsdam
Conference, covers here the end of the war in the Pacific--
and struggles with the decision to use the bomb on Japan,
which many authorities believed on the verge of collapse regarding its war-making ability.

26. FOWLER, Eric B. Radioactive Fallout, Soils, Plants,
    Foods, Man. Elsevier, 1965. 317 p.

Papers based on those presented at an American Chemical
Society symposium six years earlier. Covers the cycle of
radioactive fallout through the food chain.

27. FOWLER, John M., ed. Fallout: A Study of Super-
    bombs, Strontium 90 and Survival. Basic Books,
    1960. 235 p.

A determined effort to furnish reliable information on the kinds of afflictions and problems connected with atomic testing and nuclear war.

28. GIOVANNITTI, Len and Freed, Fred. The Decision to Drop the Bomb. Coward-McCann, 1965. 348 p.

Covers the period from FDR's death to the surrender of Japan. The authors believe that use of the bomb was a good-faith effort to end the war.

29. GLASSTONE, Samuel, ed. The Effects of Nuclear Weapons. U.S. Atomic Energy Commission, 1957. 579 p.

Updating of information first published under the same title in 1950. A comprehensive inquiry into atomic blast effects, relying on the Hiroshima and Nagasaki bombs along with data from subsequent tests. Numerous photos, charts. Covers blast effects, thermal radiation, nuclear radiation, fallout--the whole atomic menu. Put succinctly, nuclear weapons blow things apart, set fire to them, and poison them. All other discussion amplifies these three basic facts.

30. GOWING, Margaret. Britain and Atomic Energy, 1939-1945. St. Martin's, 1964. 464 p.

An official and unexciting history of the subject; covers Anglo-American atomic collaboration, the breakdown of same; the role of Canada in the bomb through uranium supply and the Montreal laboratory. Suggests that use of the bombs on Japan was "inevitable." Not a benchmark of philosophical or moral inquiry, but a highly-detailed technical and inter-organizational history.

31. _____. Independence and Deterrence: Britain and Atomic Energy, 1945-1952. St. Martin's, 1974. 2v., 553 and 559 p.

A continuation, at exhaustive and meticulous length, of Great Britain's development of the bomb and of her independent strategic nuclear force.

32. GREENE, Owen, et al. London after the Bomb. Oxford University Press, 1982. 142 p.

A critical response to the British Home Office's strangely blithe publications on civil defense. Focus on an atomically-blasted London, with attention to radiation effects, food and water contamination, breakdown of civil order, disease, lack of power, etc. Many charts, graphs and maps.

33. GROUEFF, Stephane. The Manhattan Project: The Untold Story of the Making of the Atomic Bomb. Little, 1967. 372 p.

Technical account more interesting for its omission of the meaning of the bomb and the efforts (however futile) to keep it from enslaving the modern era than for its content. There are far too many trivial conversations recreated here (" 'Aren't there any peppermints left?' Gwen asked mischievously") to which the author could not have been privy. No footnotes. Strictly for popular consumption.

34. GROVES, Leslie R. Now It Can Be Told: The Story of the Manhattan Project. Harper, 1962. 464 p.

General Groves was in charge (1942-1946) of the bomb-building Manhattan Project. This is a thorough account of the operation employing some previously-classified documents.

35. HAWKINS, David, et al. Manhattan District History, Project Y, The Los Alamos Story. Tomash, 1983. 506 p.

The official history of the U.S. atomic bomb project, completed in 1947 but not relieved of its "secret" classification until 1961, when published originally by the Los Alamos Scientific Laboratory. Covers the establishment of the Laboratory, initial bomb testing, and the period immediately following the Japanese defeat.

36. HAYNES, Richard F. The Awesome Power: Harry Truman as Commander in Chief. Louisiana State University Press, 1073. 359 p.

On Truman's performance in the title role, with special regard to his decision to drop the bombs on Japan and to the establishment of a postwar atomic energy control structure.

37. HEER, David M. After Nuclear Attack: A Demographic Inquiry. Praeger, 1965. 405 p.

What would be left of the U.S. population following a limited (very limited by current nuclear stockpile standards) attack.

38. HERKEN, Gregg. The Winning Weapon: The Atomic
    Bomb in the Cold War, 1945-1950. Knopf, 1981.
    425 p.

One of the best books on how the brief U. S. nuclear monopoly
affected the nation's foreign policy. Covers U. S. overconfi-
dence in its early atomic status and consequent over-emphasis
on the bomb's foreign policy role; how it worsened the Cold
War, led to overzealous secrecy, and spurred the arms race,
particularly after the Russian bomb test of August, 1949.

39. HERSEY, John R. Hiroshima. Knopf, 1946. 118 p.

A restrained, factual account of how the bombing affected a
half-dozen people. First published in The New Yorker.

40. HOFFMAN, M. David, ed. Readings for the Atomic
    Age. Globe Books, 1950. 406 p.

Articles by journalists, educators and scientists on the bomb
and its implications. Main selections cover the dramatic impact of the bomb, its development, the nature of atomic energy,
and speculation on the future, for better or worse. Intended
as a textbook for high school students, and one can only wish
that it had been widely adopted.

41. HOGG, Ian and Chant, Christopher. Nuclear War in the
    Eighties. Harper & Row, 1983. 224 p.

Less about war than about weapons themselves, this book features detailed, color illustrations, complete with cut-away
views, of currently deployed nuclear weapons, along with
descriptions of their capabilities.

42. HUIE, William Bradford. The Hiroshima Pilot. Put-
    nam's, 1964. 318 p.

Claude Eatherly (item 22) is generally given credit, or blame,
for serving as the pilot of the "Enola Gay" when it bombed
Hiroshima. He wasn't the pilot. He wasn't on board the
plane. Paul Tibbets was the pilot. This is a detailed examination of the web of circumstance, publicity, confusion, and
evasions which assure Eatherly his peculiar place in history.

43. IRVING, David. The German Atomic Bomb: Germany's
    Atomic Research and Allied Counter Measures. Si-
    mon & Schuster, 1967. 329 p.

Germany took an early lead in the race for the bomb with Otto Hahn's discovery of uranium fission, but, under Allied bombing pressure, sabotage (raids on the German heavy water plant in Norway), and factional differences did not finish the job. Chief sources for the book were German war files retrieved from the Atomic Energy Commission offices. Irving believes that the Germans "were in fact further advanced than either the British or the Americans publicly gave them credit for. "

44. JAPAN Broadcasting Corp., ed. Unforgettable Fire: Pictures Drawn by Atomic Bomb Survivors. Pantheon, 1981. 111 p.

A collection of paintings and drawings by Hiroshima survivors showing the effects of the bombing. The artwork is sometimes skillful, sometimes crude, but is of unrelieved and painful intensity. Divided into such sections as "The Bomb and I, " "What I Saw on That Day, " "Where is My Child? Where is My Wife?" etc. Hard to look at and impossible to forget.

45. KATZ, Arthur M. Life after Nuclear War. Ballinger, 1982. 422 p.

Based on a 1979 study for the Joint Committee on Defense Production, features a "limited" attack which takes 90 million casualties. A thorough look at what would be left, makes it plain that no nuclear war could be justified by any objectives.

46. KIRCHWEY, Freda, ed. The Atomic Era: Can It Bring Peace and Abundance? McBride, 1951. 176 p.

The author, editor of The Nation at the time, presents papers from a conference sponsored by that magazine with the intention of offering "an informed guide to the kinds of policy that may check our stumbling, headlong plunge toward atomic conflict. " Most of the contributors are academicians.

47. KNEBEL, Fletcher and Bailey, Charles W. No High Ground. Harper, 1960. 272 p.

A dramatic, journalistic account of the bomb's development and use.

48. KUNETKA, James W. City of Fire: Los Alamos and the Birth of the Atomic Age, 1943-1945. Prentice-Hall, 1978. 240 p.

Another effort to retell the tale of the birth of the bomb.
Satisfactory as a quick introduction.

49. LAMONT, Lansing. Day of Trinity. Atheneum, 1965.
     333 p.

Events leading up to, and culminating in, the first atomic
bomb test. Lansing, a Time writer, provides a quick-reading
treatment with a lot of personal detail on the atomic scientists.

50. LANG, Daniel. Early Tales of the Atomic Age. Double-
     day, 1948. 223 p.

Essays from The New Yorker on the bomb's development, the
lives of the atomic scientists, civil defense initiatives.

51. LAPP, Ralph E. Atoms and People. Harper, 1956.
     304 p.

On the making of the bomb, "Atoms for Peace, " the threat
of nuclear war, the behavior of atomic scientists, by one
who worked on bomb research and then as an adviser to the
Department of Defense on atomic energy. Lapp is critical
of the Atomic Energy Commission's extreme concern for
secrecy.

52. _____. Must We Hide? Addison-Wesley, 1949.
     182 p.

Argues that, while nasty, an atomic war would not be the
end of it all. An attempt to inform the public on the nature
of such war as it would have existed in the late 1940s or
early 1950s.

53. _____. The New Force: The Story of Atoms and
     People. Harper, 1953. 238 p.

Critical discussion of popular attitudes and misconceptions regarding the bomb; especially interesting, given Reagan administration intentions to restrict access even to unclassified
nuclear information, for Lapp's condemnation of the secrecy
surrounding the U.S. atomic program, a secrecy he describes
as a "contagion" which has done the U.S. far more harm,
both strategically and politically, than it has hindered Soviet
atomic work.

54. _____. Voyage of the Lucky Dragon. Harper, 1958.
     200 p.

The "Lucky Dragon, " a Japanese tuna trawler, was less than
100 miles from Bikini during a nuclear test. Fallout covered
the boat and its crew, who, unaware of their danger, took
no precautions. One of them died; 22 others were hospitalized
for a year. The event caused some strain in Japanese-
American relations. Lapp's main target is again the Atomic
Energy Commission's obsessive secrecy, a closed-mouthedness
which led even to the Commission's refusal to divulge to Japanese physicians important information about the nature of
the fallout affecting the fishermen.

55. LAURENCE, William L. Dawn Over Zero: The Story
 of the Atomic Bomb. Knopf, 1946. 274 p.

Laurence, a New York Times reporter, was the only journalist permitted to attend the bomb's secret New Mexico testing.
An informed record of the bomb's origination, first testing,
and initial use.

56. _____. The Hell Bomb. Knopf, 1951. 198 p.

A combination of popular exposition and technical conclusions
based on available documents and the reporter's personal
observations and interviews concerning what became the H-
bomb. Includes a summary of events and proposals in the
effort toward international control of atomic weapons, 1945-
1950.

57. _____. Men and Atoms: The Discovery, the Uses
 and the Future of Atomic Energy. Simon & Schuster,
 1959. 302 p.

Certainly an insider's view, but shows too much of the insider's willingness to be beguiled by the view from within.
One of a dwindling group believing that the atomic spies really
did play a crucial part in Soviet acquisition of the bomb.

58. LIEBOW, Averill A. Encounter with Disaster: A Medical Diary of Hiroshima, 1945. Norton, 1971.
 209 p.

Liebow was one of the U. S. Army physicians who visited
Hiroshima as a team shortly after the bombing. A straightforward account of the bomb's effects on human beings.

59. LIFTON, Robert J. Death in Life: Survivors of Hiroshima. Random House, 1968. 594 p.

The psychiatrist's outstanding work on the subject, based on
interviews with 75 survivors. Documents the "psychic numbing" of bomb victims.

● ● ●

"Five hundred bombs may be better than 100, but 50,000 are
no better than 5,000 because 5,000 would destroy all important
targets in any country. "
                                        --Atomic Scientists of Chicago,
                                            Item 3, p. 7

● ● ●

60. MARX, Joseph L. Seven Hours to Zero. Putnam's,
      1967. 254 p.

A readable work on the selection of the crew and the flight
of the "Enola Gay" to Hiroshima, ending with the dropping of
"Little Boy, " the crude proto-bomb with the pathologically
ironic name. Based on interviews with crew members.

61. MANDELBAUM, Michael. The Nuclear Revolution: In-
      ternational Politics Before and After Hiroshima.
      Cambridge University Press, 1981. 283 p.

In the course of answering the question "How have nuclear
weapons affected international politics?" the author examines
such broad subjects as cultural, institutional, and strategic
restraints on the weapons; the balance of power; the arms
race; and the "nuclear presidency. " The final chapter, "The
Bomb, Dread, and Eternity, " could easily stand alone as a
worthwhile essay on how the bomb's existence has affected
everyday life, from the ideals of youth to eschatological vision.

62. MILLER, Merle and Spitzer, Abe. We Dropped the A-
      Bomb. Crowell, 1946. 152 p.

Spitzer was the radio operator on the plane which bombed
Nagasaki. Valuable insights concerning the psychology of the
average but humanly-sensitive men who were responsible for
the final step in the bomb's delivery.

63. NAGAI, Takashi. We of Nagasaki: The Story of Survi-
      vors in an Atomic Wasteland. Duell, 1951. 189 p.

Eight narratives by acquaintances of the author, a Nagasaki

physician. The author dedicated himself to work against the bomb after the blast. See Josef Schilliger's Saint of the Atom Bomb (item 76).

64. NAKAZAWA, Keiji. Gen of Hiroshima. Educomics
    (P. O. Box 40246, San Francisco, CA 94140), 1981.

Translated from the Japanese; an effective antiwar comic series set in Hiroshima. Focuses on a young boy at the time of the bombing.

65. NATIONAL Research Council, National Academy of Sciences. Longterm Worldwide Effects of Multiple Nuclear Weapons Detonations. National Academy of Sciences, 1975. 213 p.

Discusses effects of a 10,000 megaton exchange in the northern hemisphere on climate, ecosystems, agriculture, animals, water resources, etc.

66. NEWMAN, James R. and Miller, Byron S. Control of Atomic Energy: A Study of Its Social, Economic and Political Implications. Whittlesey House, 1948. 434 p.

Analysis of the Atomic Energy Commission's powers and responsibilities. Explains the Atomic Energy Act of 1946 (the McMahon-Douglas Bill). [See item 89.]

67. O'NEILL, John J. Almighty Atom: The Real Story of Atomic Energy. Washburn, 1945. 94 p.

O'Neill's article "Enter Atomic Power" in the June, 1940 Harper's was probably the first informed journalistic revelation of the shape of nuclear things to come. The book contains a history of the work toward the release of atomic power and a blue-sky section on peaceful applications of atomic energy.

68. OSADA, Arata, ed. Children of the A-Bomb: The Testament of the Boys and Girls of Hiroshima. Putnam's, 1963. 256 p.

Osada was President of Hiroshima University in 1945, and suffered radiation sickness from the bomb. He died in 1962. He devoted the last seventeen years of his life to efforts on behalf of world peace and assistance to children injured by the bomb. The sixty-plus essays here by children who survived the bomb are generally pathetic and heartbreaking. Reissued in 1981 as Children of Hiroshima by Taylor & Francis.

69. PIRIE, Antoinette. Fall Out: Radiation Hazards from Nuclear Explosions. MacGibbon & Kee, 1958. 176 p.

What radiation did to us as a result of the nuclear tests in the 1950s. Covers bone cancer, leukemia, genetic effects, accumulation of radioactivity by plants and animals.

70. POLMAR, Norman. Strategic Weapons: An Introduction. Crane-Russak, 1982. 126 p.

Second edition of a work first published in 1975; provides information on the strategic arsenals of the U.S., the U.S.S.R., Britain, France, and China.

71. PURCELL, John. The Best-Kept Secret: The Story of the Atomic Bomb. Vanguard, 1963. 188 p.

Another journalistic account of the bomb's development.

72. ROBERTSON, John K. Atomic Artillery & the Atomic Bomb. Van Nostrand, 1945. 173 p.

A technically sound, popular treatment of the bomb and its creation. Concludes with a plea for the cause of the scientists who contributed to the bomb: "The scientist is neither more nor less guilty than his fellow-workers in other fields." Some may choose to disagree, beginning with such superficially facetious claims as "Short order cooks do not grill entire cities, " and working up from there.

73. ROSENBERG, Howard L. Atomic Soldiers: American Victims of Nuclear Experiments. Beacon Press, 1980. 192 p.

An advocate's account of the estimated quarter-million plus American soldiers exposed to radiation during the open-air bomb testing of the 1950s.

74. ROTBLAT, Joseph. Nuclear Radiation in Warfare. Taylor & Francis, 1981. 149 p.

On the biological effects of radiation, radiation from nuclear explosions, radiation casualties in war, and attacks on nuclear reactors. On shelter protection: "It appears that the large

protection factors provided by the great thicknesses of earth
or concrete will be illusory in the final outcome. " A Stockholm International Peace Research Institute Study.

75. SAFFER, Thomas H. and Kelly, Orville E. Countdown
    Zero. Putnam's, 1982. 351 p.

Another book on the "atomic soldiers. " Kelly, who died of
cancer before this account's publication, witnessed nearly two
dozen test blasts in 1958. Saffer is also an atomic test
veteran. They provide first-hand information on human reaction to nuclear explosions, and describe the official indifference to the immediate participants' welfare in the effort to
build "better" bombs.

76. SCHILLIGER, Josef. The Saint of the Atom Bomb.
    Newman Press, 1955. 144 p.

The story of Takashi Nagai, a physician and director of air
raid defense in Nagasaki. Following the bombing, Nagai
worked in behalf of Christian spiritual awakening until his
own apparently radiation-induced death a few years later.
[See also item 63.]

77. SCHOENBERGER, Walter S. Decision of Destiny. Ohio
    University Press, 1970. 330 p.

Why the U. S. dropped the bomb on Japan, with focus on Harry
Truman, whom the author paints as a person subject to the
military and its technology rather than as a calculating master
of the event.

78. SHAPLEY, James R. and Blair, Clay, Jr. The Hydro-
    gen Bomb: The Men, The Menace, The Mechanism.
    David McKay, 1954. 244 p.

A popular account of the development of, and controversy
over, the H-bomb, with emphasis on J. R. Oppenheimer and
Edward Teller. Touched by Cold War enthusiasms.

79. SMYTH, Henry DeWolf. Atomic Energy for Military
    Purposes: The Official Report on the Development
    of the Atomic Bomb Under the Auspices of the United
    States Government, 1940-1945. Princeton University
    Press, 1948. 308 p.

This is a reprint, with some additional material, of the famous "Smyth Report" of 1945. Concentrates almost exclu-

sively on technical details, and is likely to be heavy going for
most readers. Includes discussion of the "plutonium production problem, " the separation of uranium isotopes, and other
critical features of the bomb's development. Smyth chaired
the Physics Department at Princeton and was a consultant for
the "Manhattan District, " the name given by the U. S. War
Department to the bomb project.

80.   STOCKHOLM International Peace Research Institute.
      Weapons of Mass Destruction and the Environment.
      Taylor & Francis, 1977. 95 p.

A SIPRI staff exercise on how badly and how long these weapons would affect the environment. Covers geophysical and
environmental weapons, chemical and biological weapons--and
the bomb. Good twenty-page bibliography.

81.   THOMAS, Gordon and Witts, Max M.   Enola Gay.   Stein
      & Day, 1977.   327 p.

A well-researched and fascinating record of preparations for,
dropping, and aftereffects of the Hiroshima bomb. Good bibliography and index. Includes updating on many of those involved at first hand in the Hiroshima attack. Peculiar detail:
in 1976, the highlight of a Texas air show was a simulated
atomic bomb drop from a specially-restored B-29 flown by
the original Hiroshima pilot, Paul Tibbets. U. S. Army engineers concocted non-nuclear explosives to make a satis-
factorily mushroom-shaped cloud. Some in attendance were
appalled. Others thought it was just fine.

82.   TRUMBULL, Robert.   Nine Who Survived Hiroshima and
      Nagasaki.   Dutton, 1957.   148 p.

The stories of nine Japanese men who lived through both the
atomic bombings; Trumbull interviews each of these simultaneously lucky yet incredibly victimized individuals--most
businessmen--and brings out again the experiences of people
subjected to the most extreme stress.

83.   TUGWELL, Rexford G.   A Chronicle of Jeopardy: 1945-
      1955.   University of Chicago Press, 1955.   488 p.

A year-by-year meditation on the role of the bomb in human
affairs. Tugwell, then a professor at the University of Chicago, spreads his pessimism and near despair over our
atomic follies both broad and deep. While at the University
of Chicago, Tugwell served on a committee which prepared a
proposed constitution for a world government.

84. UHL, Michael and Ensign, Tod. G. I. Guinea Pigs:
    How the Pentagon Exposed Our Troops to Dangers
    More Deadly than War: Agent Orange and Atomic
    Radiation. Playboy Press, 1980. 256 p.

Another appeal on behalf of nuclear test victims exposed to
radiation in Nevada, at Bikini, and Eniwetok. Heavy on human interest. The second half of the book is devoted to the
Agent Orange fiasco.

85. U. S. Congress. Joint Committee on Atomic Energy.
    Biological and Environmental Effects of Nuclear War.
    U. S. Government Printing Office, 1959. 966 p.

The nuclear smorgasboard, served up before the Subcommittee
on Radiation, with testimony on civil defense, fallout both local and global, weather factors, pull-out maps tracing stron-
tium-90 deposits over a chronological period following a
nuclear attack, skin lesions, lethal gene mutations, inhalation
of radioactive debris, blast & thermal effects, etc.

86. _____. Joint Committee on Atomic Energy. Fallout
    from Nuclear Weapons Tests. U. S. Government
    Printing Office, 1959. 4v.

Over 2,500 pages of statements on a large number of fallout-
related issues: strontium 90 in human bones, radioactive
milk, developments in radiation biology, "permissible" exposure levels, the methods by which plants, animals, and
people absorb radioactive elements. An inquiry of international scope. The fourth volume is the index.

87. _____. Office of Technology Assessment. The Ef-
    fects of Nuclear War. Allanheld, Osmun, 1980.
    151 p.

On the immediate and after-effects of various attack scenarios,
including a single city (Detroit and Leningrad), a modest attack on oil refineries, a counterforce attack, and a total attack.

● ● ●

"All the pent-up emotions were released in those few minutes
[during the first atomic test] and all seemed to sense immediately that the explosion had far exceeded the most optimistic expectations and wildest hopes of the scientists....
Words are inadequate tools for the job of acquainting those

not present with the physical, mental and psychological effects. It had to be witnessed to be realized. "

> --from the "War Department
> Release on The New Mexico
> Test, " Item 79, p. 254.

● ● ●

88. U. S. Department of State. International Control of
Atomic Energy. Doubleday, 1946. 55 p.

A report to the Secretary of State's Committee on Atomic
Energy by Chester Barnard, J. R. Oppenheimer, Charles
Thomas, Harry Winne and David Lilienthal. Examines the
reasons for a commitment to international control, essential
characteristics of a workable plan, and outline for the plan's
organizational administration. "When fully in operation the
plan ... can establish patterns of cooperation among nations,
the extension of which may even contribute to the solution of
war itself. " Lilienthal chaired the group which prepared
this document; it is sometimes referred to as the "Lilienthal
Report. " Among its proposals: an Atomic Development
Authority with global ownership of uranium mines and facilities for the conversion of U-238 into plutonium and U-235;
licensing of atomic researchers, etc. Suggested that such
Authority be either an agency of the U. N. or an independent
international body.

89. U. S. Laws, Statutes, etc. Atomic Energy Act of 1946.
Public Law 585, 79th Congress; 60 Stat. 755-775.

"It is reasonable to anticipate ... that tapping this new source
of energy will cause profound changes in our present way of
life, " says the Act's "Declaration of Policy. " The Act provided for the Atomic Energy Commission, charged with "the
production of atomic bombs ... or other military weapons
utilizing fissionable materials"; it provided for control of
atomic information, acquisition of private property containing
"source material" (i. e. , uranium), etc.

90. UNITED States. Scientific Laboratory, Los Alamos,
New Mexico. Effects of Atomic Weapons. U. S.
Government Printing Office, 1950. 456 p.

An Atomic Energy Commission-Los Alamos Laboratory guide
to the technical considerations and physical effects of the
bomb.

91. WASSERMAN, Harvey and Solomon, Norman. Killing
    Our Own: The Disaster of America's Experience
    with Atomic Radiation. Delacorte Press, 1982.
    368 p.

A considerably-researched study, with appeal to human interest, of the effects of exposure to radiation emitted by
nuclear weapons production and testing, reactors, and uranium
mining. Includes a summary of U.S. bomb tests.

● Periodical Articles ●

92. BATES, Don G., et al. 'What a Nuclear War Would
    Do to Canada. " Canadian Forum, June 1983, p. 18+

Bates and his colleagues from the McGill Study Group for
Peace and Disarmament believe that Canadian military installations, energy resources, and population centers would
be likely Soviet targets in a U.S.-Soviet strategic war. They
calculate that a third of the Canadian population would die
immediately or within a few days of the attack. Discussion
of fallout, blast effects, etc.

93. BERNSTEIN, Barton J. 'Truman, Acheson and the H-
    bomb. " Foreign Service Journal, 60 (June 1983):
    20-23+

By making a "politically popular and bureaucratically safe"
decision for a crash program to develop the hydrogen bomb,
Truman--influenced by the Joint Chiefs and by Secretary of
State Dean Acheson--"turned away from any possibility" of
retarding the nuclear buildup, in spite of the U.S.'s already-
adequate nuclear deterrent and a vote against development of
the H-bomb by the Atomic Energy Commission.

94. BRUIN, Janet. 'Never Again: The Organization of
    Women Atomic Bomb Victims in Osaka. " Feminist
    Studies 7 (Spring 1981): 5-18.

The Women's Section, Osaka Association of A-Bomb Victims,
formed in 1967. This article consists of four self-portraits
of women survivors of Hiroshima and Nagasaki. Emphasis
on role of women as bearers of life and their consequent responsibility to work for disarmament.

95. EMMANUEL, Jorge. 'Rapid Extinction: The Conse-
    quences of a Nuclear Attack on the Philippines. "
    Southeast Asia Chronicle, April 1983, p. 18-19.

The U. S. maintains military bases in the Philippines within easy range of Soviet nuclear forces; this is a blunt statement of what would happen to the Philippines should the bases come under nuclear attack.

96. FRANCIA, Luis H. "Victims Then, Victims Now. " Bridge: Asian American Perspectives 8 (Winter 1982-83): 14-15.

Among the victims of the Hiroshima and Nagasaki blasts were over 3, 000 American citizens, expatriates stranded in Japan by the war. Although these individuals receive free medical treatment in Japan, there is no U. S. -sponsored program to assist them. An estimated 800-1000 American "hibakusha" ("A-bomb received persons") now live in the U. S. ; 450 who have declared themselves have formed the Committee of Atom Bomb Survivors in the U. S. A. Federal refusal to honor their so-far unique needs has intensified the survivors' sense of alienation.

97. KAMATA, Sadao and Salaff, Stephen. "The Atomic Bomb and the Citizens of Nagasaki. " Bulletin of Concerned Asian Scholars 14 (April-June 1982): 38-50.

Reviews the history and the bombing of the city; discusses post-bomb recovery, efforts by bomb victims to work for peace. Includes interesting account of the immediate postwar period when "almost all early works by Japanese authors dealing with Hiroshima and Nagasaki were censored. "

98. KLOCHKO, Mikhail. "Victims of Stalin's A-bomb. " New Scientist 98 (June 23, 1983): 845-849.

The author, a chemist and head of a Soviet scientific laboratory for many years, obtained political asylum in Canada in 1961. He contends here that in its haste to build a nuclear bomb, the U. S. S. R. exercised sloppy and sometimes non-existent safety precautions, from uranium mining to bomb testing, which resulted in thousands of deaths.

99. MATHER, Celia. "Sunrise in the West. " New Society 65 (Sept. 1983): 309-310.

An anecdotal review of Pacific island dwellers who suffered, and still suffer, from effects of U. S. atomic tests. Many have been forced from their homes and cannot return; the U. S. , recognizing its responsibility for radiation disease among Marshall Islanders, has set up a $150 million trust fund for the islands.

100. SCHMIDT, Jeffrey D. "Global Atmospheric Effects of Nuclear War Fires." Physics Today 35 (Oct. 1982): 17-20.

The author sets forth theory concerning the possible loading-up of the atmosphere with particulate matter from bomb-caused fires--urban, pastoral, and forest--resulting from a modest nuclear war in which the U. S. and U. S. S. R. exhaust only 25 percent of their warheads. The possibility is that close to 100 percent of sunlight could be blocked from the northern hemisphere for a long period, resulting in, among other events, starvation for most of those "surviving" the war.

● ● ●

"The war has to be brought speedily to a successful conclusion and attacks by atomic bombs may very well be an effective method of warfare. We feel, however, that such attacks on Japan could not be justified, at least not unless the terms which will be imposed after the war on Japan were made public in detail and Japan were given an opportunity to surrender."

--from a petition to the President circulated among his atomic scientist peers by Leo Szilard in July, 1945. Item 782, p. 459-460.

● ● ●

● II ●

Playing the Game:
Nuclear Strategies, Tactics and Worldviews

"A wiser rule would be to make up your mind soberly what
you want, peace or war, and then to get ready for what you
want; for what we prepare for is what we shall get."

--William Graham Sumner,
"War," 1903.   (In Sumner
Today, Yale University
Press, 1940, p. 185.)

101. ABSHIRE, David M. and Allen, Richard V., eds.
National Security: Political, Military, and Economic
Strategies in the Decade Ahead. Praeger, 1964.
1039 p.

Reports a 1963 conference sponsored by Georgetown University's Center for Strategic Studies. A good handbook of bas-
ically hardline attitudes flourishing at the time. Covers
perceptions of Soviet and Chinese strategies, as well as the
U. S. approach.

102. ALIANO, Richard A. American Defense Policy from
Eisenhower to Kennedy: The Politics of Changing
Military Requirements, 1957-1961. Ohio University
Press, 1975. 309 p.

Documents the shift in defense thinking from Eisenhower's
"massive retaliation" and "strategic sufficiency" to Kennedy's
"flexible response" and "strategic superiority." Argues that
these shifts led to two major events: U. S. intervention in
Vietnam and the Soviet strategic buildup of the late 1960s in
effort to attain parity with the U. S.

103. ARON, Raymond. The Great Debate: Theories of
Nuclear Strategy. Doubleday, 1965. 265 p.

Translated from the French. From an overview of U. S.
strategy to issues facing the Atlantic Alliance. Includes reflections on the 1962 Cuban Missile Crisis.

104. BALDWIN, Hanson. Strategy for Tomorrow. Harper
& Row, 1970. 378 p.

From the traditionally hard-nosed Center for Strategic and
International Studies at Georgetown University, this is a traditionally hard-nosed argument in favor of force based in certain traditional assumptions: because humanity has always
known war, humanity always will know war; because human
beings are innately violent, we will always be violent. This
is what Baldwin considers a "pragmatic" and "realistic" basis
for discussion of a wide variety of military issues, including
the nuclear sort.

105. BEILENSON, Laurence W. Survival and Peace in the
Nuclear Age. Regnery, 1980. 169 p.

The author believes that nuclear war is likely, but that by the
U. S. pulling its troops out of foreign countries and leaving

these nations to defend themselves, U. S. involvement in future war of any kind would be much reduced. His other ideas: treaties set the scene for betrayal, so we should avoid them; we should build a stronger strategic force; we should pursue a space-based missile defense system, and should also plunge full-speed into a serious civil defense system. For some reason he does not recognize the paradox involved in the global retraction of military forces coupled with preparation for what could easily be interpreted as an intention to launch a nuclear first-strike.

106. BERES, Louis R. Apocalypse: Nuclear Catastrophe in World Politics. University of Chicago Press, 1980. 315 p.

The ways nuclear conflict might arise, its consequences for human life, and methods that might be employed to avoid it. Covers some ground similar to that paced off by Nigel Calder in Nuclear Nightmares (item 118).

107. _____. Mimicking Sisyphus: America's Counter-vailing Nuclear Strategy. Lexington Books, 1983. 142 p.

Points out what Beres calls the "megalomanic and paranoid distortion of reality" inherent in the arms race and the fantasy that nuclear deterrence can endure forever; is particularly critical of the Reagan administration's "refractory nuclear policy"; proposes solutions which entail a comprehensive test ban, a no-first-use pledge, joint nuclear freeze, and nuclear-weapon free zones.

108. BERMAN, Robert P. and Baker, John C. Soviet Strategic Forces: Requirements and Responses. Brookings Institution, 1982. 171 p.

The authors discuss the historical development of Soviet missile forces, examine the link between technological capacity and strategic policy, and describe the boundaries within which Soviet strategic planners must work. This book is heavily oriented toward the hardware of strategy rather than toward the political considerations which also bear influence.

● ● ●

"Thus, the basic irony: nuclear weapons--the special crutch that nominally props up NATO's defenses--cannot be used

without, in all likelihood, obliterating Europe in the process."
--Daniel Ford, Item 522,
p. 103

● ● ●

109. BLACKETT, Patrick Maynard Stuart. Atomic Weapons
and East-West Relations. Cambridge University
Press, 1956. 107 p.

A set of lectures in which Blackett addresses the "lurid
thinking" characterizing the West's belief that it is imminently
at the mercy of Soviet military strength; argues that the success of the Soviet atomic program helped create a strategic
balance more conducive to peace, and contends that those in
the West who ascribe aggressive intentions to the Soviet Union
are in fact "projecting on to the Soviet Union what they thought
American policy was or perhaps should have been."

110. _____. Fear, War, and the Bomb: Military and
Political Consequences of Atomic Energy. McGraw,
1949. 244 p.

Blackett, a physicist who helped develop Britain's radar defense system in the late 1930s, argues that fears of an imminent and utterly destructive nuclear war are unreasonable.
He points out the great unlikelihood of Soviet precipitation of
global war any time soon after WW II, and urges international
cooperation in the control of atomic energy. Considerable
attention to Soviet interests here, and, indeed, Blackett has
been characterized as "pro-Soviet."

111. _____. Studies of War: Nuclear and Conventional.
Hill & Wang, 1963. 242 p.

A collection of the author's magazine articles, 1947-62. Condemns tactical nuclear weapons and is especially critical of
the academic nuclear strategists of the U.S.

112. BOTTOME, Edgar M. The Missile Gap: A Study of
the Formulation of Military and Political Policy.
Fairleigh Dickinson University Press, 1971. 265 p.

The infamous "missile gap" exploited by various U.S. politicians in the late 1950s was a myth. The Soviet Union possessed essentially no ICBM force at the time. This book analyzes the creation and debunking of the myth. Good bibliography.

113. BRACKEN, Paul. The Command and Control of Nuclear
     Forces. Yale University Press, 1983. 288 p.

How the U. S. and the Soviet Union would manage their nuclear
arsenals in a crisis. Bracken argues that in any superpower
nuclear conflict, decision-making would quickly deteriorate,
moving from centralized civilian to patchwork military control. Examines the ways in which hostile actions would be
determined at command centers, allegedly enabling retaliatory action of an "appropriate" sort.

114. BRODIE, Bernard. Escalation and the Nuclear Option.
     Princeton University Press, 1966. 151 p.

This RAND political scientist argues that the U. S. should not
forego threatening or using "tactical" nuclear weapons in limited warfare. Includes attention to the course of escalation: how a conflict edges toward the nuclear "firebreak."
Clearly written.

115. _____. Strategy in the Missile Age. Princeton
     University Press, 1959. 423 p.

"A study of the military problems and strategy from the viewpoint of national policy." Advocates strengthening conventional
forces to avoid nuclear war. Brodie is one of the clearest
writers and most persuasive logicians among the nuclear
strategists of academe; unlike Herman Kahn's books, whose
syntax approximates an instrument of physical torture, Brodie's
prose flows with his arguments. Here he argues in behalf
of deterrent theory. With a clear eye toward the future he
speaks of mobile missiles (e. g. , carried by rail) as a likely
requisite for insurance of a retaliatory force. One need not
agree with his basic assumptions--that security ultimately lies
in armaments--to admire his style.

116. BROWN, Harold. Thinking about National Security:
     Defense and Foreign Policy in a Dangerous World.
     Westview Press, 1983. 288 p.

The Secretary of Defense under President Carter looks at
present and approaching security issues, chooses deterrence
as the best policy (though arguing that it can be accomplished
with a strategic force far smaller than that envisioned under
Reagan proposals), and criticizes Western Europe and Japan
for insufficient attention to their own military requirements.

117. BROWN, Neville. Nuclear War: The Impending
     Strategic Deadlock. Praeger, 1965. 238 p.

An optimist on the possibility of containing limited nuclear wars--and a believer in their likelihood--Brown surveys the balance of terror. Dismisses prospect of nuclear prolifera- tion as not especially worrisome provided NATO and the UN endure. Covers warheads, delivery systems, sea-based de- terrence, ICBMs, etc., all of which combine, in his opinion, to form an East-West strategic deadlock.

118. CALDER, Nigel. Nuclear Nightmares: An Investiga- tion into Possible Wars. Viking Press, 1980. 168 p.

A morbidly entertaining account of four possible progressions to atomic war. Includes the routes of conventional war in Europe, nuclear proliferation, provocation to attack by seeing one's command system "decapitated," and the impulsion to- ward first-strike by fear that the other side may be planning such an act.

119. CAVE-BROWN, Anthony. Dropshot: The United States Plan for War with the Soviet Union in 1957. Dial Press/James Wade, 1978. 330 p.

The Pentagon's 1949 plan for war with Russia, including aims, assumptions, strategies. Interesting chiefly as a window on one venue of the developing Cold War worldview.

120. CLARK, Ian C. Limited Nuclear War: Political Theory and War Conventions. Princeton University Press, 1982. 266 p.

The idea that nuclear war might be fought within tacitly agreed-upon limits dominates U.S. strategic thought. Clark deals with historical forms of war limitation, models of lim- itation, forms of nuclear-war limitation, and "The Code of Nuclear Chivalry." He does not assure us that such war could remain limited. Extensive bibliography.

121. COFFEY, Joseph I. Strategic Power and National Security. University of Pittsburgh Press, 1972. 214 p.

How much and what sort of nuclear weapons do we "need," what will happen if we use them, and how we should act to avoid using them.

122. CONGRESSIONAL Quarterly, Inc. U.S. Defense Policy, 3d ed. C.Q., Inc., 1983. 248 p.

Detailed investigation of the Reagan administration's military thinking and practice, with focus on costs of the strategic arms buildup, MX and Pershing missile plans, arms control, Congressional reaction to the Freeze movement.

123. DANDO, Malcolm R. and Newman, Barrie R., eds. Nuclear Deterrence: Implications & Policy Options for the 1980s. Humanities Press, 1982. 288 p.

Essays by British, American, and Swedish authorities on deterrence, tactical nuclear weapons, conventional deterrence, etc.

124. DEITCHMAN, Seymour J. Limited War and American Defense Policy: Building and Using Military Power in a World at War. 2nd ed. M. I. T. Press, 1969. 302 p.

Dedicated to John F. Kennedy, "who created new directions in U. S. defense policy with respect to limited war," the book concentrates on nuclear weapons use in a European war.

125. DINERSTEIN, Herbert S. War and the Soviet Union: Nuclear Weapons and the Revolution in Soviet Military and Political Thinking. Praeger, 1962. 265 p.

A U. S. Air Force-sponsored study. Notable for its heavy use of material from Soviet sources. Dinerstein reaches the conclusion that if the Soviet Union felt confident that it could obliterate U. S. retaliatory ability with a first strike, it would feel rather free to do so if the situation made the move attractive. This conclusion is, perhaps, self-evident; the frequent lengthy quotations from Soviet officials may be more interesting than the author's interpretations of them.

126. DOUGLASS, Joseph, et al., eds. Soviet Strategy for Nuclear War. Hoover Institution, 1979. 160 p.

How the Soviet Union is preparing its forces for "victory" in nuclear war, or, failing the advent of war, for political persuasion.

127. ELIOT, George F. Victory without War, 1958-1961. U. S. Naval Institute, 1958. 126 p.

Convinced that the Russians could wipe out U. S. landbased missiles through ICBM attack, Eliot argues for a nuclear deterrent at sea. Straightforward propaganda in behalf of the Navy, though relieving the continent of ICBMs is not without considerable appeal now even among those committed to the doctrine of nuclear deterrence.

128. ENDICOTT, John E. Japan's Nuclear Option: Political, Technical, and Strategic Factors. Praeger, 1975. 289 p.

Reviews Japan's strategic situation, with speculation on her possible peaceful or martial relations with the U.S.S.R. and China.

129. ENTHOVEN, Alain C. and Smith, K. Wayne. How Much is Enough? Shaping the Defense Program, 1961-1969. Harper & Row, 1971. 364 p.

A tour of defense decisions and controversies of the decade, informed by admiration for the policies of Robert McNamara. Includes discussion of nuclear strategy and forces.

130. ETZIONI, Amitai. Winning without War. Doubleday, 1964. 271 p.

Nuclear brinksmanship between the superpowers may be steered away from through peaceful policies of economic competition designed to press for global influence without risk of military confrontation. See especially the concluding chapter, "International Relations in the Nuclear Age," which holds up as a model of enlightened statesmanship John F. Kennedy's June 10, 1963 American University address, a speech setting the tone for what proved prompt reduction in U.S./Soviet tensions and some genuine moves toward arms control, if not disarmament.

131. FALLOWS, James. National Defense. Random, 1981. 204 p.

One of the basic analyses of the U.S. military of the 1980s. Fallows's main point is that real defense needs have been swallowed by an obsession with high-technology, high-cost hardware that cannot be trusted. Our one "trustworthy" system is the strategic nuclear force, whose use would likely render most other concerns beside the point.

132. FIRESTONE, Bernard J. The Quest for Nuclear Stability: John F. Kennedy and the Soviet Union. Greenwood Press, 1982. 176 p.

Argues that the steps toward amelioration of the Cold War taken in Kennedy's last year in office, including the Nuclear Test Ban Treaty, set the basic design--arms control and policy intended to avoid nuclear war as a component of military policy--for his successors, until Reagan.

133. FINLETTER, Thomas K. Power and Policy: Foreign Policy and Military Power in the Hydrogen Age. Harcourt, Brace, 1954. 408 p.

Opens with a statement that by 1956 the Soviets will have nuclear superiority over the U.S. and will not hesitate to use it, follows with a call for massive build-up of U.S. strategic capacity to counter this alleged Soviet advantage (it may be hard to remember that this is Finletter writing in 1954 and not some Reagan functionary in 1983), then reverses his field in his conclusion and stresses the importance of "enforced disarmament" on a global basis.

134. FORD, Harold P. and Winters, Francis X., eds. Ethics and Nuclear Strategy. Orbis Books, 1977. 246 p.

Can we rely ethically on nuclear deterrence? Can we justify a policy embracing limited nuclear war? A collection of essays attending to the brambles of strategic, political, and technical issues revolving around these questions. Various points of view receive space; the editors argue that an ethical position and nuclear weapons are mutually exclusive.

135. FRANK, Lewis A. Soviet Nuclear Planning: A Point of View on SALT. American Enterprise Institute for Public Policy Research, 1977. 63 p.

An unusual little book written from the point of view of a hypothetical Kremlin strategist pondering how to achieve both political and military détente, yet at the same time obtain an ability to "win" a nuclear war.

136. FREEDMAN, Lawrence. The Evolution of Nuclear Strategy. St. Martin's Press, 1981. 473 p.

How nuclear weapons have affected strategic thinking. Covers the entire scope of the issue--doctrines, tactics, problems technological, political and psychological; a good study of how we reached our present uncomfortable situation.

137. _____. U.S. Intelligence and the Soviet Strategic Threat. Westview Press, 1978. 235 p.

A scholarly examination of how U. S. intelligence evaluates
"whether or when" question of Soviet intentions to launch
ICBM attack. Focuses on the question of the U. S. land-based
Minuteman missile's reputed vulnerability. (A reputation
since called into severe question itself; see, for example, the
Report of the U. S. President's Commission on Strategic
Forces, item 238.)

138. GALLOIS, Pierre. Balance of Terror: Strategy for
the Nuclear Age. Houghton, 1961. 234 p.

The author, a retired French air force general, speculates
on the state of nuclear deterrence, which he prefers to call
"dissuasion. " He believes that the vastness of the superpowers' nuclear stockpiles goes very far toward eliminating
general war altogether, since (as most familiar with the
weapons' effects would agree) the costs of such war would
far outweigh the benefits, if there were any benefits. Also
has less than alarmist things to say about nuclear weapons in
arsenals of smaller countries.

139. GARTHOFF, Raymond L. The Soviet Image of Future
War. Public Affairs Press, 1960. 137 p.

Apparently Garthoff is optimistic that the Russians are not
rash. His analysis of Soviet military ambitions, especially
regarding general war, is based on study of Soviet military
journals; some of the materials he used are included here in
an appendix. Argues that, although Soviet technological capacities have grown rapidly, Soviet strategy is essentially
conservative, acknowledges the concept of mutual deterrence,
and is unlikely to initiate a nuclear war.

140. _____ . Soviet Strategy in the Nuclear Age. Praeger, 1958. 283 p.

Based primarily on Soviet documents; an informative overview
of Soviet military thinking, including "Perspectives on Limited
War, " with a focus on limited nuclear war. Dated because
of technological changes, but far from uninteresting. A chapter on "Soviet Strategy in 1970 and Beyond" is a blend of
sharp prescience and fancy not realized by events.

141. GEORGE, Alexander L. and Smoke, Richard. Deterrence in American Foreign Policy: Theory and Practice. Columbia University Press, 1974. 666 p.

Criticizes U.S. deterrence theory and practice, employing

studies of major crises ranging from the Berlin Blockade through
the Quemoy and the Cuban Missile Crisis.

142. GEORGETOWN University. Center for Strategic Studies.
The Soviet Military Technological Challenge. Center
for Strategic Studies, 1967. 98 p.

A right-of-center panel composed of retired military officials
and academicians discuss their interpretations of numerous
elements of Soviet techno-military accomplishment and potential, including nuclear bombs and delivery systems. Apparently inspired by Soviet antiballistic missile work.

143. GOMPERT, David C., et al. Nuclear Weapons and
World Politics: Alternatives for the Future. McGraw-
Hill, 1977. 370 p.

Four pictures of strategic nuclear "regimes": they will stay
the same; the bomb exists to keep anyone from using it;
global disarmament; things get worse. The sum impression
of the essays is that the present uneasy deadlock is likely to
remain in place, or to deteriorate. See the appendix which
is "designed to help the newcomer understand the basic issues
of nuclear weapons policy." It reviews strategic concepts,
forces, and arms control, and is actually the best place to
begin reading the book.

144. GOODWIN, Geoffrey L., ed. Ethics & Nuclear Deterrence. St. Martin's Press, 1982. 208 p.

A collection of essays by British government officials and
theologians running at least a partial gamut from defense of
nuclear deterrence as the only strategy that can work to
arguments in behalf of unilateral disarmament.

145. GOURE, Leon, et al. The Role of Nuclear Forces in
Current Soviet Strategy. University of Miami, 1974.
148 p.

Argues that as the U.S. became comfortable with détente,
the U.S.S.R. never abandoned its goal of nuclear strength
and a to-the-death struggle against capitalism, and that the
Soviet nuclear buildup from the late 1960s on enabled a confident boldness in foreign policy.

146. GRAHAM, Daniel O. Shall America be Defended?
SALT II and Beyond. Arlington House, 1979. 267 p.

Arlington House is a reliable purveyor of right-wing opinion, and this book is no exception. Argues that the SALT negotiations are an avenue of appeasement, that the U.S.S.R. believes it can win a nuclear war with minimal damage to itself, and that real security lies in more and better bombs. General Graham, former head of the Defense Intelligence Agency, writes from a confirmed Cold Warrior's point of view.

147. GREEN, Philip. Deadly Logic: The Theory of Nuclear Deterrence. Ohio State University Press, 1966. 361 p.

Attacks the scenario-setting and nuclear games theories of academic strategists Herman Kahn, Thomas B. Schelling, Henry Kissinger, Albert Wohlstetter, et al., as pseudoscience bereft of moral or ethical considerations. Contends that these "authorities'" authority "is completely spurious. If the discussion of deterrence consisted solely of academic deterrence theory, then it would be of little or no value as a guide to policy."

148. HAGEN, Lawrence S., ed. The Crisis in Western Security. St. Martin's Press, 1982. 247 p.

Strategists of academe from the U.S., U.K., and Europe discuss détente's deflation and the where-do-we-go-from-here question of arms control.

149. HALLE, Louis J. Choice for Survival. Harper, 1958. 147 p.

Halle, a former planner in the State Department, counsels patience as we face the need to develop political policies which will prevent nuclear war.

150. HALPERIN, Morton H. China and the Bomb. Praeger, 1965. 166 p.

Inter-relationships of the U.S., U.S.S.R. and China, in light of China's acquisition of the bomb. Since China possessed neither a substantial bomb stockpile nor an adequate delivery system, the author believed that the U.S. Pacific nuclear force would prove a sufficient deterrent against Chinese nuclear adventurism; he left the door open for "the use of strategic nuclear weapons designed to destroy China's war-making capability" in the event of a Chinese invasion of India or Taiwan. Halperin's worldview squares with traditional military vision. In his earlier Strategy and Arms Control (see item

455) he and Thomas C. Schelling defined "arms control" as "a recognition that nearly all serious diplomacy involves ... some kind of power or force, and that a main function of military force is to influence the behavior of other countries. ... "

151. _____. Limited War in the Nuclear Age. Wiley, 1963. 191 p.

See especially chapters on "Nuclear Weapons and Local War," "Arms Control and Local War, " and "American Local-Defense Strategy. " Addresses the policy maker's "dilemma" of "how to apply or resist force to attain the objectives of the nation without running undue risks of all-out nuclear war." Note the implied assumption that there is such a thing as a "due risk" of such war. Includes a 343-item annotated bibliography of relevant books and journal articles.

152. HARKABI, Yehoshafat. Nuclear War and Nuclear Peace. Israel Program for Scientific Translations, 1966. 303 p.

Translation from Hebrew of a 1963 study with emphasis on the psychological aspects of nuclear deterrence and balance, including the paradoxical idea that the opponent's improved strategic strength--his ability to survive a first strike with sufficient retaliatory forces intact--augments one's own security.

153. HARKAVY, Robert and Kolodziej, Edward, eds. American Security Policy and Policy-Making: The Dilemmas of Using and Controlling Military Force. Lexington Books, 1980. 268 p.

Fifteen essays concerned with the subtitle problem, with chapters on the Cruise missile, anti-ballistic missile systems, arms control, and SALT negotiations.

154. HARVARD Nuclear Study Group. Living with Nuclear Weapons. Harvard University Press, 1983. 268 p.

An overview of nuclear weapons, their control, and the inevitability of having to accommodate their existence within our grasp of the world. Historical information on the nuclear arsenals, politics of strategic balance, moral implications, possible routes toward methods of greater control, and thwarting of proliferation. Contributors include Samuel P. Huntington, Joseph S. Nye, Jr. , Stanley Hoffman among others.

155. HEILBRUNN, Otto. Conventional Warfare in the Nu-
      clear Age. Praeger, 1965. 164 p.

Maintains, as do many strategic writers, that the West's
over-reliance on nuclear deterrence in Europe, in lieu of
adequate conventional forces, leads to a no-win military
choice of acquiescence to Soviet occupation or nuclear war
and extinction.

156. HERZOG, Arthur. The War-Peace Establishment.
      Harper, 1965. 271 p.

An interview-based presentation of the major varieties of
attitudes in the mid-1960s U.S. toward nuclear issues. Herzog breaks the interviewees into three groups, and those into
sub-groups. They are the "deterrers," consisting of the
strategic analysts and others who favor nuclear superiority;
the "realists," who favor less emphasis on the military and
more on traditional diplomacy; and the "experimentalists,"
who, while favoring maintenance of at least a minimum nuclear deterrent still approve of a careful unilateral disarmament; and the peace advocates, who place all emphasis on
moral and religious values.

157. HILGARTNER, Stephen, et al. Nukespeak: Nuclear
      Language, Visions, and Mindset. Sierra Club, 1982.
      282 p.

An outstanding inquiry into the nuclear establishment's public
relations campaign. Given the often neglected psychological
aspects of both nuclear power and nuclear weapons (the latter
at least regarding the public mind), a highly useful and en-
lightening book.

158. HITCH, Charles J. and McKean, Roland N., eds.
      Economics of Defense in the Nuclear Age. Harvard
      University Press, 1961. 422 p.

A study on efficient use of defense resources, among them
those dedicated to nuclear business. "In an all-out thermonuclear war," they say, "the superior economic war potential of the United States is important only to the extent that
it has been effectively diverted to security purposes before
war starts." An intriguing point of view from the standpoint
of psychological inquiry.

• • •

"The only thing we have to fear is fear itself. "
                                    -- Franklin D. Roosevelt

• • •

159. HOLST, Johan J. and Nerlich, Uwe, eds. Beyond
      Nuclear Deterrence: New Aims, New Arms. Mac-
      Donald & Jane's, 1977. 314 p.

A strategically mainstream collection of essays on changes in
the Atlantic Alliance, the political context of Western Europe's
defense, doctrinal framework for tactical nuclear weapons
use, impact of new technology, etc.

160. HORELICK, Arnold L. and Rush, Myron. Strategic
      Power and Soviet Foreign Policy. University of
      Chicago Press, 1966. 225 p.

Notable for a discussion of the U. S. S. R. 's contribution to the
Western myth of the "missile gap, " which came into being
with the Sputnik launch of 1957 and proceeded until after John
F. Kennedy's inauguration.

161. HUNTINGTON, Samuel P. The Common Defense:
      Strategic Programs in National Politics. Columbia
      University Press, 1961. 500 p.

The author, a champion of nuclear deterrence, expounds on
the complex way defense strategy develops through executive
and legislative branches of the U. S. government.

162. JACOBSEN, Carl G. The Nuclear Era: Its History,
      Its Implications. Oelgeschlager, 1982. 143 p.

Tries "to draw together the concerns, interests, and expertise
of diverse communities, from 'strategists' to 'arms control-
lers' and disarmament advocates. " Treats the emergence of
U. S. -Soviet strategic equivalence, Moscow's development into
a global power, and nuclear proliferation, among other topics.

163. KAHAN, Jerome H. Security in the Nuclear Age:
      Developing Strategic Arms Policy. Brookings Insti-
      tution, 1975. 361 p.

Traces nuclear policy from Eisenhower through the end of
the Nixon administration. Covers massive retaliation, MAD
(Mutual Assured Destruction), parity, sufficiency, and SALT.
Kahan is convinced that nuclear weapons must never be used,
and concludes with suggestions to prevent their use and to
encourage strategic stability. Contains a good analysis of the
U. S. strategic force components as they existed in 1975.

164. KAHN, Herman. On Escalation: Metaphors and
    Scenarios. Praeger, 1965. 308 p.

Kahn has established a 44-level scale of U. S. -Soviet confrontation running from routine Cold War nastiness to mutual mass
murder ("Spasm or Insensate War"); illustrates the point-
spread with examples from history and "scenarios" from his
own imagination. Considering that the whole range of possibilities could be messily exhausted in less than half an hour,
one wonders at their fine demarcation here. A provocative
book lightened--insofar as such ruminations may be lightened
--by some unintentional and eccentric black humor, e. g. , a
footnote in which Kahn discusses a sample question one might
pose a meeting of, say, the League of Women Voters, concerning the appropriate U. S. response to the unscheduled vaporization of New York City. Should we blow up Moscow,
or maybe Leningrad or Kiev? And how many cities do we
blow up until we feel satisfied that we have blown up enough
to make our point?

165. _____. On Thermonuclear War. Princeton Uni-
    versity Press, 1961. 651 p.

Contemporary devotees of the idea that "limited nuclear war"
is a serious option, survivable and even "winnable" owe a
big debt to this monstrous (in several respects) book, the
barely-edited record of Kahn's briefings to the military and
to civilian officials on his pet subject. A benchmark, along
with Henry Kissinger's Nuclear Weapons and Foreign Policy,
of the nuclear thinking which has led us to the chasm's edge.

166. _____. Thinking about the Unthinkable. Horizon
    Press, 1962. 254 p.

Further variations on the author's nuclear themes. How the
U. S. and the Soviet Union might exchange the ultimate hard-
ware--through calculation, accident, bad guesses, etc. , and
what would be left. Not much, but not to worry: life would
go on, and we would get over our sense of loss. Morally
incredible, but influential and often fascinating. Includes

"Eight 'War Surviving' Situations, " notes on civil defense
(he's for it), "escalation ladders, " etc.

167. KAPLAN, Fred. The Wizards of Armageddon. Simon
     & Schuster, 1983. 452 p.

An illumination of the strategists of both academe and government who have devised the U.S. plans for avoiding, and
fighting, nuclear war. A political scientist with journalistic
talent, Kaplan writes with both knowledge and an ability to
communicate it. Footnotes, index, and list of authorities
interviewed.

168. KAUFMANN, William W. The McNamara Strategy.
     Harper, 1964. 339 p.

An uncritical presentation of the Secretary of Defense's program. Includes coverage of McNamara's "flexible response"
theory and his advocacy of a deterrent composed of both conventional and nuclear forces.

169. _____. Military Policy and National Security.
     Princeton University Press, 1956. 274 p.

Eight essays on deterrence, limited nuclear war, civil defense, local (non-nuclear) war.

170. KELLEHER, Catherine M. Germany and the Politics
     of Nuclear Weapons. Columbia University Press,
     1975. 372 p.

How Germany's nuclear interests affect the German desire
for reunification and its relationship with the U.S. and NATO.
A scholarly treatise.

171. KENNAN, George F. Cloud of Danger: Current
     Realities of American Foreign Policy. Little, 1977.
     234 p.

Kennan, with an extensive background in Soviet studies, including service as U.S. ambassador to the Soviet Union in
the early 1950s, counters the renewed cold war hysteria of the
late 1970s and the resurgence of the U.S. as world policeman
with a reminder that the fundamental goal of the Soviet leadership is its own survival (an unlikely event should the U.S. and
U.S.S.R. annihilate one another) and that the U.S. should
concentrate its efforts in a few crucial sites: Europe and
the Soviet Union itself, and not, e.g., Central America.

172. _____ . The Nuclear Delusion: Soviet-American Relations in the Atomic Age. Pantheon Books, 1982. 208 p.

A collection of Kennan's articles on the sub-title topic, leading to the estimation of the title: true security does not reside in a dream of nuclear superiority or sabre-rattling.

173. _____ . Russia, the Atom and the West. Harper, 1958. 116 p.

An early appeal by Kennan for U.S.-Soviet relations to be founded on recognition of the necessity of "peaceful co-existence" rather than on the perilous platform of an arms race.

174. KINTNER, William R. Peace and the Strategy Conflict. Praeger, 1967. 264 p.

Kintner, a retired military man, laments America's loss of nuclear superiority, urges its reattainment, advocates a vigorous shelter program and an antiballistic missile system.

175. _____ and Scott, Harriet F., eds. The Nuclear Revolution in Soviet Military Affairs. University of Oklahoma Press, 1968. 420 p.

Translations of articles from Russian military journals of the mid-1960s purporting to show the state of Soviet military thought, especially its preoccupation with nuclear weapons. The editors believed that the Soviet armaments growth would pose a dangerous state of affairs for the U.S. in the 1970s.

176. KISSINGER, Henry A. The Necessity for Choice: Prospects of American Foreign Policy. Harper, 1961. 370 p.

Contains some revision of the author's thoughts on "limited" nuclear war's propensity for turning into the full-fledged variety, i.e., he suspects it would.

177. _____ . Nuclear Weapons and Foreign Policy. Harper, 1957. 455 p.

A major reappraisal of foreign policy considering the bomb. Covers technology, strategy, "limited" nuclear war, disarmament, the nuclear stalemate, etc. Calls for departure from the "massive retaliation" policy then in vogue and adoption of a policy emphasizing tactical nuclear weapons. The basis for this exhortation consisted of Kissinger's belief that a threat of force to counter Soviet aggression had to be meaningful; "massive retaliation" against a limited Soviet initiative could be easily dismissed as an empty threat. An extremely influential book.

178. _____. Problems of National Strategy: A Book of Readings. Praeger, 1965. 477 p.

Two dozen essays on strategic doctrines, alliances, arms control, by both scientists and bureaucrats. Contributors are generally familiar names in the area. Considerable attention to nuclear issues and the arms race. May be taken as a standard of American strategic thought of the mid-1960s.

179. KNORR, Klaus and Read, Thornton, eds. Limited Strategic War. Praeger, 1962. 258 p.

The usual array of academic strategists hold forth on what a "limited" nuclear war might be like and how it might be terminated short of general immolation. The definition of "limited" here consists of an attack on a nation's homeland which, while not so severe as to render the society utterly shredded, would yet defeat the victim's will to proceed with further military moves. Some contributors think that such attacks could be strategically advisable and intelligent. Others --including the editors--fear that general war and irrational decision making would be the likely consequences of a "limited" attack.

180. KOHL, Wilfrid L. French Nuclear Diplomacy. Princeton University Press, 1971. 412 p.

Effects of the French nuclear-war fighting capability on relations with NATO and the Soviet Union. Holds that technocrats rather than politicians were primarily responsible for France's nuclear strike force, but that politicians--notably DeGaulle-- welcomed it as political leverage during a period of deteriorating relations with the U.S.

181. LAIRD, Melvin R. A House Divided. Regnery, 1962. 179 p.

The future Secretary of Defense, arguing from a genuinely simplistic view of the world as "half slave and half free," contends that we must be unified in our resolve to pursue

nuclear bomb development and threaten use of nuclear weapons in our campaigns "to eradicate Communists from Cuba,
protect Southeast Asia, and effect the unification of Germany."

182. LANG, Daniel. Inquiry into Enoughness: Of Bombs
     and Men and Staying Alive. McGraw, 1965. 216 p.

A half-dozen essays from The New Yorker in which Lang
portrays his frustration in trying to find any U.S. government officials or functionaries able or willing to answer the
question suggested by his title: with thousands of nuclear
weapons in hand, when can we say that we have enough?
Also treats issues of nuclear testing, the British disarmament movement, and other atomic topics.

183. LAPP, Ralph E. Kill and Overkill: The Strategy of
     Annihilation. Basic Books, 1962. 197 p.

Because we can already destroy the Soviet Union several
times over, we should take the following steps to reduce the
threat of nuclear war: eliminate the ICBM force in favor of
a sea-based deterrent; cut off production of bombs; declare
outer space "out of bounds for military operations"; set up
an international communications system to help avert unintentional war; publicize the effects of nuclear war through a
U.N. study.

184. LEGAULT, Albert and Lindsey, George. Dynamics of
     Nuclear Balance. Cornell University Press, 1974.
     273 p.

An across-the-board description of nuclear weapons systems
coupled with some cursory physics and mathematical analysis.
Champions civil defense.

185. LeMAY, Curtis. America Is in Danger. Funk &
     Wagnall's, 1968. 346 p.

LeMay, the first Commander of the Strategic Air Command, may be longest remembered for suggesting that the
U.S. bomb North Vietnam "back to the Stone Age," if
not for serving as George Wallace's running mate in that
individual's campaign for the presidency in 1968. Here Le-
May expresses great dismay at the U.S.'s failure to maintain
nuclear supremacy, great faith in the fruits a vigorous arms
race would have for the U.S., and contempt for civilian med-
dling with the military.

186. LEVI, Warner. The Coming End of War. Sage Pub-
      lications, 1981. 183 p.

Levi's thesis is that "weapons wipe out war, " i. e. , the destructive power of nuclear weapons is so great that indus-
trially-developed countries possessing them will refrain from
using them, and that developing nations obtaining the bomb
will find themselves in much the same position. Coupled
with this is the technological and economic interdependence
which characterizes the affairs of developed nations--a further
barrier to war. What Levi envisions, then, is not a deliberately achieved status of peace and reduced tensions through
treaties, arms control, and disarmament, but a de facto
nuclear peace based on the common understanding that to
use the bomb against one's opponent is the equivalent of using
it against one's self. It is hard to read this as something
other than well-rationalized wishful thinking.

187. LEVINE, Robert A. The Arms Debate. Harvard
      University Press, 1963. 347 p.

Not satisfied with such simplicities as the "hawk vs. dove"
dichotomy which came to flourish a few years after this
book's publication, Levine divides us into five "schools of
arms policy" reflecting positions from pacifistic to militant
anti-communist. His analysis of the various positions is often provocative, as in his discussion of the "systemic" anti-
war stance, but could be dense reading for those unaccus-
tomed to socio-psychological writing.

188. LICKLIDER, Roy E. The Private Nuclear Strategists.
      Ohio State University Press, 1971. 213 p.

Licklider attempts to ascertain the attitudes and beliefs of
U. S. nuclear strategists not affiliated with the government
through an in-depth questionnaire to which close to 200 subjects responded. Includes discussion of the kinds of projects
the respondents would be willing to work on--a Doomsday
Machine vs. a plan for world government, e. g. Results defy
easy categorization.

189. LIDDELL HART, B. H. Deterrent or Defense: A Fresh
      Look at the West's Military Problem. Praeger, 1960.
      257 p.

Because any situation resembling nuclear parity must mean
"nuclear nullity, " i. e. , the impossibility of nuclear employment because of its self-defeating qualities, war will proceed
through other, more limited, means.

190. LIU, Leo Yueh-yun. China as a Nuclear Power in
      World Politics. Taplinger, 1972. 125 p.

Liu, a Canadian university professor, surveys the People's
Republic's nuclear position in the belief that the nation is
well on the way to becoming a major nuclear power, with a
survivable retaliatory force. Assumes that, whereas the
U. S. and Soviet Union seek strategic stability (a questionable
assumption in the early 1980s), China will be a more adventurous nuclear player. China's nuclear emergence will
further unsettle the loose world alignment of U. S. and Soviet
client states, and U. S.–Soviet guarantees of military assistance to such states threatened by the Chinese bomb will suffer reduced credibility. (Would the U. S., e. g., sacrifice
Detroit for Delhi?)

191. LOWE, George E. The Age of Deterrence. Little,
      1964. 324 p.

A liberal's analysis of defense policy, 1952-1963, arguing in
behalf of using only the force necessary to attain the desired
end. Says that Berlin and Cuban crises bear out this approach.

192. LYONS, Gene M. and Morton, Louis. Schools for
      Strategy: Education and Research in National Security
      Affairs. Praeger, 1965. 356 p.

Discussion of the various institutions involved in instruction,
research and advocacy in national security issues.

193. McCLELLAND, Charles A., ed. Nuclear Weapons,
      Missiles, and Future War: Problem for the Sixties.
      H. Chandler, 1960. 235 p.

A potpourri of essays by such opposed authors as Sidney Hook
and Bertrand Russell and others on different ends of the
ideological teeter-totter, meditating on the bomb, disarmament, "nuclear obsession," accidental war, etc.

194. McNAMARA, Robert S. The Essence of Security.
      Harper & Row, 1968. 176 p.

A collection of policy statements from public addresses and
reports to Congress. Includes a chapter on McNamara's
vision of nuclear deterrence. "The question is: what is our
determination in an era when unlimited war will mean the
death of hundreds of millions and the possible genetic impairment of a million generations to follow?" Clearly McNamara
is an optimist in his estimation that any generations might

follow unlimited nuclear war. As for his "essence, " it lies
not in overwhelming military superiority, but in political,
economic and social health.

195. MALLAN, Lloyd. Peace is a Three-Edged Sword.
    Prentice-Hall, 1964. 253 p.

And there's no need to bother putting it back in the scabbard,
either. Unrestrained fervor for military personnel, systems,
nuclear forces--and assurances that accidental atomic war is
next to impossible. (By the author of It IS Safe to Smoke,
Hawthorn, 1966.) Somehow we are not comforted.

196. MANDELBAUM, Michael. The Nuclear Future. Cor-
    nell University Press, 1983. 131 p.

Concludes in the idea that "the nuclear future will be like the
past. It will follow a middle path between nuclear war and
nuclear disarmament. " A clearly-written book for the layman covering basic issues in the nuclear weapons complex,
including the arms race, proliferation, and the anti-nuclear
weapons movement.

197. _____ . The Nuclear Question: The United States
    and Nuclear Weapons, 1946-1976. Cambridge Uni-
    versity Press, 1979. 277 p.

Deterrence, says the author, is the proper strategy for the
nuclear era; it is, in fact, the only nuclear strategy that
makes sense. Regards the Eisenhower-era "massive retaliation" doctrine as the preferred nuclear posture, considers
talk of "limited" nuclear war benighted and pointless. Includes an interpretation of the Cuban Missile Crisis maintaining that fear of the nuclear abyss led both parties to act
with restraint.

198. MARTIN, Laurence W. , ed. Strategic Thought in the
    Nuclear Age. Johns Hopkins University Press, 1979.
    233 p.

Seven pieces on the roles of military forces in the nuclear
era covering strategic intelligence and doctrine, crisis diplomacy, etc.

199. MEDARIS, John B. Countdown for Decision. Putnam's,
    1961. 303 p.

A blunt criticism of American defense and space policy by

the former head of the Army Ballistic Missile Agency; attacks reliance on nuclear retaliation instead of a conventional
deterrent as suicidal.

200. MENDL, Wolf. Deterrence and Persuasion: French
      Nuclear Armament in the Context of National Policy,
      1945-1969. Praeger, 1970. 256 p.

On the roles of scientists, politicians, and military figures.
Believes that the French nuclear program's motivations lay
not only in a perceived threat from the Soviet Union, but in
a desire to maintain military superiority over West Germany
and to demonstrate independence from U.S. policy.

201. MIKSCHE, Ferdinand O. Atomic Weapons and Armies.
      Praeger, 1955. 222 p.

On tactical atomic war in Europe. The author all but assumes
that such a war could be limited to military fronts, that cities
would not be subject to the bomb. He cautions against over-
reliance on the bomb to the exclusion of conventional forces,
however.

202. _____. Failure of Atomic Strategy, & A New
      Proposal for the Defense of the West. Praeger,
      1958. 224 p.

Favors a more unified Western European alliance, reduction
of reliance on U.S. and deterrence of an "unlikely" Soviet
invasion of Western Europe through stronger conventional
forces. Of reliance on nuclear deterrence he writes, "We
cannot give the name of strategy to the creation of a situation which would be worse than any Pyrrhic victory, the defeated all being dead and the victors left in agony. "

203. MILLS, C. Wright. Causes of World War Three.
      Simon & Schuster, 1958. 172 p.

Contending that "the strategic outlook is the idiot's outlook, "
Mills argues that "the drift and thrust toward World War III
is now part of the contemporary sensibility--and a defining
characteristic of our epoch. " Makes some specific proposals
for disarmament, but the book's real value is now, as it
was when published, as a goad to reexamination of received
ideas on running the world according to the traditional military scheme.

204. Nuclear America: A Historical Bibliography. ABC-
      Clio, 1984. 180 p.

Dozens of authors annotate over 800 articles appearing 1973-1982. Emphasis on weapons history and the arms race. Numerous foreign-language citations. A quarter of the material is post-1980.

205. O'KEEFE, Bernard J. Nuclear Hostages. Houghton Mifflin, 1983. 252 p.

O'Keefe helped develop the detonating system used on early atomic bombs, and eventually became an important military contractor. Though unapologetic about his work on the bomb, he claims that the nuclear arms race is effectively at an end through stalemate; he ridicules the notion of "limited" nuclear war, and advocates broader U.S.-Soviet cooperation in areas of mutual interest to help minimize the possibility of superpower conflict.

206. PARSON, Nels A. Missiles and the Revolution in Warfare. Harvard University Press, 1962. 245 p.

Intended as a general introduction for the layman, useful as a portrait of assumptions and expectations at the time of publication. See, e.g., chapter 10, "Strategic Missile Attack and Defense."

207. PAYNE, Keith B. Nuclear Deterrence in U.S.-Soviet Relations. Westview Press, 1982. 239 p.

Payne finds traditional U.S. deterrent policy wanting; what we need, he thinks, is a combination of defense against attack which will minimize damage along with an offensive capacity. Supposedly this combination would make for a more credible nuclear deterrent.

208. PEETERS, Paul. Massive Retaliation: The Policy and Its Critics. Regnery, 1959. 304 p.

The strategy of massive retaliation, embodying reliance on nuclear weapons as the primary deterrent against all types of aggression, is often regarded the brainchild of John Foster Dulles, Secretary of State under Eisenhower, although Admiral Arthur Radford, chairman of the Joint Chiefs of Staff, had more to do with its development than Dulles. Peeters is a convinced proponent of the policy, regards its opponents as misguided, and believes that public discussion of such topics as nuclear arms merely opens the door for foreign propagandists.

209. People of the World, Unite, for the Complete, Thorough, Total and Resolute Prohibition and Destruction of Nuclear Weapons! Foreign Languages Press,
Peking. 1963. 208 p.

In spite of the hortatory title, this book is a broadside not
against nuclear weapons, but against the Nuclear Test Ban
Treaty of 1963, to which the People's Republic was not a
party. Composed of articles and newspaper editorials to the
effect that the U.S. and Soviet Union wished to use the Treaty
for their own strategic advantage.

210. PIERRE, Andrew J. Nuclear Politics: The British
Experience with an Independent Strategic Force,
1939-1970. Oxford University Press, 1972. 378 p.

The basic book on Great Britain's decision to build a nuclear
force. Covers the period from the nation's inchoate atomic
bomb project to the quandary posed her nuclear deterrent in
the 1970s by changes in the superpower arsenals. The issue here is how jockeying for political advantage led Britain
to a dubious involvement with nuclear weapons. [See item 255].

211. PLATT, Alan. The U.S. Senate and Strategic Arms
Policy, 1969-1977. Westview Press, 1978. 129 p.

Contends that Senate involvement in policy making, from the
anti-ballistic missile system to SALT II, was more super-
ficial than influential. Well researched.

212. POSVAR, Wesley W., ed. American Defense Policy.
Johns Hopkins University Press, 1965. 471 p.

Posvar, an Air Force Colonel, was head of the Political
Science Department at the Air Force Academy. He offers
here a collection of essays on the usual themes by some
familiar names--Kahn, Kissinger, et al. Acceptable as an
introduction to mainstream defense thought of the period.

213. POWER, Thomas S. Design for Survival. Coward-
McCann, 1965. 255 p.

Power was the Strategic Air Command's Commander-in-Chief
for seven years. His "design" includes maintenance of SAC
bombers, a gung-ho civil defense plan and placement of ICBMs
in railroad cars (thus anticipating the original MX deployment
plan by nearly two decades).

• • •

"The first point to notice is that the political leaders of the
Soviet Union appear today to believe quite as deeply as our
own in the utterly catastrophic nature of general nuclear war. "
--Bernard Brodie, Item 114,
p. 43.

• • •

214. PRADOS, John. The Soviet Estimate: U. S. Intelligence Analysis & Russian Military Strength. Dial
Press, 1982. 367 p.

How the U. S. judges Soviet military strength, and how this
judgment affects U. S. policy. A fundamental work on nuclear
intelligence-gathering. Fully-researched.

215. PRANGER, Robert J. and Labrie, Roger P. Nuclear
Strategy and National Security Points of View.
American Enterprise Institute for Public Policy Re-
search, 1977. 515 p.

A handy compendium of mostly right-of-center U. S. officialdom's and academic nuclear views, with articles by Richard
Nixon and Melvin Laird on foreign policy, James Schlesinger
on strategic policy, Colin S. Gray (one of today's premier
cheerleaders of "limited" nuclear war) on strategic competition, etc.

216. QUANBECK, Alton H. and Blechman, Barry M. Strategic Forces: Issues for the Mid-Seventies. Brookings Institution, 1973. 94 p.

Analyzes strengths and weaknesses of the U. S. nuclear weapons systems, as well as those of the Soviet Union and China.
Expresses concern over the perceived vulnerability of the
U. S. Minuteman missile system which would develop toward
the end of the 1970s.

217. QUESTER, George H. Offense and Defense in the International System. Wiley, 1977. 219 p.

Historical study of technology and its interrelation with military doctrine, including approaches to nuclear management.
The last part of the book concerns arms control and the balance of power. The author is an Air Force veteran and
professor of government.

218. RAPOPORT, Anatol. <u>Strategy and Conscience.</u> Har-
     per & Row, 1964. 324 p.

Tries to deal with the refusal of nuclear strategists to enter-
tain the moral questions implicit in their work. "In stressing
the role of conscience in human affairs, the concerned people
take a more realistic position than the self-styled 'realists, '
who cannot transcend the limitations of their conceptual
scheme. " The author was on the faculty of the University
of Michigan's Mental Health Research Institute.

219. REINHARDT, George C. <u>American Strategy in the</u>
     <u>Atomic Age.</u> University of Oklahoma Press, 1955.
     236 p.

Urges "active steps which will make all-out war less likely,
and simultaneously restore to the free world the initiative in
the less than war struggle.... " This is a "Win the Cold
War" exercise advocating that the U. S. help establish multiple powers friendly to Western values which will somehow
persuade the Soviet Union to peacefully relinquish its hold on
its "slaves. "

● ● ●

"Nuclear war is stupid, stupid, stupid! If you reach for the
pushbutton, you reach for suicide!"
                                    --Nikita Khrushchev, June,
                                      1964.   Item 114, p. 44.

● ● ●

220. _____ and Kintner, William R. <u>Atomic Weapons in</u>
     <u>Land Combat.</u> Military Service Publishing Company,
     1954.   243 p.

An attempt by two former atomic weapons instructors to show
how soldiers should prepare themselves for service when nuclear blasts are going off at hand. One suggestion is that
they dig deeper foxholes. That anyone believes soldiers
could endure battlefield exposure to the effects of nuclear
bombs without losing all interest in soldierly rectitude, to say
nothing of individual sanity, is surely a testament--of some
sort--to a military mind steeped in tradition.

221. ROSE, John P. <u>The Evolution of U. S. Army Nuclear</u>
     <u>Doctrine, 1945-1980.</u> Westview Press, 1980.   252 p.

The Army ought to prepare for tactical nuclear warfare, says Major Rose, and explains why he thinks so.

222. RUSSETT, Bruce M. The Prisoners of Insecurity: Nuclear Deterrence, the Arms Race, and Arms Control. W. H. Freeman, 1983. 204 p.

For those who find Ground Zero's books on the nuclear threat too shallow, but those of the typical academic strategist too oppressive, this is a good alternative. It presents in read-able, informed prose an analysis of "security" policy (and the insecurity it provokes), arms and deterrence, the origins of arms races, arms control and the conduct of war. Wisely points out that in a democratic society it is the obligation of concerned citizens to speak out on matters of national securi-ty rather than leaving the whole business to the "experts"-- who, after all, have brought us to our present unenviable condition.

223. SCHEER, Robert. With Enough Shovels: Reagan, Bush and Nuclear War. Random House, 1982. 285 p.

A merciless flaying of the Reagan administration's reckless nuclear positions, from its incredible assertions of American strategic inferiority, its attack-inviting promotion of the no-torious "window of vulnerability" slogan, and the whole whim-sical entertainment of the "winnable" nuclear war option. In-cludes interviews and excerpted interviews with many present and former government officials.

224. SCHILLING, Warner R., et al. American Arms and a Changing Europe: Dilemmas of Deterrence and Disarmament. Columbia University Press, 1973. 218 p.

Argues for a large conventional deterrent in Europe with options for tactical nuclear weapons.

225. SCHWARZ, Urs. American Strategy: A New Perspec-tive; The Growth of Politico-Military Thinking in the United States. Doubleday, 1966. 178 p.

How military thinking and foreign policy blended into one an-other following WW II. Focus on strategic policy makers like Kissinger and Kahn.

● ● ●

"The sum made available by the [U. S.] government for the
study of uranium fission during the year 1 November 1939 to
31 October 1940 was $6, 000. "
                                        --Arthur Compton, Item 786,
                                                    p. 28.

● ● ●

226.   SLESSOR, Sir John C.   The Great Deterrent: A Col-
       lection of Lectures, Articles and Broadcasts on the
       Development of Strategic Policy in the Nuclear Age.
       Cassell, 1957.   321 p.

Close to two dozen pieces spanning as many years; the emphasis is on Great Britain.

227.   SNOW, Donald M.   Nuclear Strategy in a Dynamic
       World: American Policy in the 1980s.   University
       of Alabama Press, 1981.   332 p.

Reviews U. S. and Soviet nuclear strategies and attitudes, the
arms control process and proliferation.   Carefully documented,
more readable than most in the area.

228.   SNYDER, Glenn H.   Deterrence and Defense: Toward
       a Theory of National Security.   Princeton University
       Press, 1961.   294 p.

Do we prepare to absorb attack with a minimum amount of
damage, or do we mount so potent a retaliatory force that
attack is deterred?   These are the security choices Snyder
sees, and which he examines in small-print detail.

229.   SOKOLOVSKII, V. D. , ed.   Soviet Military Strategy.
       Prentice-Hall, 1963.   544 p.

Translated and with an analytical introduction by Herbert G.
Dinerstein, Leon Goure, and Thomas Wolfe.   Originally
issued by the Military Publishing House of the U. S. S. R. 's
Ministry of Defense.   First brought to the attention of the
public through a long review in Red Star, the Soviet military
newspaper, this book became one of the most influential of
post-war points of access to the Soviet conceptions of war
and strategy in the nuclear era.   The 78-page editors' introduction helps clarify what follows, which, of course, entails
discussion of nuclear strategy.

230. SOMERVILLE, John, ed. Soviet Marxism & Nuclear
War: An International Debate. Greenwood Press,
1981. 166 p.

A debate among Marxists begun at the 15th World Congress
of Philosophy held in Bulgaria in 1973, and continued through
correspondence and research studies. Contributors hail from
the U.S., Japan, India, Canada, Mexico, the Soviet Union,
and other countries. The introduction states that "this discussion taken as a whole marks the first and so far the only
time that the problems involved in nuclear war have been
publicly debated and explored by Marxists who hold differing
views on the subject."

231. STOCKHOLM International Peace Research Institute.
Tactical Nuclear Weapons: European Perspectives.
Taylor & Francis, 1978. 371 p.

Papers based on a 1976 SIPRI conference. Coverage of the
issues is thorough, if somewhat repetitive.

● ● ●

"They all hate us anyhow--let's drop the Big One now."
--Randy Newman, "Political
Science." Reprise
Records, 1972.

● ● ●

232. TAYLOR, Maxwell D. The Uncertain Trumpet. Harper, 1960. 203 p.

A significant book by the former U.S. Army Chief of Staff
for several reasons. Taylor derides Eisenhower's massive
retaliation policy, criticizes the inefficiency of armed services
management, sets forth the "flexible response" strategic
policy adopted under John F. Kennedy; falls headfirst into a
credulous embrace of the "missile gap"--and concludes with
a paper submitted to the journal Foreign Affairs but rejected
because of State and Defense Department objections (included
in italics through the paper) to many of Taylor's statements,
one being that vast stockpiles of nuclear bombs are not required for an efficient deterrent against attack.

233. TELLER, Edward and Latler, Albert L. Our Nuclear
Future ... Facts, Dangers and Opportunities. Cri-
terion Books, 1958. 184 p.

A condescending "illumination" for the layman of the radiation
and fallout issue by one of the century's great enthusiasts for
all things nuclear. According to Teller, we really had nothing to worry about from nuclear tests in the atmosphere;
what we really needed was "clean, flexible and easily delivered weapons of all sizes. . . . Clean nuclear weapons
would be the same as conveniently packaged high explosives.
They would be nothing more. " And besides, as we all know,
cleanliness is next to Godliness. This level of thought is
not universal in the book's treatment of atomic testing, nuclear reactors, "Danger to the Race, " and other topics, but
it is by no means unusual.

234. TUCKER, Robert W. The Just War: A Study in Con-
        temporary American Doctrine. Johns Hopkins Uni-
        versity Press, 1960. 207 p.

A good elucidation of the American doctrine of just war, which
holds that acts of war are morally acceptable if taken in response to another's initial act of aggression. Helpful as a
basis for understanding the U. S. strategic doctrine of massive retaliation which ruled the 1950s.

235. TURNER, Gordon B. and Challener, Richard D. , eds.
        National Security in the Nuclear Age: Basic Facts
        and Theories. Praeger, 1960. 293 p.

Seven academic views on deterrence and stability, limited
war, strategic and political implications of missiles, and
NATO; editor Gordon sets the tone when he writes that American strategists "must resist those strong pressures emanating
from traditional American conceptions about war and peace
which may well sweep us over the precipice of world destruction. "

236. TWINING, Nathan F. Neither Liberty Nor Safety: A
        Hard Look at U. S. Military Policy and Strategy.
        Holt, 1966. 320 p.

Books promising a "hard look" at anything usually bear a
dismal predictability with them, especially when the object
scrutinized involves the military. This one is no exception.
Air Force General Twining proffers a zealous brief for nuclear supremacy in the face of communist "immorality. "

237. U. S. President's Air Policy Commission. Survival in
        the Air Age: A Report. Government Printing Office,
        1948. 166 p.

Popularly known as "The Finletter Report, " after Commission
Chairman Thomas K. Finletter. Addresses all phases of
aviation, but leads off with discussion of strategic security,
and envisions the need for "an air arm ... capable of dealing
with a possible atomic attack on this country at January 1,
1953. " A useful example of establishmentarian focus on the
threat of war, and preparation for war, rather than on the
possibilities of peace and international cooperation.

238.   U. S. President's Commission on Strategic Forces.
       Report.   Department of Defense (?), 1983.   P?

Issued on a small scale on April 11, 1983, this is one of the
most significant "public" documents of the decade.   It is also
one of the most difficult to obtain; I was unable to acquire a
copy by the time I prepared this entry, and have based my
remarks on excerpts (see, e. g. , the New York Times of
April 12, 1983) and discussion of the item in secondary
sources.   The report of the commission chaired by General
Brent Scowcroft (and often referred to as the "Scowcroft
Commission Report"), it effectively repeals the Reagan administration "Window of Vulnerability" claims regarding
existing U. S. land-based missiles and their alleged suscepti-
bility to destruction by a Soviet first strike.   The commission
advises development of the MX missile, with its development
linked to general support for arms control, and recommends
placement of the MX in existing Minuteman silos.

At this date (mid-November, 1983), the report is, according
to a telephone call to the Government Printing Office, not
available from that source; a call to the U. S. Library of
Congress indicates that the nation's chief library of record
does not have this document, either--this in spite of President Reagan's April 19, 1983 statement that the report was
"immediately released ... to the public. " Stories have circulated of librarians spending months trying to obtain copies
of the "Scowcroft Commission Report" from a variety of
federal sources ranging from the White House to the Pentagon.   The most likely source for it may be the Defense Department's Division of Public Correspondence.

The deduction that the report has been suppressed because of
its contradiction of a fundamental Reagan administration assumption and policy plank is, unfortunately, inescapable.

239.   VAN CLEAVE, William R. and Cohen, S. T.   Tactical
       Nuclear Weapons: An Examination of the Issues.
       MacDonald & Jane's, 1978.   119 p.

Maybe it's revealing that in a book on such issues, there are no entries in the index under "ethics" or "morality." Maybe it's not. At any rate, the issues, as they are identified here, include warhead technology, tactical doctrine and strategy, etc. Maybe it's comforting that "Civilian casualties, enhanced radiation warheads and," receives an index entry. But maybe it isn't.

● ● ●

"It's a job like any other--you wear a uniform at McDonald's, too."

> --An ICBM turnkey operator, interviewed by National Public Radio, April 8, 1983.

● ● ●

240. _____ and Thompson, W. Scott, eds. Strategic Options for the Early Eighties: What Can be Done? Automated Graphic Systems, 1979. 200 p.

Announces that U.S. ability to defend itself has declined precipitously; calls for something that looks a great deal like the Reagan buildup: Cruise missiles, the B-1, a mobile land-based missile, civil defense, etc.

241. WALTERS, Robert E. The Nuclear Trap: An Escape Route. Penguin, 1974. 215 p.

Calls the decision to base Western strategy upon nuclear arms "one of the great blunders of history." This criticism stems from the author's analysis of what he regards the U.S.'s inept evaluation of geopolitical realities. Urges a complete rethinking of defense practices, with greater exploitation of the sea, especially by submarines of both military and commercial purposes, a central point in his program.

242. WIESELTIER, Leon. Nuclear War, Nuclear Peace. Holt, Rinehart & Winston, 1983. 128 p.

Based on the author's essay in the January 10-17, 1983 New Republic, this is a pragmatic and concisely argued defense of the deterrence doctrine. Points out the absurdity of "winnable" nuclear war opinionating.

243. WONG-FRASER, Agatha S. Y. The Political Utility of

Nuclear Weapons: Expectations & Experience. University Press of America, 1980. 343 p.

A study of the benefits accruing from possession of nuclear weapons in a nuclear armed crowd, given the continuing basis of international conduct in conflict and threat. One of the questions: does proliferation carry with it certain "advantages" in spreading the nuclear capability beyond the superpowers?

244. ZUCKERMAN, Solly. Nuclear Illusion and Reality. Viking, 1982. 154 p.

A very good argument by the British authority on the driving forces of the arms race (he metes out considerable responsibility to the scientific sector), the questionable utility of a "deterrent" that, if used, would probably result in the deaths of those it was meant to protect, the desirability of a comprehensive nuclear test ban and an end to the nuclearistic worldview.

245. ZUMWALT, Elmo and Thompson, W. Scott, eds. National Security in the 1980s: From Weakness to Strength. Transaction, 1980. 524 p.

The sub-title tells the tale. Essays in a Reaganite vein on ways of counteracting alleged U.S. military "inferiority."

● ● ●

"One may well shudder ... over the lack of historical sense in an assumption of continuing enmity. Europe and the United States have seen enough changes of alliances during the past 150 years to suggest that it seems a folly to risk global or European incineration for an inevitably temporary set of alliances...."

> --James O'Connell, New Scientist June 16, 1983, p. 800.

● ● ●

● Periodical Articles ●

246. AGNELLI, Giovanni. "The Strategic Role of the Western Business Community." Washington Quarterly 3 (Winter 1980): 126-132.

The West should engage in more efficient military cooperation, but the real source of security lies in economic strength.
Through economic methods and multinational corporations, the
West can encourage democratic growth in the Third World,
the most likely focus of East-West conflict.

247. BUNDY, McGeorge; McNamara, Robert S.; Kennan,
      George F. and Smith, Gerard. "Nuclear Weapons
      and the Atlantic Alliance." Foreign Affairs 60
      (Spring 1982): 753-768.

The authors call on NATO to reject the policy of a first-use
option for nuclear weapons on the grounds that any use of
such weapons in Europe would damage life and property to an
intolerable degree and entail a major risk of escalation into
general nuclear war. They believe that the West's conventional deterrent has been under-rated, and could be brought
up to highly effective levels without the exorbitant expense
most nuclear deterrent advocates foresee.

248. CHOMSKY, Noam. "The Middle East and the Probabil-
      ity of Nuclear War." Socialist Review 13 (July-Aug.
      1983): 7-33.

Dissects the U.S./Israel/Palestinian complex and probes it
for routes to nuclear war. Cites reports that Israel threatened to use nuclear weapons during 1973 war unless the U.S.
provided massive shipment of conventional arms, and that
Israel and South Africa have jointly developed tactical nuclear
weapons. Argues that as long as the U.S. remains committed
to an aggressive yet isolationist Israel, "the prospects are
for further tragedy."

249. COHEN, Sam. "Accepting Nuclear Weapons." Foreign
      Service Journal 60 (Sept. 1983): 18 +

Argues that, in spite of the Cruise and Pershing II, NATO
has shifted to the idea of conventional deterrence that the
Soviets plan to counter with tactical nuclear weapons. Makes
no effort to demonstrate that Soviets actually intend to invade
Western Europe.

250. DEAN, Roy. "The Alliance and Nuclear Weapons."
      Atlantic Community Quarterly 21 (Summer 1983):
      118-124.

The author, director of the Arms Control and Disarmament
Research Unit of the British Foreign and Commonwealth Office,

stresses the need for U.S.-Western European unity in nuclear matters, and criticizes fears of nuclear war as understandable but unwarranted.

251. DEUTSCH, Morton. "The Prevention of World War III: A Psychological Perspective." Political Psychology 4 (March 1983): 3-31.

Characterizes the U.S. and Soviet Union as otherwise rational states trapped in the pathology of nuclearism. On the psychological dynamics contributing to the overall situation. Suggests ways to defuse the bomb, including proscription of first-use, removal of first-strike weapons from each nation's arsenal, rapid independence of the U.S. from Middle Eastern oil, etc.

252. "Documents: U.S. Nuclear War Against the Soviet Union." Counterspy 7 (Dec. 1982): 57+

Discusses documents revealing U.S. nuclear attitudes and options toward the Soviet Union in 1948, 1950, 1957, 1980 and 1982. E.g., the 1950 "Harrow" plan directed the U.S. Air Force to take nuclear action unilaterally against the U.S.S.R. in the event of "sudden hostilities."

253. "Documents: U.S. Nuclear War Plans for Europe." Counterspy 7 (March 1983): 53-58.

Exposition of U.S. military plans for "limited" nuclear war in Europe, first revealed in West Germany's Stern in 1970. The CIA has variously called these documents "forgeries" and "a mixture of authentic and altered U.S. war plans."

254. DUNN, Keith A. and Staudenmaier, Col. William O. "Strategy for Survival." Foreign Policy No. 52 (Fall 1983): 22-42.

Analyzes various defense strategies, then proposes a "new strategy" for the U.S. wherein "the only purpose of nuclear weapons must be to protect interests absolutely essential to U.S. survival," with a dedication to avoiding superpower conflict over relatively trivial issues and spurning reliance on nuclear threats and war-widening concepts.

255. FREEDMAN, Lawrence. "Britain: The 1st Ex-Nuclear Power." International Security 6 (Fall 1981): 80-104.

Evaluates the diplomatic, economic and strategic considerations on which hinge Great Britain's status as a nuclear weapons power. The debatable utility of the nation's small deterrent force and the financial costs of maintaining it lead to
doubts about its long-term status. No unilateral nuclear disarmament appears imminent, but the above concerns, coupled
with the attractions of unilateralism in a nuclear-obsessed
world, suggest possible action in this direction.

256. FRIED, John H. E. "Law and Nuclear War. " Bulletin
of the Atomic Scientists 38 (June-July 1982): 67-68.

Although there is no international treaty outlawing nuclear
war, first-use of nuclear weapons "is forbidden by fundamental general treaty rules which the nations of the world
have universally pledged to obey. "

257. GARTHOFF, Raymond L. "The NATO Decision on
Theater Nuclear Forces. " Political Science Quarterly 98 (Summer 1983): 197-214.

Garthoff examines the relations "between intra-alliance and
inter-adversary considerations" involving deployment of the
Euromissiles; believes that what was meant to reinforce Alliance unity and further deter Soviet aggression "has now
however become an issue within the Alliance and may even
become a test of European reassurance to a hard-line American administration. "

258. _____. "The Soviet SS-20 Decision. " Survival:
The International Journal for Strategic Studies 25
(May-June 1983): 110-119.

States that Soviet deployment of the long-range tactical nuclear
missile in Eastern Europe stemmed from technical capacity
and routine force modernization consistent with SALT requirements. Believes that the Soviets saw NATO decision to
respond with a tactical nuclear build-up "not as a justified
(or even as a misguided) response, but as a hostile initiative. " Concludes that the tactical forces reduce the security
of both sides. Garthoff writes with a grasp of technical,
political and psychological issues unusual in nuclear literature.

259. GELB, Norman. "Britain's Nuclear Debate. " New
Leader 66 (March 7, 1983): 8-9.

A brief survey of the nuclear scene at the official level and
among antinuclear leadership. British strategists standing

between Thatcher hardliners and antinuclear unilateralists may exert the greatest influence on long-term nuclear policy. Such strategists include Field Marshal Lord Carver and Lord Solly Zuckerman.

260. GELBER, H. G. "Australia, the U. S. and the Strategic Balance: Some Comments on the Joint Facilities." Australian Outlook 36 (August 1982): 12-21.

An overview of Australian defense needs and the presence of U. S. military forces on the continent. Presents the U. S. - Australian military relation as an open question for public debate between those who wish to abstain from superpower involvements, with their consequent risks of nuclear war, and those who regard Australian defense requirements as warranting the acceptance of such risks.

261. GLIKSMAN, Alex. "Under the Nuclear Gun: Three Keys to Europe's Bombs." Foreign Policy No. 39 (Summer 1980): 40-57.

Because Western Europe is uneasy over the reliability of the U. S. "nuclear umbrella," a new mode of nuclear co-responsibility is required. Proposes that individual European states possess warhead launching capability (the first key), and that these states and the U. S. possess duplicate keys for detonating the warheads. This would improve U. S. and European nuclear cooperation, it is said.

262. GRAY, Colin S. and Payne, Keith. "Under the Nuclear Gun: Victory is Possible." Foreign Policy No. 39 (Summer 1980): 14-27.

A blow in behalf of "limited" nuclear war. The authors think that the policy of deterrence is irresponsible, that what the U. S. ought to do is prepare to fight and "win" a nuclear war.

263. GUERTNER, Gary. "Nuclear War in Suburbia." Orbis 26 (Spring 1982): 46-69.

Speculates on the manner of a Soviet-Warsaw Pact invasion of West Germany; believes that tactical advantages would lead invaders to a city-hugging process; discusses tactical nuclear weapons, including neutron bombs. The mass urbanization of Western Europe puts strictures on the utility of nuclear weapons of any kind. The difficulty the Soviets would have in quickly securing Western Europe while maintaining control

over Eastern Europe contributes to the unlikelihood of invasion.

264. HOWARD, Michael E. "On Fighting a Nuclear War. "
International Security 5 (Spring 1981): 3-17.

Howard counterposes the traditional conception of nuclear deterrent with the presently fashionable notion of nuclear war-
fighting for the sake of political objectives, using Bernard
Brodie as a proponent of the former, Colin S. Gray (item
262) as advocate of the latter. Argues that though nuclear
war might achieve its object, "I doubt whether the survivors
on either side would very greatly care. " Believes that only
adequate conventional forces can serve as a deterrent that
could be employed in a non-suicidal way.

265. JONES, David R. "Nuclear War and Soviet Policy. "
International Perspectives (Nov 1982): 17-20.

Through analysis of current Soviet military writing, concludes
that the Soviet strategic policy is very similar to the for-
merly well-established U.S. deterrent policy abandoned by the
Reagan administration in the glow of "winnable" and protracted
nuclear wars. The irony is that--with the Soviets evidently
finally acknowledging that nuclear war is not an extension of
politics by other means--as the U.S. long contended--the
U.S. now wishes to assert the opposite. Jones edits the
Soviet Armed Forces Review Annual at Dalhousie University
in Halifax.

266. JOSEPH, Paul. "From Mad to Nuts: The Growing
Danger of Nuclear War. " Socialist Review 61 (Jan
1982): 13-56.

Reviews U.S. strategic policy from MAD (Mutually Assured
Destruction) to NUTs (Nuclear Utilization Target Selection).
NUT spokesmen believe in the possibility of containing nuclear
war at either a tactical or limited strategic level. The
greater threat of war posed by the NUT approach, together
with the increased tensions of the new Cold War, can be reduced through an American peace movement recognizing arms
control efforts as too important to link with other foreign
policy issues, and by forcing 1984 Democratic presidential
contender to commit himself to lowering the nuclear war
threat.

267. KAPLAN, Fred. "Bombs Awry. " Inquiry: A Libertarian Review 4 (Oct. 5, 1981): 6-8.

Explains the "bias" factor in missile guidance--the forces of
nature which would act to throw an ICBM off course. The
notion of extraordinary missile accuracy, one of the arguments used by the Reagan administration to propound the
"Window of Vulnerability" myth, is itself a myth, and makes
the MX missile superfluous.

268. KAVKA, Gregory S. "Deterrence, Utility, and Ra-
     tional Choice." Theory and Decision 12 (March 1980):
     41-60.

Argues that nuclear deterrence is morally defensible from a
standpoint of utilitarian ethics, i. e. , it is better to risk a
great disaster, nuclear war, than to submit to a smaller
disaster, domination by another superpower.

269. KEENY, Spurgeon M. , Jr. and Panofsky, Wolfgang
     K. H. "MAD Versus NUTS: Can Doctrine on Weap-
     onry Remedy the Mutual Hostage Relationship of the
     Superpowers?" Foreign Affairs 60 (Winter 1981/82):
     287-304.

The "limited" nuclear war-fighting possibilities envisioned by
NUTS advocates (item 266) allegedly offer a chance to avoid
MAD, mutual assured destruction. The authors contend that
NUTS is, if not crazy, then deluded, for the hostage state of
potential MADness still exists, and any attempt to go NUTS
would probably soon go MAD.

270. LACKEY, Douglas P. "Missiles and Morals: A Utili-
     tarian Look at Nuclear Deterrence." Philosophy &
     Public Affairs 11 (Summer 1982): 189-231.

Compares the probabilities of nuclear disaster contingent upon
three strategic policies: superiority, equivalence, and unilateral disarmament, and finds the latter preferable from a
utilitarian viewpoint. It is the least probable to lead to
nuclear war, either intentional or accidental.

271. McGEEHAN, Robert. "East-West Strategic Stability. "
     Contemporary Review 243 (July 1983): 8-14.

A nuclear deterrent advocate's analysis of the title issue.
Although pessimistic about the prospects for disarmament and
evidently content that, because of their mutual ability to
destroy each other war between the superpowers "is even
more improbable than it is unthinkable, " the author condemns
recent American Cold War "rhetorical belligerence" and the
"groundless American assertion" of strategic inferiority.

272. _____. "Europe and America in the Year of the Missiles." International Journal 38 (Winter 1982-83): 147-162.

Calls the European anti-nuclear movement "NATO's most threatening adversary." Analyzes the effects of the movement, along with erratic U. S. short-term policies, on stability of the Atlantic Alliance. A good statement of the conservative European position on deterrence.

273. McNAMARA, Robert S. "The Military Role of Nuclear Weapons: Perceptions and Misperceptions." Foreign Affairs 62 (Fall 1983): 59-80.

The former Secretary of Defense argues that nuclear weapons are militarily useless, since even "tactical" use would probably precipitate general war; their use as a deterrent increases the probability of nuclear war; McNamara argues in favor of improved conventional deterrence, nuclear-free zone in Europe, major cuts in nuclear weapons deployed in Europe. Includes discussion of Soviet perceptions of NATO policy.

274. MALCOLMSON, Robert W. "Dilemmas of the Nuclear Age." Queen's Quarterly 90 (Spring 1983): 16-28.

The central dilemma of nuclear weapons is that by threatening to use them on the enemy (which is the essence of deterrence) one threatens one's self with equal or greater affliction. "Deterrence theory ... strives to preserve peace and stability by asserting a willingness to act suicidally." Calls for close attention to the self-serving jargon and displacement of ill intent engaged in by both Soviets and U. S.

275. MANN, Paul S. "Panel Reexamines ICBM Vulnerability." Aviation Week and Space Technology 115 (July 13, 1981): 141 +

Reports on studies conducted under auspices of the Townes Committee (Charles Townes, chairman) set up by Defense Secretary Caspar Weinberger to examine MX basing proposals. The study receiving the most notice is that of J. Edward Anderson, who contends that the much-ballyhooed accuracy of ICBMs cannot be counted upon in an actual war situation, and that even a Soviet first strike on Minuteman silos could not destroy half of them. A fairly stunning report, considering this magazine's role as a forum for a general hard-line military outlook.

276. MOUNTBATTEN, Louis. "A Military Commander Surveys the Nuclear Arms Race." International Security 4 (Winter 1979/80): 3-5.

Dismisses the idea that tactical nuclear war could be prevented from reaching the strategic level; tactical warfare must be avoided through a military balance of forces between West and East.

277. "NATO C^3/EW/I." Armed Forces Journal International 120 (Dec 1982): 52-75.

The title makes clear the intended audience for this story-- one that has the jargon down pat. "C^3I" stands for "Command, Control, Communications & Intelligence." "EW" is "Electronic Warfare." There is, according to a Lockheed ad in this issue, an "Electronic Warfare community" consisting of "intelligence analysts, pilots, system builders, and key component suppliers." This collection of pieces under the acronymic rubric poses electronic combat as NATO's "warfare of the future" in which the "problem of nuclear war" consists mostly of the way nuclear blasts would render the whole electronic baggage useless. It is hard to escape the feeling when perusing this material that the so-called "Electronic Warfare community" can hardly wait to try out their toys.

278. "The New Missile Crisis." Inquiry: A Libertarian Review 6 (Feb 1983): 4.

Points out the U.S. failure to recognize the reason for the Soviet refusal to distinguish between strategic and "tactical" nuclear weapons. U.S. "tactical" weapons--the Cruise and Pershing II--could easily be employed in a strategic first strike on the U.S.S.R. Thus, a Pershing attack from West Germany would be the equivalent of an ICBM attack from the continental U.S., and would probably be responded to in the same way. Advocates withdrawal of U.S. forces from Europe.

279. RATHJENS, George and Ruina, Jack. "Nuclear Doctrine and Rationality." Daedalus 110 (Winter 1981): 179-189.

The authors discuss the U.S.-Soviet ability to destroy each other, nuclear-warfighting strategies, anti-ballistic missile systems, etc. They believe that we should pursue SALT, chiefly in hopes of reducing political tensions, though SALT will not provide a "fix" to nuclear dangers and to "unfortunate" international events.

280. REGEHR, Ernie. "From Deterrence to Intimidation. "
Our Generation 15 (Fall 1982): 50-55.

Regehr, an instructor at the University of Waterloo's Institute
of Peace and Conflict Studies, describes the expanding role of
nuclear weapons, now filling such capacities as deterring
limited military initiatives and for demonstration of national
resolve. Believes that Canada should reject all involvement
with the Cruise missile, support a Freeze and no-first-use
pledge, continue support for a comprehensive test ban and
ban on tests of warhead delivery vehicles.

281. REVENAL, Earl C. "Under the Nuclear Gun: Doing
Nothing. " Foreign Policy No. 39 (Summer 1980):
28-39.

The best response to the Soviet invasion of Afghanistan and a
possible future threat to the Middle East oil supply does not
include military measures. A military response would be
too costly, regarding lives of American soldiers, and, in the
case of the oil, would be a likely provocation to nuclear war,
which would be harder for U.S. citizens to endure than an
oil shortage.

282. ROSENBLUM, Simon. "MXing Up American Foreign
Policy. " Canadian Forum, May 1983, p. 16 +

The U.S. , believes the author, is a power in decline which
seeks to reassert itself not through diplomacy or "a meaningful political-economic approach to revolutionary upheavals and
North-South conflicts, " but through an expansion of nuclear
weapons from the role of deterrent to "coercion and intimidation. " U.S. development of first-strike weapons is intended
to allow the country greater freedom regarding intervention in
developing countries without risking confrontation with the
Soviet Union.

283. ROSENBERG, David A. " 'A Smoking Radiation Ruin
at the End of Two Hours': Documents on American
Plans for Nuclear War with the Soviet Union, 1954-
1955. " International Security 6 (Winter, 1981-82):
3-38.

Considers material contained in two declassified mid-1950s
U.S. defense documents in light of President Carter's Presidential Directive 59 "limited nuclear war" strategy.

• • •

"I know of no plan which gives reasonable assurance that nuclear weapons can be used beneficially in NATO's defense. "

--Robert S. McNamara,
Item 273, p. 72.

• • •

284. RUSSETT, Bruce and Deluca, Donald R. "Theater Nuclear Forces: Public Opinion in Western Europe. " Political Science Quarterly 98 (Summer 1983): 179-196.

An illuminating collection of graphs based on opinion polls, coupled with explanatory material, on a variety of war- and peace-related issues, including pacifism, attitudes toward use of nuclear weapons (fewer than 20 percent of the British favor resort to nuclear weapons in the event of an overwhelming Soviet conventional attack), etc. Concludes that NATO governments cannot ignore popular fears if the alliance is to survive.

285. SCHNEIDER, Barry R. "Invitation to a Nuclear Beheading. " Across the Board 20 (July-Aug. 1983): 8-16.

On the likely effort of the Soviets to destroy U.S. command centers, especially Washington, in the event of nuclear war. Because of the destruction of leadership, "Once begun, a nuclear exchange [i.e., "war"] between the superpowers is likely to be massive and virtually uncontrollable. "

286. SLOCOMBE, Walter. "The Countervailing Strategy. " International Security 5 (Spring 1981): 18-27.

Attacks on many fronts the change in U.S. strategic policy from that of deterrence to the concept of "limited" nuclear war, a change given White House imprimatur with Carter's Presidential Directive 59 (July 25, 1980), which changed U.S. strategic targeting priorities from economic and civilian to military. Like many others, Slocombe argues that this is a provocative first-strike strategy.

287. STEWART, Blair. "The Scowcroft Commission and the 'Window of Coercion. ' " Strategic Review 11 (Summer 1983): 21-27.

The author, who has an extensive background in development of U. S. strategic missiles, praises the Scowcroft Commission for recommending silo deployment of the MX, for such deployment would ward off dreaded "asymmetries" of strategic balance and "close the window" through which the Soviets might pull nuclear blackmail or worse. An interesting interpretation of the Commission's report, which pointed out that existing land-based U. S. missiles are not susceptible to an effective Soviet first strike. See item 238.

288. SZANTO. "Real Intelligence: The World According to Andropov. " CoEvolution Quarterly (No. 37, Spring 1983): 126-129.

An evaluation of Soviet intentions under Andropov, whom the author, employing the pseudonym above, describes as "a sophisticated and formidable player of geopolitical games" compared to the simplistic and nostalgic Reagan. The point: for the nuclear weapons Freeze to amount to more than mere moral outrage, it must recognize the nature of the games, and prove neither a pawn of Moscow nor a victim of Reagan.

289. TOLKUNOV, Lev. " 'Psychological War'--A Symptom of Nuclear Pathology. " Co-Existence: An International Journal 19 (Oct 1982): 142-157.

A pro-Soviet essay on the U. S. military buildup, the public statements of U. S. officials about nuclear war's reputed winability, and the Western propaganda campaign against the U. S. S. R. Some of this is transparently self-serving, but some of it is also perceptibly sincere. Useful for those trying to piece together the Soviet worldview.

290. TUCKER, Jonathan B. "Strategic Command and Control: America's Achilles Heel?" Technology Review 86 (Aug. -Sept. 1983): 38+

Discusses vulnerability of strategic command system in the event of nuclear war, with the resulting probability that authority over nuclear weapons launching has been delegated at relatively low levels by both the U. S. and Soviets. Tucker believes that strategic balance would be better served if both nations possessed invulnerable command systems, thus reducing the provocation to attempt a "decapitating" first-strike.

291. WEEDE, Erich. "Extended Deterrence by Superpower Alliance. " Journal of Conflict Resolution 27 (June 1983): 231-254.

Although Weede is not optimistic about the future of nuclear deterrence as a preventive of war, he finds here through empirical study of military conflicts on a global basis that nuclear deterrence has historically reduced the risk of war.

292.   ZUCKERMAN, Solly.   "Nuclear Weapons in Europe:
         Doctrines and Strategies. "   Bulletin of Peace Pro-
         posals 14 (No. 2, 1983):   115-118.

An interview with Lord Zuckerman, who argues that "modern-ization" of European nuclear forces has no military meaning given the present overwhelming deterrence in Western Europe's favor; accuses the Pentagon of "brainwashing" smaller NATO countries into acceptance of the Cruise and Pershing II; has similar opinions of other current nuclear issues advanced by the West.

•   •   •

"No government or social system is so evil that its people must be considered lacking in virtue.   As Americans, we find communism profoundly repugnant as a negation of personal freedom and dignity.   But we can still hail the Russian people for their many achievements--in science and space, in economic and industrial growth, in culture and in acts of courage. "

> --John F. Kennedy, in his
> American University Ad-
> dress, June 10, 1963.

•   •   •

● III ●

Upping the Ante: The Arms Race

"When history sifts the ashes it will almost inevitably turn
out that World War II taught but one lesson of transcendental
importance. It is this: that with unlimited money to spend,
we can buy an answer to any scientific problem. We laid
two billion dollars on the line and bought an atomic bomb."

--J. D. Ratcliff, Item 20,
p. xlii.

293. BAKER, David. The Shape of Wars to Come. Stein
     & Day, 1981. 262 p.

An essay written from a point of view within the "star wars"
syndrome, following the line that the U. S. S. R. is well ahead
of the U. S. in pursuit of ICBM-neutralizing particle-beam and
other space-to-earth systems.

294. BALDWIN, Hanson W. The Great Arms Race: A
     Comparison of U. S. and Soviet Power Today. Prae-
     ger, 1958. 116 p.

New York Times military editor Baldwin offers an immediately post-Sputnik "attempt to evaluate American strengths and
weaknesses vis-a-vis Soviet Russia in as measured a manner
as possible. " Marches point-by-point through the two nations'
military and civilian resources. Covers missiles, aircraft,
armies, etc. , and tries to ascertain who has the "lead. " Not
hysterical, unlike a good deal of popular opinionating following the Soviet space triumph.

295. BARNABY, Charles F. Arms Uncontrolled. Harvard
     University Press, 1975. 232 p.

A SIPRI (Stockholm International Peace Research Institute)
study surveying the global nature of the arms race, tactical
and strategic weapons systems and nuclear proliferation. Includes a table (p. 200, 201) showing year by year atomic
tests--atmospheric, underground and underwater--conducted
by the first five nations to join the "nuclear club. " As of
1973, these club-members had performed close to 1, 000
nuclear bomb tests on or in the planet.

296. _____ . Prospects for Peace. Pergamon, 1980.
     105 p.

We are drifting toward nuclear war by becoming accustomed
to "living with the bomb, " through conflict over energy supplies, nuclear proliferation, growing military spending, and
especially through the uncontrolled arms race between the
U. S. and the Soviet Union. Examines the roles of public
opinion, scientists, churches and trade unions in exerting
pressure toward relief from the nuclear threat.

297. BEARD, Edmund. Developing the ICBM: A Study in
     Bureaucratic Politics. Columbia University Press,
     1976, 273 p.

Focuses on the military aspects--the bureaucratic intrigue and factional rivalries, especially in the Air Force, 1945-1958-- which affected the ICBM's development.

298. BETTS, Richard K. , ed. Cruise Missiles: Technology, Strategy, Politics. Brookings Institution, 1981. 612 p.

An exhaustive collection of papers on the Cruise, evaluating it from almost every conceivable angle: economic, political, technological, strategic--and from a variety of attitudes. See particularly the chapter by James Foster and Bruce Bennett, which makes the Cruise's utility look dubious from any military vantage.

299. BOBROW, Davis B. , ed. Weapons Systems Decisions: Political and Psychological Perspectives on Continental Defense. Praeger, 1969. 282 p.

The sociological jargon is off-putting, but this compilation of material resulting from studies by various social scientists in 1965 does offer some insights into mid-1960s thinking on U. S. perceptions of the military ambitions and attitudes of the U. S. S. R. and China. Lack of an index hurts.

300. BOTTOME, Edgar M. The Balance of Terror: A Guide to the Arms Race. Beacon Press, 1971. 215 p.

Argues that the U. S. has been "fundamentally responsible for every major escalation of the arms race. " Surveys such components of the race as the B-36 and the hydrogen bomb, tactical nuclear weapons, strategic thinking, etc. Of special interest: "The Missile Gap: A Study in Myth Creation. " Many authorities now contend that at the height of the notorious "missile gap" non-issue, the U. S. S. R. possessed anywhere from four to a dozen ICBMs. Bottome analyzes Soviet nuclear strategy pertinent to the "gap, " the gap's budgetary, partisan and military effects, and effects abroad.

• • •

"It's a boy!"

> --Edward Teller, excited over a successful bomb test at Eniwetok. Item 819, p. 542.

• • •

301. BRODIE, Bernard and Brodie, Fawn. From Crossbow
      to H-Bomb. Indiana University Press, 1973. 320 p.

"A history, " says the introduction, "of the application of
science to war. " The last three chapters cover the "nuclear
revolution. "

302. CARLTON, David and Schaerf, Carlo, eds. Dynamics
      of the Arms Race. Wiley, 1975. 244 p.

Nuclear, chemical and biological warfare. Articles on MIRV
(Multiple Independently Targetable Re-entry Vehicles), SALT,
anti-submarine war, verification of arms control, etc. Contributors include both well and lesser-known authors who represent a wide range of positions, from national-security
first advocates to quasi-pacifists.

303. CHAPMAN, John L. Atlas: The Story of a Missile.
      Harper, 1960. 190 p.

The Atlas was the first U.S. ICBM. Chapman, editorial
board member of the aeronautics firm which built the missile,
provides a detailed history.

304. CLARK, Ronald W. The Greatest Power on Earth:
      The International Race for Nuclear Supremacy. Har-
      per & Row, 1981. 342 p.

A readable history of the bomb and related issues.

305. CLEMENS, Walter C. The Arms Race and Sino-Soviet
      Relations. Hoover Institution on War, Revolution and
      Peace, 1968. 335 p.

How China's possession of the bomb affects the course of
East-West arms control and disarmament. Detailed study of
Soviet and Chinese positions regarding Marxist-Leninist doctrine on questions concerning the inevitability of war, disarmament, containment vs. détente; also covers nuclear proliferation, nuclear testing and other issues connected with
China's "nuclear club" status.

306. COHEN, S. T. The Neutron Bomb: Political, Tech-
      nological and Military Issues. Institute for Foreign
      Policy Analysis, Inc. , 1978. 95 p.

The neutron bomb, more properly called an enhanced radiation bomb, has long been the focus of intense debate. Those

who favor it see it as an effective "anti-personnel" weapon
of limited geographic impact which would serve to heighten
deterrence of attack and to reduce likelihood of having to rely
on "tactical" nuclear bombs. Those who oppose it do so on
two basic grounds: the belief that because it is a nuclear
weapon, its use would encourage prompt escalation to tactical
nuclear warfare, and that its mode of action--killing through
radiation--causes death of such intense and lingering agony
that it belongs in the same class of "banned" weapons as
poison gas. (By far the most shallow argument from any
direction regarding the neutron bomb, yet one frequently used
by its opponents, is that it constitutes "the ultimate capitalist
weapon" in that it destroys life with minimal damage to property. This is nonsense. The radius of property damage
from a neutron bomb would be close to that of a Nagasaki-
size nuclear bomb. Property in the vicinity of a neutron
bomb burst would be every bit as thoroughly demolished as
any life forms unlucky enough to be present.)

Cohen, the bomb's chief developer, provides a history of the
weapon, including coverage of political debate, effects and
military applications.

307. _____ . The Truth about the Neutron Bomb: The
Inventor of the Bomb Speaks Out. William Morrow,
1983. 226 p.

Cohen claims that "our strategic nuclear capabilities are weak
and inadequate, " that the neutron bomb's public reputation is
a fraud (see above annotation), and that it wouldn't make any
difference anyway in the Western European arsenal, since in
any attack on Western Europe the U. S. S. R. would erase neutron repositories with its own nuclear bombs. Europe, thinks
Cohen, is indefensible because the Europeans are not interested in defending themselves. Pleads for stronger defense of the continental U. S. ; includes a dismissal of radiation poisoning as an affliction whose discomforts have been
overstated. This last argument is quite unconvincing.

308. COLLINS, John M. America and Soviet Military Trends:
Since the Cuban Missile Crisis. Center for Strategic
Studies, 1978. 496 p.

A study of weapons, systems, and strategy by a defense
specialist in the American Congressional Research Service;
extensive attention to compared strengths of U. S. and Soviet
Union, of NATO and the Warsaw Pact.

309. COX, Arthur M. The Dynamics of Détente: How to End the Arms Race. Norton, 1976. 256 p.

An introduction to the arms race; explains nuclear weapons systems, U. S. defense policy (which Cox believes is based on outmoded views), and proposes that the U. S. can only end the arms race by settling for parity with the Soviet Union.

310. _____. Russian Roulette: The Superpower Game. Times Books, 1982. 248 p.

Attacks wishful calls for U. S. nuclear superiority, assails the U. S. S. R. for Third-World adventurism as a provocation to superpower crisis, castigates the Reagan administration's lackadaisical approach to arms control, and gives Soviet Americanologist Georgy Arbatov a chapter to elucidate the Soviet view of arms control.

311. EDWARDS, John. Superweapon: The Making of the MX. W. W. Norton, 1982. 287 p.

Identifies technological change as the reason for the MX's existence. Based to a large extent on interviews with scientists, politicians and military officials, the book presents the history of the missile from its introduction in 1970 through the early 1980s. Edwards opposes the weapon as a threat to mutual deterrence. [See also item 328.]

312. FELD, Bernard T., et. al. Impact of New Technologies on the Arms Race: A Pugwash Monograph. MIT Press, 1971. 379 p.

Covers then-new nuclear bomb technology, ballistic missile guidance, safeguards of nuclear materials, anti-ballistic missile systems among other hardware issues. The Pugwash Conferences on Science and World Affairs have been held periodically since their inception in 1957 as the result of an appeal by Bertrand Russell, Albert Einstein, and other scientists to the scientific community regarding the dangers of nuclear war.

● ● ●

"Unless the whole military establishment is geared to nuclear tactics, nuclear war becomes a highly dangerous adventure. "
--Henry Kissinger, Item 177, p. 197.

● ● ●

313.   GANTZ, Lieut. Col. Kenneth F., ed. The United States
        Air Force Report on the Ballistic Missile: Its Tech-
        nology, Logistics and Strategy. Doubleday, 1958.
        338 p.

First published in Air University Quarterly Review, this study
covers the Air Force's missile development, but not that of
the Navy. A quantity of shifty obscurantism can be found,
e. g., the destruction of cities is referred to as the "neutrali-
zation of complete target systems." As for the missiles' use,
the aim and hope is for deterrence alone. "Although not in-
dicated in the foreseeable future, public opinion in support of
a world authority may bring about an eventual understanding
and acceptance of the implications of the ballistic missile era.
The United States, by all means, should encourage any over-
tures in this direction."

314.   GRAHAM, Daniel O. High Frontier. TOR, 1983.
        314 p.

An excited campaign for a space-based anti-ballistic missile
system designed to close the U. S.'s "window of vulnerability"
to Soviet first strike so widely advertised by the Reagan administration, and then slammed shut by the Scowcroft Commission, which proclaimed the U. S. land-based deterrent in
firm and reliable condition. Introduction by, of all people,
Robert Heinlein.

315.   GRAY, Colin S. The MX ICBM and National Security.
        Praeger, 1981. 173 p.

Gray is a charter member of the "we can win a nuclear war
with only 20 million dead" school; here he offers probably the
best available argument for development of the MX, which is
not to say that it is a good argument. Does include a good
bibliography, however.

316.   GREENWOOD, Ted. Making the MIRV: A Study of
        Defense Decision Making. Ballinger, 1975. 237 p.

Revision of a doctoral dissertation attending to technological,
organizational, political, and other aspects involved in the
procurement of the MIRV warhead. Among the author's concluding points: weapons innovation cannot survive without political support; the critical moment in the life of a weapons
system is the entry into engineering development; the technological community plays an important part in the weapons acquisition process; the Arms Control and Disarmament Agency
and special interest groups are not of prime influence.

317. GRIFFITHS, Franklyn and Polyani, John C., eds.
The Dangers of Nuclear War: A Pugwash Symposium.
University of Toronto Press, 1979. 197 p.

Ten position papers from the 30th Pugwash conference; the
conclusion is that the danger of nuclear war is increasing
greatly because of both the superpower arms race and because of nuclear proliferation.

318. HOLLOWAY, David. The Soviet Union and the Arms
Race. Yale University Press, 1983. 211 p.

Examines the role of the military in the Soviet system, especially that of the nuclear forces. Contends that the prime
objective of the U.S.S.R. regarding nuclear arms is to avoid
nuclear war, for, though it would conduct such war to the
best of its ability, Soviet leaders recognize that even a nom-
inally-victorious nuclear war contender would be left in a
catastrophic situation. Influence on the Soviet economic system of the arms race is also crucial; the race has become
a brake on the Soviet non-military sector. Urges that the
West use this fact to its advantage, since, in a period of
deteriorating relations, it affords a route of possible amelioration. Makes it clear that the ability of the Soviet state to
suppress public demand for consumer goods to divert resources to the military should not be underestimated.

319. LAPP, Ralph E. Arms Beyond Doubt: The Tyranny
of Weapons Technology. Cowles, 1970. 210 p.

Khrushchev once remarked that "what the scientists have in
their briefcases is terrifying," and Lapp agrees. Possibilities of technology push military and civilian officials into the
embrace of weapons--the ABM, the MIRV, etc.--which do not
enhance strength as much as they threaten stability.

320. LENS, Sidney. The Day Before Doomsday: An Ana-
tomy of the Nuclear Arms Race. Doubleday, 1977.
274 p.

Reviews the arms race, points to its logical conclusion (global
extinction) and urges the public to press its leaders for a halt
to the race.

321. McGUIRE, Martin C. Secrecy and the Arms Race: A
Theory of the Accumulation of Strategic Weapons and
How Secrecy Affects It. Harvard University Press,
1965. 249 p.

The theory is based to considerable extent in mathematics and will deter the non-mathematically oriented; there is, however, enough comprehensible reflection on the nature, uses, and desirability of secrecy and its relation to armaments to reward the diligent layman's investigation.

322. MOSS, Norman. Men Who Play God: The Story of the H-Bomb and How the World Came to Live with It. Harper & Row, 1968. 352 p.

"So Far" might well be the last two words of the subtitle. An enjoyable (for its genre) history covering development of and political and strategic reaction to the "superbomb." "At some point," writes Moss, "the superpowers will probably have to agree to reduce their forces to a minimum-deterrence level.... [S]uch an arms control agreement would have to come in a détente atmosphere...." Lacks documentation, unfortunately, but has a good index.

323. MOULTON, Harland B. From Superiority to Parity: The United States and the Strategic Arms Race, 1961-1971. Greenwood Press, 1974. 333 p.

Further argument that U.S.-proclaimed missile and bomber "gaps" were fictitious; maintains that "superiority" in nuclear weapons provides no real political or military advantage.

324. MYRDAL, Alva. The Game of Disarmament: How the United States and Russia Run the Arms Race. Pantheon, 1977. 397 p.

Myrdal spent over a decade as Sweden's representative in multilateral disarmament talks. Accuses the U.S. and the U.S.S.R. of tacit collusion in perpetuating the arms race; is particularly concerned that Europe may be sacrificed in a "limited" nuclear war. Makes several proposals on how the arms race may be stopped.

● ● ●

"In a sense I feel sometimes in my anti-nuclear and peace work like a German standing outside Auschwitz protesting the construction of the ovens."
                                                    --Mavis Belisle, Item 611,
                                                         p. 33.

● ● ●

325. PLATE, Thomas G. Understanding Doomsday: A
Guide to the Arms Race for Hawks, Doves and People. Simon & Schuster, 1971. 221 p.

A good introduction with still-vital insights. Points out that
the arms race is not fueled so much by international crises as
it is by a grasping at short-term political and economic gains
"in the back yards of Moscow and Washington" enabled by a
continuation of the arms race.

326. RITCHIE, David. Spacewar. Atheneum, 1982. 224 p.

An historical overview, with implications of things to come, of
the employment of outer space as a battle forum and as a post
for observation of one's opponents' terrestrial business. Significant background for an informed attitude toward present
exhilaration in some circles over the prospects of moving the
arms race into orbit. Includes a long bibliography.

327. SALKELD, Robert. War and Space. Prentice-Hall,
1970. 195 p.

An authority on space with opinions on Soviet intentions and
capacities urges that the U.S. turn to space as a setting for
a nuclear deterrent.

328. SCOVILLE, Herbert. MX: Prescription for Disaster.
MIT Press, 1981. 231 p.

One of the most intelligently-argued books of the 1980s concerning not only the likely destabilizing consequences of the
original MX deployment plan, but the arms race and the issue
of strategic balance in general. Scoville is a former Assistant Director of the U.S. Arms Control and Disarmament
Agency.

329. SHERWIN, Martin J. A World Destroyed: The Atomic
Bomb and the Grand Alliance. Knopf, 1975. 315 p.

As the record relentlessly shows, most scientists who developed the bomb promptly recognized the overriding need for
international control of nuclear energy and weapons. Sherwin
analyzes the Anglo-American effort to freeze the U.S.S.R. out
of the nuclear picture, an effort which, he contends, was a
major impetus toward the Cold War and the arms race. Shows
how Roosevelt neglected to rely on advice of such scientists
as Vannevar Bush and Neils Bohr, who regarded schemes to
retain the U.S. atomic monopoly in the postwar period as

hopeless and self-defeating. One of the best books available on the interplay among scientists concerned with long-term prospects and government officials concerned with short-term political gain.

330. TOBIAS, Sheila, et al. What Kinds of Guns are They Buying for Your Butter? A Beginner's Guide to Defense, Weaponry, and Military Spending. Morrow, 1982. 428 p.

An excellent overview of strategic weapons, their evolution, the "logic" of nuclear deterrence, attempts to control the arms race, defense controversies of the 1980s (the MX, the B-1 bomber, anti-satellite warfare); good glossary.

331. YORK, Herbert. Race to Oblivion: A Participant's View of the Arms Race. Simon & Schuster, 1970. 256 p.

York helped develop the A-bomb, was the first director of defense research and engineering for the Department of Defense; he discusses past and present weapons-development mistakes that he believes have spun the arms race out of control. "All of us, " he writes, "not just the current 'in' group of experts and technicians, must involve ourselves in creating the policies and making the decisions necessary" to avoid the destination the title refers to.

• • •

"This present monstrous catastrophe is the outcome of forty-three years of skilful, industrious, systematic world armament. Only by a disarmament as systematic, as skilful and as devoted may we hope to achieve centuries of peace. "

--H. G. Wells in "The Peace of the World, " The Works of H. G. Wells, vol. 21, Scribner's, 1926.

• • •

• Periodical Articles •

332. "Burdens of Militarization. " International Social Science Journal 25 (No. 1, 1983).

This issue of the Unesco-published journal concentrates on the issues of military research and development, the impact of militarization on the Third World, and prospects for conversion from war to peace-oriented economies.

333. CANTOR, Ileen. "Lost in Space." SANE World: A Newsletter of Action on Disarmament and the Peace Race 21 (Oct. 1982): 1-2.

Brief coverage of the military move to space, with a focus on the economic costs, dangers and complications posed for arms control.

334. FRANK, Jerome D. "Prenuclear-age Leaders and the Nuclear Arms Race." American Journal of Ortho-psychiatry 52 (Oct. 1982): 630-637.

In spite of their status as revolutionary weapons, nuclear arms tend to be visualized by national leaders and their followers in the context of a future world war along conventional lines. Discussion of routes toward diminished world tension through international cooperation.

335. GALBRAITH, John Kenneth. "The Economics of the Arms Race--and After." Bulletin of the Atomic Scientists 37 (June-July 1981): 13-16.

Argues that the arms race, pursued under the illusion that it enables protection of the political and socio-economic system, not only endangers that system by increasing the risks of nuclear war, but meanwhile damages it by drawing off resources for military pursuits which could have gone into civilian interests. No economic system, capitalist or communist, could survive nuclear war.

336. GORDON, Michael R. "Highly Touted Assault Breaker Weapon Caught Up in Internal Pentagon Debate." National Journal 15 (Oct. 22, 1983): 2152-2157.

The "Assault Breaker" is a complex system combining aerial radar, ground control, and "smart" munitions designed to slow a Soviet tank attack on Western Europe without resorting to nuclear weapons. Although supported in many circles, the system has not won the Pentagon's confidence in its ability to perform under actual battle conditions. This is a detailed discussion of one brand of "high tech" conventional weapon.

337. GSPONER, Andre. "The Neutron Bomb and the Other New Limited Nuclear War Weapons." Bulletin of Peace Proposals 13 (No. 3, 1982): 221-225.

Summarizes the effects of blast, heat, electromagnetic pulse and radiation, of the various kinds of nuclear bombs, including the neutron and other "second generation" weapons. Also brief discussion of laser, micro-wave, and particle-beam development and applications.

338. HALLINAN, Conn. "Reagan Plans for 'Death Stars'. " People's World 46 (April 2, 1983): 3.

An essay in this Berkeley, California based Marxist-Socialist paper accusing the Reagan administration of jingoistic preparation for initiating nuclear attack on the Soviet Union through space-war research and development.

339. KAKU, Michio. "Wasting Space: Countdown to a First Strike. " Progressive 47 (June 1983): 19-22.

Critical examination of the Reagan administration's space-war visions. The author regards them as part of the Reaganites' overall plan to insure a "successful" first strike against the Soviet Union through revised ICBM targeting, antimissile weapons and civil defense.

340. KLARE, Michael T. "Conventional Arms Sales: Stoking the Nuclear Fire. " MERIP Reports 13 (Feb. 1983): 3-4.

Claims that transfers of non-nuclear munitions to the Middle East have heightened the likelihood of nuclear war three ways: 1) by increasing the intensity of wars, thus pushing participants to nuclear use to escape defeat; 2) conventional weapons --e. g. , missiles--provide delivery means for nuclear warheads; 3) the fate of the arms recipient is bound to the arms supplier, thus increasing the risk of superpower confrontation in any Middle East war.

341. MACK, John E. "The Perception of U. S. Soviet Intentions and Other Psychological Dimensions of the Nuclear Arms Race. " American Journal of Orthopsychiatry 52 (Oct. 1982): 590-599.

In light of U. S. stimulation of the nuclear arms race suggests that those in the mental health field need to pay closer attention to the medical consequences of nuclear war, the way those in authority conceive of their responsibilities, and the effect of the nuclear threat on children.

342. MEDVEDEV, Roy and Medvedev, Zhores. "The U. S. S. R.

and the Arms Race. " New Left Review 1 (Nov.
1981): 5-22.

A significant essay by the two Soviet dissidents, who treat
U. S. -Soviet relations, the U. S. failure to acknowledge its
irretrievable loss of control over the Third World, the hope
and responsibilities of the peace/antinuclear movement in
Western Europe (which they consider the major barrier to a
full-blown new Cold War). Maintains that Soviet conservatism
has prevented development of a "military industrial complex"
with the autonomy flaunted by that of the U. S., and that every
important escalation of the nuclear arms race has been at the
initiative of the U. S.

343.   MILLER, Steven E.   "The Politics of Saving the MX. "
        New Leader 66 (May 2, 1983): 5-7.

The author, assistant director of Harvard's Center for Science
and International Affairs, dissects recommendations of the
Scowcroft Commission, which advised producing 100 MX
missiles for placement in Minuteman silos. Shows the Scowcroft recommendations as calculated for broad political appeal, but holding out promises unlikely to prove of substance.
Highly doubtful about the advisability of the MX.

344.   PAINE, Christopher.   "On the Beach: The RDF and
        the Arms Race. " MERIP Reports 13 (Jan. 1983):
        3-11.

"Is it possible for the Rapid Deployment Force to storm the
beaches of the Persian Gulf without leaving all of us on the
brink of nuclear annihilation?" asks Paine. Portrays the
Force as a trigger to set off first nuclear use by the U. S.
should the Force become hopelessly overmatched, which is
the strong possibility should it see action.

345.   "Paying Lip Service to Peace. " Northern Sun News 6
        (Sept. 1983): 2 +

NSN, an antinuclear tabloid from Minneapolis, features news
and criticism on all nuclear fronts. This editorial condemns
the Reagan administration's cliché fixation on the "Soviet
threat" as a rationale for speeding up the arms race with the
Cruise and Pershing II missiles.

● IV ●

All God's Children Got Bombs:
Nuclear Weapons Proliferation

The bombings of Hiroshima and Nagasaki "proved beyond peradventure that life in an international society whose members were competing in the production of atomic weapons would be intolerably precarious. "

--James Phinney Baxter,
1946. Item 780, p. 448.

346. BARNABY, Charles F., ed. Preventing the Spread of Nuclear Weapons. Souvenir, 1969. 374 p.

Valuable for contributions by Eastern European and Soviet physicists among the 45 representatives at a 1968 London meeting. On technical, political aspects and safeguards.

347. BEATON, Leonard. Must the Bomb Spread? Penguin Books, 1966. 147 p.

Addresses the general problem's technical and political aspects, the spread of plutonium, etc. " ... [I]t may be doubted if any viable system of international security could be successfully sustained. The best that could be hoped for would be a situation so intolerable to everyone that an organized world security system would become unavoidable" given rampant nuclear proliferation.

348. BOARDMAN, Robert and Keeley, James, eds. Nuclear Exports & World Politics. St. Martin's Press, 1983. 256 p.

Essays by the editors and others on nuclear export policies, the nuclear politics of France, West Germany, Canada and Australia, etc.

349. BRENNER, Michael J. Nuclear Power and Non-Proliferation: The Remaking of U.S. Policy. Cambridge University Press, 1981. 324 p.

Deals with the problem as it has stood since 1974, the year India obtained the bomb, when the demand for nuclear power began to grow because of the oil crisis, and when fuel-producing technologies applicable to weapons-development became commercialized. Based on observation and extensive interviews, focuses in detail on actions of the Ford and Carter administrations.

350. BUCHAN, Alastair, ed. World of Nuclear Powers? Prentice-Hall, 1966. 176 p.

Studies preliminary to the International Assembly on Nuclear Weapons, held in Scarborough, Canada in 1966. Difficulties in preventing proliferation, problems for international order raised by such proliferation; measures smaller powers might take to enhance security given superpower failure to reach accord on the issue. Harvard Government Professor Stanley Hoffman's essay on "Nuclear Proliferation and World Politics" is a useful introduction to the title topic and to a variety of nuclear psychological considerations.

351. CERVENKA, Zdenek and Rogers, Barbara. The Nuclear Axis: Secret Collaboration between West Germany and South Africa. Times Books, 1978. 464 p.

Maintains that sub-rosa assistance to South African nuclear scientists by West Germany has put the bomb within South Africa's grasp.

352. DeVOLPI, Alexander. Proliferation, Plutonium & Policy: Institutional & Technological Impediments to Nuclear Weapons Propagation. Pergamon, 1979. 361 p.

The author, a nuclear physicist, refers to the specter of proliferation as our "nuclear agony," but believes that "all but a few more nations" can be prevented from acquiring the bomb. Addresses the seriousness of proliferation, possible countermeasures, suggested policy decisions. The computer-produced camera-ready text makes for difficult reading.

353. DUNN, Lewis A. Controlling the Bomb: Nuclear Proliferation in the 1980s. Yale University Press, 1982. 209 p.

Proliferation is inevitable, but can be slowed and controlled; assumes that the U.S. must bear primary responsibility for achieving control.

354. DURIE, Sheila and Edwards, Rob. Fueling the Nuclear Arms Race: The Links between Nuclear Power and Nuclear Weapons. Pluto Press, 1982. 130 p.

A British parallel to the power/bomb link demonstrated most prominently in the U.S. by Amory Lovins. Contends that nuclear power has two faces inextricably joined, one "peaceful," the other martial; "unless all nuclear technologies are recognised as potential weapons technologies, permanent and total disarmament will remain illusory."

355. EDELHERTZ, Herbert and Walsh, Marilyn. The White-Collar Challenge to Nuclear Safeguards. Lexington Books, 1978. 101 p.

Explores the challenge to proliferation safeguards "presented by the so-called white-collar adversary who would employ guile and deception rather than force to achieve unauthorized objectives with respect to nuclear materials. " Following general background on white-collar crime, deals with the "Conceptual Schema of White-Collar Threats to the Nuclear Industry. " Argues that present safeguard systems are poorly attuned to coping with the white-collar threat.

356. EPSTEIN, William. The Last Chance: Nuclear Pro-
     liferation and Arms Control. Free Press, 1976.
     341 p.

Identifies Argentina, Canada, West Germany, Israel, Italy, Japan, South Africa, Sweden and Taiwan as on the verge of joining the "Nuclear Club. " (Argentina announced in Novem-ber of 1983 that it has the ability to build the bomb). Ep-stein worked on arms control for the U.N. for a quarter century. He believes that proliferation is an issue that can-not be dealt with apart from the superpower arms race.

● ● ●

For, oh, two or three months. ...

"People in a postwar world following a large war would for a time have to get by on a much lower standard of living than that to which they were accustomed. "
                                        --Herman Kahn, Item 167,
                                              p. 87.

● ● ●

357. GRAHAM, Thomas W. and Evers, Ridgely C. Bib-
     liography: Nuclear Proliferation. U.S. Government
     Printing Office, 1978. 159 p.

An annotated bibliography of books, periodical articles, U.S. documents and other materials. Includes a subject index.

358. GUHIN, Michael A. Nuclear Paradox: Security Risks
     of the Peaceful Atom. American Enterprise Institute
     for Public Policy Research, 1976. 77 p.

Dire and doomsday forecasts, writes Guhin, need not be in-voked to point out that problems of nuclear weapons prolifera-tion, given the spread of nuclear power, require serious at-tention. Surveys the extent of the problem, and discusses ap-proaches to security risks. Includes selected bibliography.

359. HEFFERNAN, Patrick, et al. The First Nuclear World
     War: A New Vision of National Security to Stop the
     Spread of the Bomb. Morrow, 1983. 437 p.

Nuclear weapons proliferation, abetted by civilian nuclear installations, all but guarantees nuclear war. The authors' remedy is the "soft path" alternative to nuclear power, including wind and solar energy.

360. IMAI, Ryukichi and Rowen, Henry. Nuclear Energy Proliferation: Japanese and American Views. Westview Press, 1980. 194 p.

Imai manages the Japan Atomic Power Co., Rowen is a former Deputy Assistant Secretary of Defense. The two divide the book between them, and thus illustrate conflicting international views on the proliferation threat posed by nuclear power, and on measures that might be taken to reduce the danger.

361. JASANI, Bhupendra, ed. Nuclear Proliferation Problems. MIT Press, 1974. 312 p.

Proceedings of a SIPRI-sponsored conference held in 1973. In four main parts: "Nuclear Technology, " "NPT [Non-Proliferation Treaty] Safeguards, " "Cooperation in the Peaceful Applications of Nuclear, " and "Security Problems of Non-Nuclear Weapon States. " Within these parts various authors cover nuclear fuel fabrication plants and programs in different countries, uranium enrichment and weapons proliferation, weapon research and development, and the NPT safeguards in the context of previously-agreed upon treaties regarding nuclear weapons.

362. JENSEN, Lloyd. Return from the Nuclear Brink: National Interest and the Nuclear Nonproliferation Treaty. Lexington Books, 1974. 150 p.

The title is deceptive, for Jensen sees considerable difficulty in persuading nations close to the bomb to refrain from carrying through their projects. Written within a political scientist's framework of hypothesis testing; argues that nations which did not sign the NPT, first approved by the U.N. General Assembly in 1968, either lack allegiance to the U.S. or the Soviet Union, or are involved in regional disputes, as are India and Pakistan.

363. KAPUR, Ashok. India's Nuclear Option: Atomic Diplomacy and Decision Making. Praeger, 1976. 295 p.

Investigates India's nuclear behavior from the 1950s to the 1970s; says that India sets forth to the world an image of cer-

tainty in decision making, but that internally its national policy is marked by failure to react to external factors in the
nation's security and by a tendency of Indian scientists to
provide scientific advice that will be welcome in the pre-
vailing political atmosphere. Good study of India as a nuclear "power in the middle. "

364. _____ . International Nuclear Proliferation: Multilateral Diplomacy & Regional Aspects. Praeger,
1979. 387 p.

On proliferation in general (definitions, political background,
diplomacy, nuclear safeguards) and in particular places:
South Asia, South Africa, Japan, Brazil and Argentina.

365. LAWRENCE, Robert M. and Larus, Joel, eds. Nuclear Proliferation: Phase Two. University Press
of Kansas. 1974. 275 p.

Nine essays on proliferation issues, most dealing with a specific nation, including Australia, West Germany, India, Israel,
Japan and South Africa. "Phase II" refers to proliferation
following the 1970 Nonproliferation Treaty.

366. LEACHMAN, Robert B. and Althoff, Philip, eds.
Preventing Nuclear Theft: Guidelines for Industry
and Government. Praeger, 1972. 377 p.

Proceedings of a 1971 symposium at Kansas State University.
Lack of an index (typical of symposia collections) is a draw-
back, but the table of contents is good. In the major section
treats safeguards generally; the national safeguard system;
the international system; thefts, criminology, the nuclear fuel
cycle, and so on.

367. LOVINS, Amory B. and Lovins, L. Hunter. Energy/
War: Breaking the Nuclear Link. Harper & Row,
1981. 164 p.

"In an era when the total explosive power released in World
War II is encapsulated in single bombs that can fit beneath a
bed, the conviction grows: We shall all blow each other up;
the only question is when. " --The devil's advocate, speaking
in the introduction. How "peaceful" reactors fuel the weapons
buildup. How to implement a non-nuclear future.

368. MARKEY, Edward J. Nuclear Peril: The Politics of
Nuclear Proliferation. Ballinger, 1982. 183 p.

An antinuclear Congressman contends that to help prevent nuclear oblivion the U.S. should 1) establish itself as a non-proliferation leader; 2) more actively work toward a halt of the superpower arms race; 3) dismantle its nuclear power installations; and 4) get out of the nuclear export business.

369. MELLER, Eberhard, ed. Internationalization: An Alternative to Nuclear Proliferation? Oelgeschlager, 1980. 159 p.

A collection of papers from the Salzberg Seminar on American Studies (1978), whose basic argument is that international control of nuclear fuel is a better counter to weapons proliferation than are independent supplier-purchaser arrangements.

370. OVERHOLT, William H., ed. Asia's Nuclear Future. Westview Press, 1978. 285 p.

Nuclear weapons conditions or potentials in China, Japan, Taiwan, S. Korea, Indonesia, the Philippines, Australia, India, Pakistan and Iran. Concludes with the editor's essay "A U.S. Nuclear Posture for Asia," "which would demonstrate to key countries which are potential nuclear powers that the U.S. is moving toward less, rather than more, reliance on nuclear weapons--in accordance with promises made in the Nonproliferation Treaty."

371. PAJAK, Roger F. Nuclear Proliferation in the Middle East: Implications for the Superpowers. National Defense University Press, 1982. 117 p.

The author states that because the nuclear "code of conduct," involving policy, rhetoric, technology, and communication, which stands between U.S.-Soviet nuclear confrontation does not apply among Middle Eastern nations, this area's instability has been further heightened by the imminent--or existing-- nuclear weapons capability of several of the states. Offers some remedial suggestions, such as a joint U.S.-Soviet security guarantee for all Mid-East nations, "perhaps built around a nuclear-free zone."

372. POTTER, William C. Nuclear Power & Nonproliferation: An Interdisciplinary Perspective. Oelgeschlager, 1982. 281 p.

Provides an overview of and historical context for the proliferation difficulty; examines nuclear power technology, economics, and politics, as well as strategies for containing proliferation. Stresses "the multicausal nature of the spread of nuclear weapons and the need to tailor nonproliferation measures to specific cases." Has a nice annotated bibliography.

373. QUESTER, George H., ed. Nuclear Proliferation: Breaking the Chain. University of Wisconsin Press, 1981. 245 p.

Eleven essays on the topic. "Preventing Proliferation: The Impact on International Politics," is a possible antidote from despair over the proliferation issue.

374. _____ . Politics of Nuclear Proliferation. Johns Hopkins University Press, 1973. 249 p.

Quester obtained data for this book from conversations with individuals familiar with the nuclear decision-making process in various then non-nuclear nations, from India to South Africa. Useful for probing official thinking processes.

375. ROCHLIN, Gene I. Plutonium, Power, and Politics: International Arrangements for the Disposition of Spent Nuclear Fuel. University of California Press, 1979. 397 p.

"There are no 'solutions,' whether technical, institutional, or political to nuclear proliferation." The best we can expect is continued effort to make the acquisition of nuclear weapons politically unattractive, and to safeguard the nuclear fuel cycle effectively. A dense, scholarly work.

● ● ●

"All God's children got guns!"
                                                    --The Marx Brothers,
                                                       Duck Soup, 1933.

● ● ●

376. SANDERS, Benjamin. Safeguards Against Nuclear Proliferation. MIT Press, 1975. 114 p.

A discussion of the International Atomic Energy Agency's proliferation safeguards system.

377. SCHOETTLE, Enid. Postures for Non-Proliferation: Arms Limitation and Security Policies to Minimize Nuclear Proliferation. Taylor & Francis, 1979. 168 p.

A SIPRI study covering various policies, especially of nuclear-weapons states, along with discussion of negotiations on the Non-Proliferation Treaty, 1965-1968.

378. SESHAGIRI, Narasimhiah. The Bomb! Fallout of
India's Nuclear Explosion. Vikas Publishing House,
1975. 147 p.

India exploded her first nuclear bomb on May 18, 1974. This
chronicle of the Indian bomb by a scientist close to the event
is marked by what is either a stupefying naïveté, or by a
barefaced duplicity, for the author asserts that the Indian
weapon is a "Peace Bomb" (a lot of those around, aren't
there?) intended only as a constructive tool for the likes of
mining, harbor-building, and such. "That explains the immense technological possibilities of nuclear explosives. And
the advantage of possessing a store of nuclear bombs." Not
that you might want to intimidate your neighbors--Pakistan,
say, or maybe China--a touch. No, no, nothing like that.
These bombs are for peace! A totally incredible book serving
to illustrate the lengths we will go to deny the obvious.

379. SHAKER, Mohamed I. The Nuclear Non-Proliferation
Treaty: Origin & Implementation, 1959-1979. Oceana, 1980. 3v.

Probably the most comprehensive record of the NPT available
in one source. Covers historical background, drafting, negotiations, obligations, and privileges of parties to the Treaty,
etc. Long bibliography and index; useful for any in-depth
study of the Treaty, if not the whole issue of proliferation.

380. STOCKHOLM International Peace Research Institute.
Nuclear Energy & Nuclear Weapon Proliferation.
Taylor & Francis, 1979. 462 p.

Papers presented at a Stockholm symposium in late 1978;
covers fuel cycles, enrichment, reprocessing, waste disposal,
safeguards technology, and much more. Calls for the "sensi-
tive parts of the fuel cycle" to be managed on an international
scale and operated under authority of an international agency;
establishment of an international repository for spent fuels;
support of nations desiring to pursue non-nuclear energy.

381. WALKER, William B. and Lonnroth, Mans. Nuclear
Power Struggles: Industrial Competition and Proliferation Control. Allen & Unwin, 1983. 204 p.

Analyzes the implications for the goal of non-proliferation re-
siding in major nuclear industry developments; the risk that
nuclear trade standards will be ignored as recession-plagued
suppliers deal with purchasers unlikely to feel constrained by
the Non-Proliferation Treaty; the decline of the U.S. nuclear

program and the leadership in the industry moving to France,
West Germany and Japan--thus removing the center of geopolitical authority from the geographical center of nuclear production.   A scholarly exegesis of a generally-overlooked as-
pect of the weapons proliferation problem.

382.   WEISSMAN, Steve and Krosney, Herbert.   The Islamic
       Bomb: The Nuclear Threat to Israel and the Middle
       East.   Times Books, 1981.   339 p.

A journalistic study of the Middle East nuclear situation,
covering the interests and intentions of Libya, Pakistan,
Israel, India and Iraq.   Based on the authors' travels and
interviews in the region.   No list of sources--many could
not be revealed without endangering them--but a good index.

383.   WENTZ, Walter B.   Nuclear Proliferation.   Public
       Affairs Press, 1968.   216 p.

Because the goal of preventing proliferation is a lost cause,
the U. S. should see to it that nations sympathetic to the U. S.
worldview are provided the bomb.   At the time, Wentz argued
that India, Japan, and Australia should be helped along to nuclear status, and that they should control their weapons independently.

384.   WILLRICH, Mason, ed.   International Safeguards and
       Nuclear Industry.   Johns Hopkins University Press,
       1973.   307 p.

Ten essays on the need for international safeguards against
proliferation of the bomb as a result of plutonium diversion
from peaceful reactors.

385.   WILLRICH, Mason and Taylor, Theodore B.   Nuclear
       Theft: Risks and Safeguards.   Ballinger, 1974.   252 p.

The authors urge that global precautions against theft of nuclear materials by criminal or political terrorists be taken
immediately.   They point out that less than 18 pounds of
reactor-grade plutonium is necessary to build a small nuclear
bomb.   Willrich has written extensively on legal aspects of
nuclear power; Taylor designed bombs for seven years at Los
Alamos.   Includes various scenarios for terrorist theft of nuclear materials, atomic blackmail, and demolition.

386.   WOHLSTETTER, Albert, et al.   Nuclear Policies:
       Fuel Without the Bomb.   Ballinger, 1978.   107 p.

Five essays which grew from studies of nuclear non-proliferation conducted by the California Seminar on Arms Control and
Foreign Policy. Attention to U.S. aid and the Indian bomb,
plutonium commerce, international controls.

387. _____ . Swords from Plowshares: The Military Po-
     tential of Civilian Nuclear Energy. University of
     Chicago Press, 1979. 228 p.

Claims that peacefully-oriented nuclear power applications
"provided the essential expeditor, and in many cases the necessary cover, for gaining capabilities to make the bomb."
Shows the interrelationship of peaceful and military uses of
nuclear technology, discusses "Life in a Nuclear Armed
Crowd," and some ways of keeping proliferation activities in
check.

388. YAGER, Joseph A. International Cooperation in Nuclear
     Energy. Brookings Institution, 1981. 226 p.

How to keep fissionable by-products out of the hands of those
who would employ them for military or terrorist ends.

● Periodical Articles ●

389. AGNEW, Harold M. "Leasing: A Solution to Nuclear
     Proliferation." Bulletin of the Atomic Scientists 38
     (Feb. 1982): 40-41.

Recommends leasing of fuel as solution to weapons proliferation. "If the supplier nation simply leased fuel ... and if the
fuel then reverted to the supplier after it had served its purpose, there would be no problem about what the receiving nation might do with the residual plutonium."

390. De MESQUITA, Bruce B. and Riker, William H. "An
     Assessment of the Merits of Selective Nuclear Pro-
     liferation." Journal of Conflict Resolution 26 (June
     1982): 283-306.

An interesting if far from convincing argument that nuclear
deterrence is likely to work in a conflict between nuclear
powers, but that, between nuclear and non-nuclear powers,
the latter may well come to know the effects of the bomb.
Enhanced global stability and prospects for peace may be obtained, if ironically, by judicious nuclear armament of non-
nuclear nations.

391. GOHEEN, Robert F. "Problems of Proliferation: U. S. Policy and the Third World. " World Politics 35 (Jan. 1983): 194-215.

Argues that the only substantial proliferation of nuclear weapons has taken place in the "vertical" sense, i. e. , in the superpower arsenals, and that failure of U. S. and Soviet efforts to control their own nuclear weapons development makes efforts to persuade other nations to do so ineffective. The U. S. must react to differing regional circumstances with greater sensitivity if it hopes to slow horizontal weapons spread, including such considerations as nationalism, technological capacity, and perceived security requirements. Superpower cooperation is the essential ingredient in any non-proliferation "regime. "

392. HOLDREN, John P. "Nuclear Power and Nuclear Weapons: The Connection is Dangerous. " Bulletin of the Atomic Scientists 39 (Jan. 1983): 40-45.

Examines what the author sees as the undeniable link between the peaceful and warlike atoms; "a nuclear power program makes it possible to mask weapons intentions through all the early stages and perhaps even into the stockpiling phase. "

393. INTRILIGATOR, Michael D. and Brito, Dagobert L. "Nuclear Proliferation and the Possibility of Nuclear War. " Public Choice 37 (No. 2, 1982): 247-260.

Nuclear nations should be more concerned with preventing accidental or "irrational" nuclear war (interesting assumption lodged in that phrase!) than with prevention of proliferation. Although a few additional nuclear states increase the chance of nuclear war, many such states would diminish it, for any act of nuclear aggression could be countered from a wide variety of sources. Includes statistical material on nuclear war probability analysis.

394. LOVINS, Amory B. "Nuclear Weapons and Power Reactor Plutonium. " Nature 283 (Feb. 28, 1980): 817-823.

Challenges the assertion commonly advanced by nuclear power advocates that reactor-grade plutonium cannot be employed to make powerful, reliable bombs. Features discussion of the different grades of plutonium.

395. _____, et al. "Nuclear Power and Nuclear Bombs." Foreign Affairs 58 (Summer 1980): 1137-1177.

The authors voice approval of the downturn in nuclear power research and development; contend that alternative energy sources are the best way of escaping from reliance on fossil fuels and from the proliferation threat.

396. NOGEE, Joseph L. "Soviet Nuclear Proliferation Policy: Dilemmas and Contradictions. " Orbis 24 (Winter 1981): 751-769.

Moscow has so far sought to maintain non-proliferation with strict controls over recipients of its nuclear technology. The Soviet desire to develop fast-breeder reactors, support of peaceful nuclear blasts, and sale of nuclear technology to volatile states (e. g. , Libya) casts Soviet commitment to non-proliferation in a paradoxical light.

397. "The Nonproliferation Predicament. " Society 30 (Sept. - Oct. 1983): 30-60.

Seven essays on nuclear proliferation, including work on "the peaceful atom, " "problem countries, " arms control and other topics.

398. "Nuclear Proliferation and World War III. " Nature 285 (June 12, 1980): 427-428.

An editorial pointing out that the most immediate threat to peace is not the possibility that other nations may obtain nuclear weapons, but that those which now possess them will use them. Though skeptical of the efficacy of treaties, does not altogether dismiss their merits.

399. NYE, Joseph S. "Nuclear Proliferation in the 1980s: Political Solutions. " Bulletin of the Atomic Scientists 38 (Aug. -Sept. 1982): 30-32.

One of four articles on proliferation in this issue. (The others deal with Reagan's "non-policy, " Argentina's impetus toward the bomb from the Falklands crisis, and the likelihood of nuclear development in Black Africa as a response to the South African bomb.) Nye states: "Political wisdom begins with efforts to maintain the existing [nonproliferation] regime.... [I]t is not perfect, just better than the possible alternatives. "

400. "The Politics of Nuclear Proliferation: A Discussion with Gene I. Rochlin. " Center Magazine 13 (May- June 1980): 28-35.

Further international efforts, including non-proliferation
treaties, are necessary to stop the spread of nuclear weapons.
Rochlin leads off this article with a summary of the proliferation problem; several other authorities respond to and expand
on the points he makes.

401. QUESTER, George H. "Nuclear Proliferation in Latin
      America. " Current History 81 (Feb. 1982): 52-55.

Investment in various civilian nuclear programs, as in Brazil
and Argentina, facilitates nuclear weapons manufacture; the
latter, with Chile, have not ratified the Nuclear Non-Proliferation Treaty. Quester outlines the stances of the Carter and
Reagan administrations toward Latin American proliferation,
along with inter-state relations in South America which affect
their nuclear interests.

402. _____, ed. "Nuclear Proliferation: Breaking the
      Chain. " International Organization 35 (Winter 1981).

This 240-page issue is devoted to an analysis of the many
issues connected with the bomb's spread, with articles "meant
to go beyond the conventional wisdom, or to contradict it, in
a look across the horizon. " With essays by Quester, Lewis
A. Dunn, Robert E. Harkavy, Irvin C. Bupp and others, this
is a good contribution to the literature. Some of the specific
topics: maintenance of non-proliferation, non-proliferation in
Latin America, and the rivalry between India and Pakistan.

403. SALAFF, Stephen. "The Plutonium Connection: Energy
      and Arms. " Bulletin of the Atomic Scientists 36
      (Sept. 1980): 18-23.

The U.S.-developed "Purex" system of reprocessing spent
reactor fuel to procure bomb-grade plutonium, coupled with
a lack of harmony among nuclear power nations over proliferation risks and safeguards threatens military work under
the guise of peaceful nuclear power programs.

404. SPIEWAK, I. and Barkenbus, J.N. "Nuclear Prolifera-
      tion and Nuclear Power: A Review of the NASAP and
      INFCE Studies. " Nuclear Safety 21 (Nov.-Dec. 1980):
      691-702.

Summarizes the work to date of the Nonproliferation Alternative Systems Assessment Program and the International Nuclear Fuel Cycle Evaluation, both efforts to review the options
for development of nuclear fuel cycles with an eye to the proliferation issue.

405. SPINRAD, Bernard. "Nuclear Power and Nuclear Weapons: The Connection is Tenuous." Bulletin of the Atomic Scientists 39 (Feb. 1983): 42-47.

Argues that nuclear weapons manufacture presents no insurmountable technical barriers regardless of access to diverted nuclear fuel, and that nuclear power actually reduces the risk of nuclear war by easing competition over energy sources.

● ● ●

"Men have gained control over forces of nature to such an extent that with their help they would have no difficulty in exterminating one another to the last man. They know this, and hence comes a large part of their current unrest, their unhappiness and their mood of anxiety."
                                        --Sigmund Freud, 1930.
                                        Civilization and Its Dis-
                                        contents, Norton, 1961,
                                        p. 92.

● ● ●

• V •

Trying To Keep It in Hand: Arms Control

"I am a dedicated believer in putting all the talent and vigor
and patience and persistence that our storehouse has to offer
in controlling the arms race.   If it is not somewhat brought
under control, atomic arms will sooner or later be used. "

> --General Bruce K. Hollo-
> way (Ret.), U. S. Strategic
> Air Command.   Item 295,
> p. 196.

406. BARNET, Richard J. Who Wants Disarmament? Beacon Press, 1960. 141 p.

Barnet, a staff member of Harvard's Russian Research Center, summarizes attitudes, arguments and proposals of both East and West since 1946 regarding disarmament and a halt to bomb tests. His outlook is not bright.

407. BARTON, John H. The Politics of Peace: An Evaluation of Arms Control. Stanford University Press, 1981. 257 p.

Because of traditional barriers to arms control, including nationalistic ambition and perceived threats from abroad, arms control can only succeed if based in "transnational" popular attitudes favoring arms restraint. Maintains that a greater international authority than the U.N. must be developed in conjunction with this popular support.

408. _____ and Imai, Ryukichi, eds. Arms Control II: A New Approach to International Security. Oelgeschlager, 1981. 328 p.

A collection of articles pointing toward the need for a new ˙ and broader concept of arms control, with special attention to changing technology and regional conflicts, the former because it tends to change military doctrine, the latter because they have proved almost completely irrelevant to the U.S. - Soviet conflict from which standing ideas about arms control emerged.

409. BECHHOEFER, Bernhard G. Postwar Negotiations for Arms Control. Brookings Institution, 1961. 641 p.

A well-documented history of disarmament proposals and negotiations, 1946-1958.

410. BENOIT, Emile, and Boulding, Kenneth E., eds. Disarmament and the Economy. Harper, 1963. 310 p.

Fifteen economists grapple with the question of how to disarm without damaging the economy. It may be hard to believe that some consider this a "problem," but it is so.

411. BERMAN, Harold J. and Maggs, Peter B. Disarmament Inspection Under Soviet Law. Oceana, 1968. 154 p.

The authors are optimistic that Soviet law can accommodate inspection. Includes many pertinent documents.

412. BLOOMFIELD, Lincoln P., et al. Khrushchev and the Arms Race: Soviet Interests in Arms Control and Disarmament, 1954-1964. MIT Press, 1966. 338 p.

A good statement of U.S. perceptions of Soviet interests, and vice-versa. Good bibliography and supplementary chapter on "Sources for the Study of Soviet Disarmament Policy."

413. BURNS, E. L. M. Megamurder. Pantheon, 1967. 297 p.

Canadian Lieutenant-General Burns believes that, because the duty of the military to protect civilian society has been made all but impossible through nuclear weapons, military authorities should pursue limited disarmament. "If the mass of nuclear weapons [which] now exists is used in war, it will mean the killing of millions of women, children and old men, who bear no arms and who bear no responsibility for warlike decisions.... Is it wrong to call this not war, but megamurder?"

414. BURNS, Richard D., ed. Arms Control and Disarmament: A Bibliography. ABC-Clio, 1977. 430 p.

Edited by the director of the Center for the Study of Armament and Disarmament, California State University/Los Angeles. Relies for material on the Center's files, which include both academic and popular sources. Citations (close to 9, 000) are grouped according to subject. The first part covers bibliographical sources, works on arms control and disarmament, verification, etc.; the second covers various treaties and proposals. Many foreign-language items cited in the latter part.

415. BURT, Richard A., ed. Arms Control & Defense Postures in the 1980s. Westview, 1982. 230 p.

Essays addressing, among other topics, the problem of defining defense policy and arms control; a nuclear test ban; Soviet strategic policy; tactical nuclear weapons; the arms race in space; institutional impediments to arms control, etc. The authors represent generally middle-of-the-road to right-of-center U.S. establishment thinking.

416. CLARKE, Duncan L. The Politics of Arms Control:

The Role and Effectiveness of the U.S. Arms Control
and Disarmament Agency. Free Press, 1979.
277 p.

Origins, operations, bureaucratic relations among the Agency,
the Executive Branch, Congress, and interest groups.

417. CLEMENS, Walter C. The Superpowers and Arms
Control: From Cold War to Interdependence. Heath,
1973. 192 p.

The two nations can avoid military confrontation and successfully pursue arms control. Written from the traditional
Catholic point of view toward arms control, contains prescrip-
tions for action by both countries which neither is likely to
follow. Well-researched, however.

418. CLOUGH, Ralph N., et al. The United States, China
and Arms Control. Brookings Institution, 1975.
153 p.

Argues that China (the People's Republic) should participate
in arms control talks, that the U.S. and China should make a
reciprocal "no first use" pledge on nuclear weapons, and that
a nuclear-free zone be established in the Korean peninsula.

419. DEAN, Arthur H. Test Ban and Disarmament: The
Path of Negotiation. Harper, 1966. 153 p.

Dean represented the U.S. at the Geneva disarmament talks
which led to the Limited Nuclear Test Ban Treaty of 1963.
He considers here issues of verification, diplomatic tactics,
etc.

420. DIVINE, Robert A. Blowing on the Wind: The Nuclear
Test Ban Debate, 1954-1960. Oxford University
Press, 1978. 393 p.

A thorough history of the chain of building possibilities,
dashed hopes, and rebuilding which led to the partial Test
Ban Treaty of 1963. Attention focuses on the health issue in
bomb testing, rather than the more significant, and more
long-run, issue of arms control, of which the Test Ban still
stands as the paramount (if partial) achievement.

421. DOUGHERTY, James E. and Lehman, J. F., eds.
Arms Control for the Late Sixties. Van Nostrand,
1967. 265 p.

Articles by Herman Kahn, William Kintner, Edward Teller,
James R. Schlesinger and company addressing political,
technical and strategic issues.

422. DRAPER, Theodore. Present History. Random, 1983.
      458 p.

Includes two significant articles reprinted from the New York
Review of Books. In "How Not to Think about a Nuclear
War, " Draper tries to return the thoughtful reader's atten-
tion--diverted by Jonathan Schell's apocalyptic and near hopeless message in Fate of the Earth--to consideration of the
most likely achievable method of securing peace in spite of
the nuclear presence. Following Lord Zuckerman's Nuclear
Illusion and Reality, he advocates a total halt in weapons research and development, since new weapons are merely re-
dundant in the deterrence scheme. In "Dear Mr. Weinberger, " Draper responds to the Reagan Secretary of Defense's
unpersuasive assertion that the Reagan administration does
not envision and prepare for a "winnable" nuclear war.

423. DRELL, Sidney D. Facing the Threat of Nuclear
      Weapons. University of Washington Press, 1983.
      120 p.

A theoretical physicist's examination of the nuclear threat,
with attention to the weapons' effects on policy, possible arms
control measures, the significance of public opinion and the
role of scientific advice in policy-making. Includes an open
letter by Soviet dissident Andrei Sakharov responding to the
issues Drell raises.

424. DUPUY, Trevor N. and Hammerman, Gay M. A
      Documentary History of Arms Control and Disarma-
      ment. Dupuy/Bowker, 1973. 629 p.

158 texts of arms control documents from 6th century China
to SALT accords of 1972. More than half the material per-
tains to post-WWII efforts to control nuclear and other contemporary weapons.

425. EDWARDS, David V. Arms Control in International
      Politics. Holt, 1969. 200 p.

An overview of various factors in arms control. Lengthy
bibliography.

426. EPSTEIN, William. Disarmament: Twenty-Five Years

of Effort. Canadian Institute of International Affairs, 1971. 97 p.

A concise picture of post-1945 efforts at disarmament. Factual and easy to understand; includes several relevant documents, such as the text of the atmospheric Test Ban Treaty of 1963.

427. ETZIONI, Amitai. The Hard Way to Peace: A New Strategy. Collier, 1962. 285 p.

Evaluates nuclear strategies of Truman, Eisenhower, and Kennedy, the "balance of terror," Pentagon policies. Favors arms reduction. Believes that rational arms control in the present is the best course to take as we await the development of "supranationalism," the author's term for a global society which would obviate war between nations.

428. FORBES, Henry W. Strategy of Disarmament. Public Affairs Press, 1962. 158 p.

Discounts almost entirely the possibility of disarmament, contends in opposition to many scholars of war that preparation for war does not cause war--and advocates conventional, limited-war fighting preparedness.

429. GEYER, Alan F. The Idea of Disarmament: Rethinking the Unthinkable. Brethren Press, 1982. 256 p.

This book, like Herman Kahn's books, "is concerned with making the unthinkable thinkable and with the metaphors and scenarios that will encourage thinkability. But it starts from a different direction: its purpose is to make disarmament thinkable." This is not the routine, and impossible to achieve, call for beating swords into plowshares this instant, but for a politically realistic reversal of the arms race. Highly critical of U.S. disarmament policy.

430. HADLEY, Arthur T. The Nation's Safety and Arms Control. Viking, 1961. 160 p.

Points out the threat of accidental war; argues that a reliable second strike force on both sides is the most attainable form of nuclear security, and urges a build-up of conventional forces by the West to reduce reliance on nuclear arms. He makes some concrete proposals toward effecting his view of global stability, such as a fixed number of nuclear weapons on either side.

431. HALPERIN, Morton H. and Perkins, Dwight H. Communist China and Arms Control. Praeger, 1965.
191 p.

How China's possession of the bomb affected her place in
world politics and military affairs. Discusses China's dis-
dain for the Test Ban Treaty of 1963 (regarded in Peking as
a Russian excuse for not sharing nuclear technology with
China), questions of proliferation, Chinese attitudes toward
arms control and nuclear war (the Chinese line at the time
was that the nation would survive such war).

432. HENKIN, Louis. Arms Control and Inspection in
American Law. Columbia University Press, 1958.
289 p.

Examines problems that arms control and inspection could
raise under U.S. law and the Constitution.

433. _____, ed. Arms Control: Issues for the Public.
Prentice-Hall, 1962. 207 p.

Overview and history of the issues, including inspection,
security questions, national interests, disarmament since
1945, etc.

434. INDEPENDENT Commission on Disarmament and Security
Issues. Common Security: A Blueprint for Survival.
Simon & Schuster, 1982. 202 p.

The Commission, chaired by Swedish Prime Minister Olof
Palme, consisted of representatives from NATO, the U.S.S.R.,
Eastern Europe, and Third World nations concerned about the
arms race and nuclear proliferation. Includes remedial proposals. A good source for a concise introduction to many
disarmament issues, with considerable attention to the nuclear
dimension.

435. INTERNATIONAL Atomic Energy Agency. International
Treaties Relating to Nuclear Control & Disarmament.
IAEA, 1975. 78 p.

Texts of treaties from the Antarctic Treaty (1959) through
a treaty of 1971 forbidding placement of nuclear weapons on
the ocean floor.

436. KAPLAN, Morton A., ed. SALT: Problems and
Prospects. General Learning Press, 1973. 251 p.

On SALT and the international system, comparison of U. S. and Soviet strategic policies, historical precedents, technological aspects and the language of arms negotiation.

437. KINTNER, William R. and Pfaltzgraff, Robert L. , eds. SALT: Implications for Arms Control in the 1970s. University of Pittsburgh Press, 1973. 447 p.

On the political, military, and bureaucratic features of the SALT talks.

438. LABRIE, Roger P. , ed. SALT Handbook: Key Documents and Issues, 1972-1979. American Enterprise Institute for Public Policy Research, 1979. 736 p.

Traces the history of the SALT talks. Statements and testimony from many officials of both the U. S. and the Soviet Union. Includes a good glossary and index.

439. LARSON, Arthur, ed. A Warless World. McGraw, 1963. 209 p.

Articles by Arnold Toynbee, Walter Millis, Kenneth E. Boulding, and others on the economics, psychology, and politics of the world following successful disarmament. Includes an appendix on "The Russian Idea of a World Without Arms," a discussion held in Moscow in 1962.

440. LARSON, Thomas B. Disarmament and Soviet Policy, 1964-1968. Prentice-Hall, 1969. 250 p.

In spite of post-Khrushchev hard line and dissatisfaction with strategic balance, Soviets are still interested in negotiation. Includes nuclear chronology, 1964-1967.

441. LEFEVER, Ernest W. , ed. Arms and Arms Control: A Symposium. Praeger, 1962. 334 p.

Close to thirty reprinted essays from politicians (Kennedy, Khrushchev), philosophers (Bertrand Russell) and scientists. On testing, disarmament, "peaceful coexistence, " etc.

442. LIEBERMAN, Joseph I. The Scorpion and the Tarantula: The Struggle to Control Atomic Weapons, 1945-1949. Houghton Mifflin, 1970. 460 p.

"The story of a disastrous failure of statecraft, " the book

chronicles "the futile efforts to control atomic weapons during
the first years of the nuclear age while America was still the
world's only nuclear power." A well-documented history of
the early nuclear charade; relies heavily on papers of Bernard
Baruch and Secretary of War Henry L. Stimson. Baruch's
revision of the Lilienthal report concerning proposals for the
international control of atomic energy (item 88) assured that
the Soviet Union would veto it when presented to the United
Nations in mid-1946, which is, in fact, what ensued. Lieberman's coverage of U.S. failure to deal adequately with the
Soviet point of view is an important part of his book.

443.   McBRIDE, James H.   The Test Ban Treaty: Military,
       Technological, and Political Implications.   Regnery,
       1967.   197 p.

Follows in the Edward Teller mode of a bomb aficionado who
believes that little but good can come from further nuclear
testing; contends that the Test Ban of 1963 provided nothing
but opportunities for Soviet military advances. What the Test
Ban did was a variety of things, none of which support Mc-
Bride's position. It cleaned up the atmosphere, bringing an
immediate reduction in health-threatening radioactive pollu-
tants resulting from open-air testing; it demonstrated that the
U.S. and the Soviet Union are capable of recognizing and
acting upon a mutually beneficial policy; and (unfortunately)
it drove nuclear testing below ground, where it has flourished
since 1963.

444.   MELMAN, Seymour, ed.   Inspection for Disarmament.
       Columbia University Press, 1958.   291 p.

Twenty contributors--authorities in nuclear arms and inspec-
tion--discuss inspection methods, secret weapons production,
and other topics related to disarmament. The consensus is
that a workable inspection system, though difficult to devise,
is obtainable. Since this book's publication, the major task
of inspection to determine compliance with arms control agreements has been performed by satellite, a method which,
though imperfect, allows sidestepping of the "sovereignty"
issues involved in on-site inspection.

445.   MILLIS, Walter.   An End to Arms.   Atheneum, 1965.
       301 p.

Guerilla warfare may continue, but Millis believes that the
price of nuclear war is too high to risk. He foresees greater
international supervision of arms by the 1980s, and regards

some form of useful world government as more than likely. Considerable emphasis on the Test Ban of 1963 as a sign of things to come.

446. MORRIS, Robert. Disarmament: Weapon of Conquest. Bookmailer, 1963. 148 p.

Characterizes disarmament as merely another Red tool of deceit. Diverting far-right paranoia.

447. NEWHOUSE, John. Cold Dawn: The Story of SALT. Holt, 1973. 302 p.

The Strategic Arms Limitation Talks began under Lyndon Johnson. This is a detailed history and analysis of their conduct as they led to the SALT accords of 1972. Newhouse relies on materials generally unavailable to other writers at the time.

448. NOEL-BAKER, Philip. The Arms Race: A Programme for World Disarmament. Stevens, 1958. 580 p.

A rather optimistic work holding that problems of inspection connected with disarmament would be resolved to a great extent by actual general disarmament. Nations must, however, seek political rapprochement at the same time as they pursue arms agreements.

449. NUTTING, Anthony. Disarmament: An Outline of the Negotiations. Oxford University Press, 1959. 51 p.

Covers major-power disarmament talks, 1945-1958. Factually presented; shows the nuclear stalemate in the beginning.

450. PANOFSKY, Wolfgang K. H. Arms Control and SALT II. University of Washington Press, 1979. 75 p.

The author's investigation of SALT II leads him to conclude that its terms would enhance U. S. and global security. Answers criticism of the proposed treaty from both left and right.

451. PAYNE, Samuel B., Jr. The Soviet Union and SALT. MIT Press, 1980. 224 p.

A highly useful and concise book for examination not only of Soviet attitudes toward strategic arms limitation, but for the U. S. S. R. 's nuclear outlook in general. Based on a large number of Soviet books and articles, includes many excerpts from same.

452. PLATT, Alan and Weiler, Lawrence D., eds. Congress and Arms Control. Westview Press, 1978. 227 p.

Ten essays by Congressional members and arms control authorities on a variety of issues regarding the title topic. The assumption is generally that further involvement of Congress in arms control negotiations and weapons systems acquisition would prove beneficial, since it would open the subjects to broader and deeper scrutiny.

453. RANGER, Robin. Arms and Politics, 1958-1978: Arms Control in a Changing Political Context. Macmillan of Canada, 1979. 280 p.

Argues that the U.S. and the Soviet Union stress two different approaches to arms control: the former technological, the latter political.

454. SAATY, Thomas L. Mathematical Models of Arms Control and Disarmament: Application of Mathematical Structures in Politics. Wiley, 1968. 190 p.

An attempt to show that applied mathematics techniques, such as games theory, can be useful as tools toward arms control. Not for the neophyte.

455. SCHELLING, Thomas C. and Halperin, Morton H. Strategy and Arms Control. Twentieth Century Fund, 1961. 148 p.

Work on arms control by a duo whose one-half (Halperin) later thought that it would be a good idea to encourage Chinese adherence to U.S. desires by reminding them of their pitiful nuclear arsenal next to that of the U.S. Somehow the paradox does not encourage a sympathetic reception to this book.

456. SEABORG, Glenn T. Kennedy, Khrushchev and the Test Ban. University of California Press, 1981. 320 p.

A good history by a participant; the author was chairman of the Committee on Atmospheric Testing, and chairman of the Atomic Energy Commission under Kennedy. He concludes his account of the Limited Test Ban Treaty of August 5, 1963, with a plea for a comprehensive ban.

457. SINGER, J. David. Deterrence, Arms Control, and
     Disarmament: Toward a Synthesis in National Secur-
     ity Policy. Ohio State University Press, 1962.
     275 p.

"Our armament policy, " writes Singer, "should be designed
to carry the nation through the dangerous but imperative
transition from deterrence to disarmament, with arms control
providing the bond and bridge between the two. " A pessi-
mist's guide to disarmament; probably realistic, and well
written. Includes a long, unannotated bibliography.

458. SLOCOMBE, Walter. Controlling Strategic Nuclear
     Weapons. Foreign Policy Association, 1975. 63 p.

The author, a former assistant for the National Security Council, discusses basic concepts of arms control, strategic balance, and related issues the U.S. must face.

459. SMITH, Gerard. Doubletalk: The Story of the First
     Strategic Arms Limitation Talks. Doubleday, 1980.
     556 p.

Smith was the chief U.S. negotiator at the talks. Firsthand
diplomatic history of the negotiations at Vienna and Helsinki.
Less than lively, but has no real competitors for the territory it covers.

● ● ●

"I have no faith in the so-called controlled use of atomic
weapons.... I would not recommend the use of any atomic
weapon, no matter how small, when both sides have the
power to destroy the world. "
                                    --Admiral Charles R. Brown,
                                     1958. Item 189, p. 83.

● ● ●

460. SPANIER, John W. and Nogee, Joseph L. Politics of
     Disarmament: A Study in Soviet-American Games-
     manship. Praeger, 1962. 226 p.

Presents the familiar argument that "arms control" can best
be lodged in mutual U.S. and Soviet possession of an "invulnerable" second-strike nuclear force. Investigates the cynical
nature of East-West arms negotiations, with each side advancing proposals for political advantage that it knows the other
cannot accept.

461. STOCKHOLM International Peace Research Institute. Armaments and Disarmament in the Nuclear Age: A Handbook. Humanities Press, 1976. 308 p.

Collects conclusions of previous SIPRI papers to mark the Institute's 10th anniversary. A good overview of facts and issues. Extensive coverage of nuclear weapons, along with chemical and biological warfare. Also treats armament dynamics, economic consequences of the arms race, and conventional weapons.

462. _____. World Armaments and Disarmament: SIPRI Yearbook. Various publishers, 1972-

Began life in 1968 as the SIPRI Yearbook of World Armaments and Disarmament; this annual reviews the year's main nuclear events, covers developments in proliferation, nuclear policies; also covers a wide variety of other global military issues.

463. STONE, Jeremy J. Containing the Arms Race: Some Specific Proposals. MIT Press, 1966. 252 p.

Pro and con reflections on manned bombers, anti-missile systems, anti-submarine warfare. Concerns the U. S. -Soviet situations, little attention to sideshow arms races around the planet.

464. UNITED Nations. Department of Political and Security Council Affairs. United Nations Disarmament Year-book. United Nations, 1976.

A broad review of the year's work in disarmament, both in and outside of the United Nations. Deals with nuclear disarmament as well as other varieties. Frequent citations to other U. N. material. Includes treaty drafts and other relevant documents.

465. _____. Secretary General. Basic Problems of Disarmament. United Nations, 1970. 265 p.

Contains three reports prepared at the request of the General Assembly in the 1960s: the "Economic and Social Consequences of Disarmament," the "Effects of the Possible Use of Nuclear Weapons and the Security and Economic Implications for States of the Acquisition and Further Development of these Weapons," and a concluding report on chemical and bacteriological weapons.

466. U. S. Arms Control and Disarmament Agency. Arms
      Control and Disarmament Agreements: Texts and
      Histories of Negotiations. U. S. Government Printing
      Office, 1972-

In close to 300 pages the 1982 edition, the fifth, contains the
texts of the Geneva Protocol of 1925 and, "in chronological
order, all major arms control agreements concluded after
World War II in which the United States has been a participant. " A brief introductory statement precedes each agreement.

467. _____. Documents on Disarmament. U. S. Govern-
      ment Printing Office, 1961- . Annual.

This annual is running well behind the times; the latest volume
is for 1979, and was issued in mid-1982. At a massive bulk
of nearly 900 pages, the 1979 annual contains texts of documents from various international sources, the United Nations,
and the U. S. A fine-print, 10-page bibliography of U. S. and
U. N. -published materials for the year will help the researcher track down elusive items. Includes a subject index.
Treatment for previous years is similar.

468. VOSS, Earl H. Nuclear Ambush: The Test-Ban Trap.
      Regnery, 1963. 612 p.

There is a bumper sticker which has been around for several
years; occasionally flourished by gun lovers, it reads, "I'll
give up my gun when they pry it out of my cold, dead fin-
gers. " Mr. Voss probably sports one of these on his ve-
hicle. If not, he should. This is an exhausting campaign
against the Test Ban Treaty based on the belief that the
whole movement toward it was cleverly engineered through
Soviet psychological manipulation. The hazards of testing
are minimal, Voss argues, compared to those lurking in the
nuclear underdog's posture. No doubt he was highly relieved
when testing continued underground. God forbid that the bombs
might not go off if we fired them!

469. WADSWORTH, James J. The Price of Peace. Praeger,
      1962. 127 p.

The author was a chief delegate for the U. S. at the United
Nations disarmament sessions, 1958-1961. Here he proposes
a gradual reduction in nuclear arms, because, though peace
costs a good deal, the bill for nuclear war would be beyond

paying. Arguments interchangeable with many other books urging disarmament along traditional lines.

470. WAINHOUSE, David W. Arms Control Agreements: Designs for Verification and Organization. Johns Hopkins University Press, 1968. 179 p.

Consists of a detailed discussion of organizational arrangements for verifying arms control and of designs for an international arms control organization.

471. WARBURG, James P. Disarmament: The Challenge of the 1960s. Doubleday, 1961. 288 p.

The challenge remains. Warburg sought disarmament on a general and fundamental basis, rather than on the piecemeal manner most arms control and disarmament professionals prefer. Complete disarmament is preferable because of problems connected with tradeoffs in partial disarmament. (Is an SS-20 worth two Pershings? Is a Cruise worth a Backfire?)

472. WILLRICH, Mason and Rhinelander, John B., eds. SALT: The Moscow Agreements and Beyond. Free Press, 1974. 361 p.

Essays on SALT I and related topics, including the path toward the agreements, a survey of strategic arsenals, verification, European and Asian perspectives, and prospects for future arms limitation. Also contains ten appendices providing the texts of various agreements between the U.S. and U.S.S.R., such as the ABM Treaty, an Accident Measures Agreement on measures to reduce the risk of accidental nuclear war, and others.

473. WOLFE, Thomas W. The SALT Experience. Ballinger, 1979. 405 p.

A history of the Strategic Arms Limitation Talks, 1968-1979, with a qualified judgment of SALT's effects on the arms race.

474. WOLFERS, Arnold, et al. The United States in a Disarmed World: A Study of the U.S. Outline for General and Complete Disarmament. Johns Hopkins University Press, 1966. 236 p.

A critical analysis of disarmament methods and enforcement. A work commissioned by the U.S. Arms Control and Disarmament Agency.

475. YEFREMOV, Aleksandr E. Nuclear Disarmament. Progress Publishers, 1979. 313 p.

A valuable book because it allows Western readers further understanding of Soviet attitudes regarding the nuclear threat. Some of the attitudes are between the lines, and the propaganda tradition is running (if in relatively low gear), but this history of Soviet involvement in attempts at arms control and disarmament since WW II is detailed and worth some attention.

476. ZILE, Zigurds L., et al. The Soviet Legal System & Arms Inspection: A Case Study in Policy Implementation. Praeger, 1972. 394 p.

Considers the effects various points of Soviet law would have on international arms inspectors in the Soviet Union. Originally prepared for the U. S. Arms Control and Disarmament Agency.

● Periodical Articles ●

477. "The Armament Syndrome: The Future in Jeopardy." Development No. 1 (1982): 80 p.

An issue on problems of and proposals for disarmament. Reviews the arms race, the SALT process, military-dominated Third World governments; also covers reconversion of armaments industries, peace education, satellite monitoring and many other issues. (This is the journal of the Society for International Development, with headquarters in Rome.)

478. BERG, Per and Lodgaard, Sverre. "Disengagement Zones: A Step Towards Meaningful Defence?" Journal of Peace Research 20 (No. 1, 1983): 5-15.

Speculates on the possibility of raising the nuclear threshold in Europe through removal of nuclear weapons from a zone or zones cutting through the continent. Covers such points as the depth of the zone, the relationship between nuclear disengagement and conventional force rearrangements, benefits of conventional defense, etc.

479. BLECHMAN, Barry M. and Moore, Mark R. "A Nuclear-Weapon-Free Zone in Europe." Scientific American 248 (April 1983): 37-43.

Proposes a zone free of all nuclear weapons covering the eastern half of West Germany, the western half of East Germany, and the western portion of Czechoslovakia as a deterrent, in the event of war, to use of nuclear weapons and the risk of rapid escalation. Cites agreements on nuclear-free Antarctic and Latin America as precedents. (The U. S. S. R. has endorsed the idea of nuclear-free Germanys.)

480. CORDES, Colleen. "Arms Debate Focuses on U. S. - Soviet Trust. " APA Monitor 14 (June 1983): 9+

A short but useful introduction to some of the psychological factors involved in arms negotiations, including the way unspoken assumptions about "the enemy" color policy, how each side sees the same issue in different ways, respective "good guys/bad guys" thinking employed by both nations, projection of own worst qualities onto the other, etc.

481. DeWITT, Hugh E. and Barker, Robert B. "Debate on a Comprehensive Nuclear Weapons Test Ban. " Physics Today 36 (Aug. 1983): 24-34.

DeWitt argues for, Barker against a comprehensive ban. DeWitt: "Some form of comprehensive test ban treaty that ends nuclear testing is both feasible and vital to the security of the world"; Barker: "The weapons designers have done a good job throughout the history of the U. S. nuclear stockpile, but perfection has escaped them. " (Alas.)

482. DIWAKAR, R. R. and Agrawal, Mahendra, eds. "Disarmament and Human Survival. " Gandhi Marg: Monthly Journal of the Gandhi Peace Foundation 4 (May-June 1982): 444 p.

A special disarmament issue with articles on the military mindset, the economics of militarism, nuclear proliferation, the European peace movement, disarmament and non-alignment and much else. Contributors are an international lot. Published in India.

483. DRELL, Sidney D. "Arms Control: Is There Still Hope?" Daedalus 109 (Fall 1980): 177-188.

Surveys the growth of the nuclear stockpile; believes that nuclear weapons are good for nothing but preventing their own employment; encourages stricter attention by the U. S. to arms control as a vital component of national security. This issue of Daedalus is entirely devoted to "U. S. Defense Policy in the

1980s, " and includes articles on strategic stability, deterrence, superpower relations with China, etc.

484. FREEDMAN, Lawrence. "Arms Control: No Hiding
      Place. " SAIS Review 3 (Winter-Spring 1983): 3-11.

Arms control "will no longer provide a hiding place" from
the real problems of East-West relations or Western Europe's
defense; arms control talks in the foreseeable future will proceed under adverse political conditions. Suggests that a debate on NATO strategy resolved "possibly on a basis of reduced dependence on nuclear weapons" would make arms
control easier to pursue.

485. GORDON, Michael R. and Labrie, Roger P. "The
      Press Rewrites SALT II. " Columbia Journalism Review 22 (July-Aug. 1983): 39-40.

The authors point out numerous inaccuracies and failures of
comprehension in U.S. press stories on the so-far unratified
SALT II treaty, especially concerning reports of alleged Soviet
non-compliance.

486. HAMILTON, John A. "To Link or Not to Link. "
      Foreign Policy No. 44 (Fall 1981): 127-144.

Argues that, in spite of historical precedents in which nations associated bargaining behavior in one area with issues
in another area, the overwhelming importance of nuclear arms
negotiations makes their linkage with other issues undesirable.

487. HARDIN, Russell. "Unilateral Versus Mutual Disarmament. " Philosophy & Public Affairs 12 (Summer
      1983): 236-254.

A criticism of Douglas Lackey's argument (item 270) for unilateral disarmament, turning chiefly on Lackey's analysis of
the effects of unilateralism. Hardin agrees with Lackey that
a nuclear-disarmed U.S. would probably not be subjected to
Soviet rule, but believes that resulting Soviet influence on
U.S. conduct would be considerable. Regards mutual disarmament--"at least down to deterrent levels"--as a better prospect for peace and justice than "a nuclear Pax Romana" attained by either side, in no small measure because such a
supreme position would be dangerous and probably impossible
to attain.

488. HULETT, L.S. "Carter, SALT II and Détente II. "

Australian Journal of Politics and History 28 (No. 2,
1982): 190-200.

On the weakness of the "Mutual Assured Destruction" strategy,
the weakness being the suicidal nature of a retaliatory blow
following a first strike on one's military targets. Criticizes
SALT as a de facto cover for Soviet strategic and political
advantage.

489. JACOBSEN, Carl G. "East-West Relations at the Cross-
        Roads. " Journal of Peace Research 20 (No. 2, 1983):
        101-106.

Calls 1983 "a make or break year for arms control. " Holds
Soviet arms control offers by Andropov far more conciliatory
than U.S. /Reagan initiatives or responses (claims that some
Andropov offers, e. g. , of a 25 percent reduction and equality
in warheads would have been "music to the ears" of Nixon,
Ford and Carter.) U.S. insistence on Pershing II deployment
"torpedoes any and all possibility of agreement with Moscow. "

490. KATSUMI, Takeoka. "Nuclear Disarmament for De-
        fense. " Japan Echo 10 (Summer 1983): 25-33.

A former official of the Japanese Defense Agency describes
his apprehension at the likelihood of any Japanese-Soviet conflict escalating to nuclear levels given the present over-
reliance on nuclear deterrence; fears that any Soviet-U.S.
conflict in the region under present strategic policy would
drag Japan into war. Urges greater reliance on conventional
deterrence, and continued Japanese decline of the nuclear
weapons option.

491. KAVKA, Gregory S. "Doubts about Unilateral Nuclear
        Disarmament. " Philosophy & Public Affairs 12 (Sum-
        mer 1983): 255-260.

Another criticism of Douglas Lackey's 1982 essay (item 270)
on unilateralism. Believes that Lackey's estimate of the
Soviet threat is inadequate; that less likelihood of nuclear use
exists under a system of deterrence than under unilateralism;
also that advocacy of unilateralism weakens reception of overall disarmament arguments in the U.S.

492. KREPON, Michael. "Assessing Strategic Arms Reduc-
        tion Proposals. " World Politics 35 (Jan. 1983): 216-
        244.

Reviews eight alternatives for "deep cuts" in strategic arsenals. Considers the Reagan administration uncooperative on
the framework of negotiation, accuses it of setting up "extra-
ordinarily difficult negotiating objectives, " and that it has
shown little desire to offer "carrots as well as sticks" which
might lead to an agreement with Moscow. Anticipates long,
bitter and unsatisfactory negotiations if these practices continue.

493. LINEBAUGH, David and Peters, Alexander. "Restart-
      ing START. " Foreign Service Journal 60 (Jan. 1983):
      26-31.

The authors state that more nuclear weapons will not, contra
Reagan administration claims, serve as "bargaining chips"
but merely make it more difficult to achieve mutual reductions. Discussion of various alternatives to current U. S.
position; suggests mutual reductions to 5, 000 warheads or
fewer, a ban on deployment of new missiles, and a ban on
flight-testing of counterforce weapons, among other points.

494. MILLETT, Stephen M. "Forward-Based Nuclear Weap-
      ons and SALT I. " Political Science Quarterly 98
      (Spring 1983): 79-97.

How U. S. -Soviet variances in perception of NATO missiles
(the U. S. considers them "tactical, " the Soviets a strategic
threat to their homeland) affected SALT I negotiations. Describes both nations' perceptions as "highly subjective and
self-serving, " a habitual vision which both would do well to
abandon.

495. " 'New Proposals' Reveal Discord. " Beijing Review
      26 (Oct. 17, 1983): 10-11.

A short analysis of Soviet and U. S. arms reductions proposals
in Geneva. Accuses both nations of a lack of sincerity in
negotiations, and seeking not balance but advantage over one
another in the contest for dominance in Europe.

496. SCHNEIDER, Barry R. "Verify. " Across the Board
      20 (April 1983): 10-21.

On the importance of establishing reliable verification procedures to insure compliance with arms agreements, "so that
neither side can cheat in a game that could destroy the world."

497. SIGAL, Leon V. "Kennan's Cuts. " Foreign Policy No.
      44 (Fall 1981): 70-81.

Deep cuts in nuclear armaments advocated by George F. Kennan will not appeal to the Soviet Union. A gradual reduction of nuclear arms, including a comprehensive test ban, is the best way to proceed, if not the most immediately appealing.

498.   "The Soviet-American Arms Race and Arms Control. " Current History: A World Affairs Journal 82 (May 1983).

This issue focuses on the title topics, which receive analysis through separate articles on the Reagan administration's nuclear strategy, Soviet-American diplomacy, arms control negotiations, etc. , along with current documents on arms control proposals.

499.   STEINBRUNER, John.   "Fears of War, Programs for Peace. "   Brookings Review (Fall 1982):   6-10.

Reviews arms control negotiations and treaties (SALT and SALT II), reaction of Reagan administration to antinuclear weapons movement in U. S. , the probability of continued nuclear parity between the U. S. and the Soviet Union; expresses approval of public pressure on U. S. officials, believing that it serves "the cause of international stability. "

500.   ULLMAN, Richard H.   "Out of the Euromissile Mire." Foreign Policy No. 50 (Spring 1983):   39-52.

Covers various superpower proposals regarding the Euromissile situation in a worthwhile overview of "NATO's nuclear dilemma. "   Regards the Pershing II as a threat to crisis stability; suggests that the West not dismiss certain Soviet proposals out-of-hand.

501.   YORK, Herbert F.   "Bilateral Negotiations and the Arms Race. "   Scientific American 249 (Oct. 1983): 149-160.

A historical review of U. S. -Soviet arms negotiations examining the different perceptions each has of the process, areas of conflicting assumptions and requirements (e. g. , U. S. insistence on more territorially invasive means of verification than the Soviets will even discuss), and domestic political impediments in both countries (e. g. , the quadrennial U. S. presidential election and the Soviet absence of public pressure groups.)

● ● ●

"One hears a great deal about hope. It is hope naked, hope pure, hope unalloyed with anything hard enough to point to as an actual reason. At this point in our history, it seems clear, optimism must be blind. We have built thousands of nuclear warheads, and we hope they won't be used.

Is this the best we can do?"

--Thomas Powers, Item 954, p. 124-125.

● ● ●

● VI ●

To Banish the Nuclear Specter: The Peace Movement

"The message of this new peace movement is: count on
nothing--not on good will, or critical intelligence, and certainly not on the people in power.   The only thing we can
count on is ourselves and grassroots collective action. "

--Suzanne Gordon, Item 576,
        p. 23.

502. ADAMS, Ruth and Cullen, Susan, eds. The Final
     Epidemic: Physicians and Scientists on Nuclear
     War. Educational Foundation for Nuclear Science,
     1981. 254 p.

Essays by a large number of authorities in public health and
armaments policy on the various aspects of the arms race
and the threat of nuclear war; the final chapter, "Treatment,"
includes suggested attitudes and measures for preventing "the
final epidemic. "

503. ALBERT, Michael and Dellinger, David, eds. Beyond
     Survival: New Directions for the Disarmament Move-
     ment. South End Press, 1983. 366 p.

A collection of essays whose general intention is to help the
disarmament movement "broaden and deepen at the same
time, " both to bring those into the movement who have traditionally stood apart from activism or unconventional views,
and to dissect in greater detail the social basis of the nuclear
threat. Contributors include the editors, Noam Chomsky,
Holly Sklar, and others on "Lessons from the Sixties, " "Fem-
inism and Militarism, " interventionism, etc. A good compilation of the views of the contemporary U.S. left.

504. AMERICAN Library Association. Social Responsibili-
     ties Round Table. Task Force on Peace Informa-
     tion Exchange. Peace Research and Activists Groups:
     A North American Directory. The Task Force,
     1982. 35 p.

An alphabetical listing of peace groups in the U.S. and Canada, including many specifically devoted to antinuclearism.
Entries provide addresses, telephone numbers, contact persons. Geographical index.

505. ARONOW, Sault, et al., eds. The Fallen Sky: Medical
     Consequences of Thermonuclear War. Hill & Wang,
     1963. 134 p.

The first major statement by Physicians for Social Responsibility on the likely aftereffects of nuclear war: psychological
breakdown; biological ruin; epidemic disease. Generally
ignored after its publication. Those who place their faith in
fire and their hopes in "civil defense" might find the chapters "Psychiatric Considerations for Shelters" and "The Illusion of Civil Defense" appropriate reading.

506. BARASH, David P. and Lipton, Judith E. Stop Nuclear War! A Handbook. Grove Press, 1982. 396 p.

A good introduction to the psychology of the arms race, the effects of nuclear war, the various ways such a war could start, the civil defense illusion and other topics; includes well-taken advice on what individuals and the U. S. can do to reduce the threat of nuclear war. Appendixes provide lists of pertinent organizations and other publications.

507. BENNETT, John C., ed. Nuclear Weapons and the Conflict of Conscience. Scribner, 1962. 191 p.

Essays by Bennett, Erich Fromm, and others leading to the view that nuclear weapons' use is unjustified and immoral under any circumstances.

508. BIGELOW, Albert. Voyage of the Golden Rule: An Experiment with Truth. Doubleday, 1960, 286 p.

Bigelow, a Quaker, attempted in 1958 to sail a small boat, with the help of three companions, into the Eniwetok atomic test site at a time scheduled for a blast. The motive: nonviolent protest of nuclear weapons. Inspiring at times, but suffers from a desire to tell everything, whether heroic or trivial.

509. BOULTON, David, ed. Voices from the Crowd, Against the H-Bomb. Peter Owen, 1964. 185 p.

Over thirty short statements from British anti-nuclear and disarmament advocates of the late 1950s and early '60s, including J. B. Priestly, Alex Comfort, Philip Toynbee, Alan Sillitoe, John Osborne, and many others. A lively, provocative collection.

510. BRADLEY, David J. No Place to Hide. Little, Brown, 1948. 182 p.

The author, a physician, served as a radiological monitor at the two atomic tests at Bikini Island in the summer of 1946. His message is evident in the title: the bomb is lethal, and the future precarious. The book is his diary of his stay at Bikini. He draws four main lessons from his atomic observations: 1) There is no defense against atomic weapons; 2) There are no adequate methods of decontamination; 3) No adequate medical or public health services are available for people in atomic attack areas; 4) the bomb "and its unborn relatives" may poison the land for centuries through radioactivity.

511. BRIGGS, Raymond. When the Wind Blows. Schocken Books, 1982. 38 p.

A brilliantly-conceived and executed comic strip tale of a meek English couple slowly succumbing to radiation death at their countryside home following a nuclear war. The pathos is heightened by their recollection of WW II: "It was nice in the War, really...." Some images from this book--like those of an ICBM standing erect and ready for ignition, and of a gigantic nuclear submarine sliding through the ocean like a mutant beast--are chilling and unforgettable. Brings home the war that threatens in a most convincing way.

512. CALDICOTT, Helen. Nuclear Madness: What You Can Do. Autumn Press, 1978. 120 p.

Caldicott is one of the most prominent antinuclear figures in the U.S.; she opposes both nuclear power and weapons with great vehemence and conviction, and can be very persuasive, as she is here.

513. CHIVIAN, Eric, et al., eds. Last Aid: The Medical Dimensions of Nuclear War. W.H. Freeman, 1982. 338 p.

Composed primarily of papers presented at the First Congress of International Physicians for the Prevention of Nuclear War, held in 1981 in Washington, D.C. Covers physical and psychological effects of nuclear bombing, epidemics among survivors, radiation, etc. Many photographs. A good treatment. Includes index, bibliography.

514. CLARK, Grenville. Plan for Peace. Harper, 1950. 83 p.

Contends that "disarmament is the crux of the problem of world order, and that only disarmament in all arms and by all nations will suffice." Disarmament is to be achieved under the authority of a "World Federation," "whose membership shall include every country and whose authority, though strictly limited, shall bind all the nations." Along the way reflects on what we might expect from a third world war.

515. COLE, Paul M. and Taylor, William J., eds. The Nuclear Freeze Debate: Arms Control Issues for the 1980s. Westview Press, 1983. 245 p.

Elucidations of some of the issues connected with the Nuclear Freeze movement. Essays cover Congressional attitudes toward the Freeze, European anti-nuclear sentiments, questions of Freeze verification, the role of U.S. churches in the nuclear debate, and reaction of the Reagan administration to the issues.

516. COUSINS, Norman. In Place of Folly. Harper, 1961. 224 p.

Cousins argues that we must turn to world government if we are to escape self-destruction with the bomb.

517. _____. Modern Man is Obsolete. Viking, 1945. 59 p.

An expanded version of the author's much-noted Saturday Review (Aug. 18, 1945) editorial in which he points out the urgent necessity for "the transformation or adjustment from national man to world man" to prevent nuclear war.

518. DAVIS, Barbara N., ed. Voices for Peace Anthology. Voices for Peace, Rochester, N.Y., 1983. 47 p.

A nice collection of poems attempting to come to terms with peace movement issues, many directly concerned with nuclearism. Work by both prominent and little-known writers.

519. DRINAN, Robert F. Beyond the Nuclear Freeze. Seabury, 1983. 170 p.

The former Congressman regards the Freeze movement as a desperate public call that policy makers would do well to heed. Surveys the nuclear area, finds cause for alarm at the Reagan administration's attitude regarding arms control; in his final chapter discusses possible ways to avert nuclear war.

520. EPSTEIN, William and Toyoda, T., eds. A New Design for Nuclear Disarmament. Bertrand Russell Peace Foundation, 1977. 338 p.

Papers from the 25th Pugwash Conference held in Kyoto, Japan, 1975, focusing on the need for disarmament. The concluding report calls for a complete nuclear test moratorium, negotiations to eliminate strategic delivery systems, removal of tactical nuclear weapons from border areas, etc.

521. FEDERATION of American Scientists. Seeds of Promise: The First Real Hearings on the Nuclear Arms Freeze. Brick House Publishing Company, 1983. 213 p.

The transcripts of late-1982 hearings in Washington, D. C. in which a panel selected by the F. A. S. leads witnesses Randall Forsberg, Richard Garwin, Paul C. Warnke, and Robert Dean to discuss a wide variety of questions related to the proposal for a mutual U. S. -Soviet freeze on nuclear weapons. The witnesses and panelists speak from various points of view: Forsberg is one of the originators of the National Freeze Campaign, Dean a Reagan administration spokesman. A good introduction in an easy to follow question-answer format.

522. FORD, Daniel F. , et. al. Beyond the Freeze: Steps to Avoid Nuclear War. Beacon Press, 1982. 132 p.

A straightforward, readable book from the Union of Concerned Scientists, gives a clear picture of the arms race and the Reagan administration's "we can prevail" nuclear policy, then makes some worthwhile suggestions on how to avoid nuclear war.

● ● ●

"The freeze movement is an indication that the public has lost its faith in the priests who have directed nuclear policy for all these years. It is a sign of the liveliness of American democracy. "
> --William Colby, former
> CIA Director and Freeze
> advocate. Item 580, p. 6.

● ● ●

523. GIANGRANDE, Carole. The Nuclear North: The People, the Regions and the Arms Race. House of Anansi Press, 1983. 231 p.

The author, a Canadian Broadcasting Corporation employee and professional interviewer, spoke with many Canadians involved in or affected by the country's role in nuclear weapons. Covers the Cruise missile issue (partially built and tested in Canada), the link between Saskatchewan uranium and weapons production, political considerations, the Canadian nuclear power program and proliferation, and the Canadian peace movement. Includes an interesting discussion of the after-math of the Direct Action group bombing of the Litton plant responsible for the Cruise guidance system. The attention to the effects of the arms race on Canada's native population is an exception to the usual rule of the nuclear thumb, which is to ignore these people.

524. GOLLANCZ, Victor. The Devil's Repertoire: Or, Nuclear Bombing and the Life of Man. Doubleday, 1959. 192 p.

The English publisher makes a plea for unilateral disarma-ment, based in his belief that any use of nuclear weapons would represent the exercise of utter evil.

525. GROUND Zero. Nuclear War: What's in it for You? Pocket Books, 1982. 272 p.

For the citizen who can stand to read only one book on the topic, this may be the one, because it's all here in a readily-digestible form. An overview of the arms race, what hap-pens when a nuclear bomb goes off (particularly to the people in its vicinity), glossary of terms, basic questions answered --and much-needed counsel on how one citizen can help re-verse the arms race and diminish the nuclear threat.

526. _____. What About the Russians--and Nuclear War? Pocket Books, 1983. 237 p.

A useful and popularly-written overview of Russian history and of post-Hiroshima nuclear bargaining, strategy and psy-chology. Aimed at clarifying Soviet ambitions and actions.

527. HELLER, Steven, ed. War Heads: Cartoonists Draw the Line. Penguin Books, 1983. 96 p.

Anti-bomb and anti-war cartoons by close to 100 artists. Some of these are fairly whimsical: Mark Stevens's "My MX Missile Plan" shows a group of missiles pointed harmlessly straight down into the earth; some of it is very strong and angry stuff, such as "The De-Creation of Man by Reagan," in which Gerald Scarfe portrays Reagan--with echoes of Michelangelo and Mickey Mouse--reaching for the bomb button.

528. JASPERS, Karl. The Future of Mankind. University of Chicago Press, 1961. 342 p.

First published in Germany under the title The Atom Bomb and the Future of Man. A meditation by one of the great contemporary philosophers on the choice humanity faces between destruction or a fundamental change in political behavior and moral attitudes.

529. KEYES, Ken. The Hundredth Monkey. Vision Books, 1982. 176 p.

An easily-read, persuasive, and encouraging polemic which cites many authorities on the dementia of the arms race and the close-at-hand quality of nuclear war as long as the race proceeds. Argues that every individual's attitude toward the bomb matters, and that global suicide is not inevitable. A uniquely-conceived and hopeful book suitable for both adolescents and adults who are not inclined to read weighty books on the subject. This book is weighty, but bears its weight lightly.

530. KING-HALL, Sir Stephen. Defense in the Nuclear Age. Fellowship of Reconciliation, 1961. 234 p.

Advocates unilateral nuclear disarmament by Great Britain. Argues that the Soviet Union would be hesitant to summarily crush the independence of a non-communist state which still retained the option of resistance by conventional means.

● ● ●

"We shall go forward trusting in Thee, knowing that we are in Thy care now and forever. In the name of Jesus Christ. Amen. "

--Chaplain's prayer for the
"Enola Gay" crew before
the flight to Hiroshima.
Item 81, p. 238.

● ● ●

531. LANGOR, Victor and Thomas, Walter. Nuclear War Funbook. Holt, 1982. 128 p.

An anti-nuclear tract in the form of a child's game book, the Funbook, with illustrations by Brent Richardson, is based on Langer's belief that we're "better active now than radioactive later!" Like Raymond Briggs's When the Wind Blows (item 511), this book removes speculation about nuclear war from the realm of academic abstraction into our own back yards-- literally. Includes a flip-book animation of a family's atomic incineration in their yard. Grim and ugly, but not uninspired.

532. LIFTON, Robert J. and Falk, Richard. Indefensible
Weapons: The Political & Psychological Case against
Nuclearism. Basic Books, 1982. 301 p.

Lifton examines the way "nuclearism" asserts itself in the
worldview of the average person, gulled by official assurances
and personal hope into trusting in the bomb for "security";
Falk looks at the ways the U.S. and the Soviets pursue a
similar self-defeating and dangerous mindset on a global level.
The message, as Dexter Masters put it in 1946, is "One
World or None." [See item 533.]

533. MASTERS, Dexter and Way, Katharine, eds. One
World or None: A Report to the Public on the Full
Meaning of the Atomic Bomb. McGraw, 1946.
79 p.

Eighteen essays, most by scientists--including J.R. Oppenheimer, Niels Bohr, and Albert Einstein, among others--
which combine to present a single message: if war is not
abolished, humanity will be. A brief but highly significant
early effort against the bomb's dominion.

534. MATTES, Kitty Campbell. In Your Hands: A Citizen's
Guide to the Arms Race. Parents for Peace, Ithaca,
N.Y., 1981. 56 p.

A very basic, easily-grasped set of arguments briefly covering such aspects of the arms race as weapons, economics,
consequences of war, treaties, etc. Would be useful at highschool or junior-high school levels.

535. MYRDAL, Alva, et al. Dynamics of European Nuclear
Disarmament. Dufour Editions, 1982. 306 p.

In the book's title essay Myrdal discusses the desirability of
a nuclear-weapons free Western Europe, an argument spurred
by fears that the forthcoming deployment of medium-range
missiles there helps set the stage for a U.S.-Soviet nuclear
war on European ground. Other essays by European nuclear
disarmament advocates provide further amplification of these
and other nuclear issues.

536. PARKIN, Frank. Middle Class Radicalism: The Social Bases of the British Campaign for Nuclear Disarmament. Praeger, 1968. 207 p.

A sociological study whose ideas could be valuable in an

analysis of the antinuclear movement of the 1980s, which far surpasses the scope of the earlier disarmament movement, but which is still fundamentally of the middle class.

537. PAULING, Linus C. No More War! Dodd, 1958.
254 p.

Pauling lays the facts of nuclear devastation on the line, and pleads for disarmament. "The time has now come, " he writes, "for morality to take its proper place in the conduct of world affairs; the time has now come for the nations of the world to submit to the just regulation of their conduct by international law. "

538. Preventing Euroshima. Mobilization for Survival, 1983. 40 p.

A guide to organizing local action against Cruise and Pershing II missile deployment. Information and suggestions on public meetings, peace camps, etc.

539. REYNOLDS, Earle. The Forbidden Voyage. McKay, 1961. 281 p.

Reynolds, his wife and two children tried to complete the course first attempted by the "Golden Rule" (item 508) by sailing into a nuclear test zone in the Pacific. Told in diary form. The author was a member of the U. S. Atomic Bomb Casualty Commission which studied the aftermath of the Hiroshima blast. Reynolds undertook the voyage, prematurely terminated by arrest and trial, partly because he was convinced that the Atomic Energy Commission was hiding from the public the truth about radioactive fallout.

540. RUSSELL, Bertrand A. Common Sense and Nuclear Warfare. Allen & Unwin, 1959. 93 p.

Russell once said that, following the bombing of Japan, he could scarcely walk the streets of London without seeing a vision of the great city laid waste by atomic bombs. Here he speaks to both East and West with a plea for disarmament and peaceful co-existence based on the belief that the destruction of civilization is not merited by any conceivable political or military goal.

541. _____. Has Man a Future? Simon & Schuster, 1962. 128 p.

If the arms race continues, the answer is no. If world government can be obtained, yes. In the meantime, nothing can justify the use of nuclear weapons.

542. SCHELL, Jonathan. The Fate of the Earth. Knopf, 1982. 244 p.

So far the decade's most influential work on the prospect of nuclear war. Schell has taken criticism from many sources, both left and right, for imagining only the worst case and for an allegedly naïve worldview, yet the worst case is what probably the majority of nuclear weapons authorities expect should the weapons ever be used again, and Schell's call for a revision of our whole manner of seeing the world is not that far from Einstein's appeal in the same vein nearly forth years earlier. In spite of its detractors, the book has been a point of departure for many readers in their effort to understand the nuclear threat.

● ● ●

''There are at the present time two great nations in the world, which started from different points, but seem to tend towards the same end. I allude to the Russians and the Americans. ''
--Alexis de Tocqueville,
1835. Democracy in
America, Knopf, 1956,
vol. 1, p. 434.

● ● ●

543. SCHWEITZER, Albert. Peace or Atomic War? Holt, 1958. 47 p.

The texts of three radio broadcasts from Oslo in 1958 in which Schweitzer called for prompt disarmament.

544. _____. Teaching of Reverence for Life. Holt, Rinehart & Winston, 1965. 63 p.

Six essays based on Schweitzer's uncompromising objections to nuclear weapons and the prospect of their further use.

545. SCOVILLE, Herbert and Osborn, Robert. Missile Madness. Houghton, 1970. 93 p.

Notable chiefly for cartoonist Osborn's nearly 50 illustrations depicting steps awaiting us on the road to nuclear ruin if the nuclear nations do not control their worst inclinations.

546. SWING, Raymond. In the Name of Sanity. Harper,
      1946. 116 p.

Urges world unity, international government and the abolition
of war as the only alternative to the destruction of civilization.

547. TAYLOR, Richard and Pritchard, Colin. The Protest
      Makers: The British Nuclear Disarmament Move-
      ment of 1958-1965 Twenty Years On. Pergamon
      Press, 1980. 190 p.

A political and sociological study based on two sources: a
questionnaire completed by more than 400 antinuclear activists, and detailed interviews with over twenty movement
leaders. The questionnaire is included.

548. THOMPSON, E. P. Beyond the Cold War: A New Ap-
      proach to the Arms Race and Nuclear Annihilation.
      Pantheon, 1982. 198 p.

Thompson, probably the chief English representative in
Europe's antinuclear movement, is certainly the optimist,
but his program for European unity against the newly-
invigorated arms race seems based more on wishful thinking
than distasteful reality. This collection of pieces on E. N. D.
(European Nuclear Disarmament) is not without some valuable
ideas, however.

549. _____ and Smith, Dan, eds. Protest and Survive.
      Monthly Review Press, 1981. 216 p.

Eleven essays on arms control, the arms race, the nuclear
threat, and disarmament.

550. TOYNBEE, Philip, ed. The Fearful Choice: A De-
      bate on Nuclear Policy. V. Gollancz, 1958. 112 p.

A compilation of opinions revolving around Toynbee's advocacy
of unilateral nuclear disarmament.

551. WALLIS, Jim, ed. Waging Peace: A Handbook for
      the Struggle Against Nuclear Arms. Harper & Row,
      1982. 304 p.

A nice collection of essays on nuclear matters for Christian
activists. Background on the global strategic situation, the
role of faith, witnessing for peace.

● Periodical Articles ●

552. ADLER, Alice. "A Call for Disarmament." Gray
Panther Network, July 1982, p. 13.

"As Gray Panthers, we passionately care about humanity's
survival." A column on the June 12, 1982 disarmament rally
in New York City and the desirability of a nuclear Freeze.

553. _____. "Attempts to Thaw Freeze Movement Fail."
Gray Panther Network, Jan. 1983, p. 13+

Description of right-wing attack on the Freeze movement,
discusses various antinuclear actions around the country.
The author is founder of the Gray Panthers of Chicago, a
chapter of the national organization of older citizens.

554. "An All-American Movement." Inquiry: A Libertarian
Review 5 (June 1982): 3.

Argues that the nuclear freeze movement has grown "too
large too fast to be molded, manipulated, or extinguished by
any outside group. It has transcended the left/right paradigm
and has left both these camps to watch from the sidelines."
Criticizes Reagan administration attempts to portray--with
complete cynicism--Freeze advocates as Kremlin dupes.

555. ATHANASIOU, Tom. "A Cure for the Common Cold
War: The European Resistance to the New Missiles
and the American Peace Movement." Radical America 16 (July-Oct. 1982): 21-34.

Discusses various factions involved in the Euromissile protests and laments the insufficiently radical U.S. movement
for the Freeze. Is distressed over the "great orthodoxy" of
the Freeze and the disregard its supporters seem to have for
basic issues of war, peace, poverty, etc.

556. BERES, Louis Rene. "Embracing Omnicide: President Reagan and the Strategic Mythmakers." Hudson
Review 36 (Spring 1983): 18-29.

An angry, bewildered tirade against the Reagan nuclear policies as a combination of stupid opportunism, psychopathology,
and the sheer inability to think. One of the most pointed and
passionate objections to the Reaganite worldview that one could
hope to find.

557. _____. "Tilting Toward Thanatos: America's 'Countervailing' Nuclear Strategy. " World Politics 34 (Oct. 1981): 25-46.

Criticizes the policy of limited nuclear warfighting across a broad spectrum; argues for greater public awareness of the nuclear threat, further efforts toward nonproliferation, a mutual U. S. -Soviet "no first use" pledge, and a comprehensive nuclear test ban.

558. _____. "Victory Is Not Possible: A Rejoinder to the Strategic Mythmakers. " Policy Studies Review 2 (Feb. 1983): 359-369.

Attacks current U. S. strategic policy for embracing the "limited" and "winnable" nuclear war syndrome. Believes that the only likely result of this shift in U. S. doctrine is heightened Soviet nervousness regarding U. S. first-strike intentions. Nuclear "victory" is a pipe dream which overlooks the consequences of death, injury, disease, and other effects that nuclear war would bring.

559. BOYTE, Harry C. "The Formation of the New Peace Movement: A Communitarian Perspective. " Social Policy 13 (Summer 1982): 4-8.

On the grass roots origins of the peace and the pro-Freeze movement; emphasis on community organizing, the right and responsibility of citizens to take local action; characterizes the movement as transcending narrow ideological interests, and thus impossible for government to control.

560. BRADFORD, George. "Norman Mayer and the Missile X. " Fifth Estate 17 (Winter 1982): 7+

Mr. Mayer seized the Washington Monument in December, 1982, and threatened to blow it up as a protest against the MX missile. He possessed no explosives, and was shot to death by the police. Bradford holds Mayer's action as a desperate effort to awaken a dozing public to the danger their silence encourages.

561. BRUBAKER, Bob. "Direct Action Bombs Litton. " Fifth Estate 17 (Winter 1982): 4+

An account of the Oct. 14, 1982 bomb blast which destroyed part of the Litton Systems Canada Ltd. plant in Rexdale, Ontario, home of the guidance system for the Cruise missile.

The group Direct Action claimed responsibility for the bombing, which injured seven. The author is ambivalent about D. A. 's tactics.

562. "But War's Not the Remedy. " Industrial Worker 79 (July 1982): 1.

An editorial calling for the average person, who has "far too little to say" about world events, "to develop that little to the full. " The alternative is "for a few heads of state to demolish forever in a few hours our hopes for a happy and prosperous Planet Earth. "

563. CHALFONT, Alun. "The Great Unilateralist Illusion. " Encounter 40 (April 1983): 18-38.

Attacks the British Campaign for Nuclear Disarmament as a deluded movement which has willingly rallied around the slogan "Ignorance is Strength" from Orwell's 1984. Cites the usual arguments raised against unilateral disarmament, including prospects for "Finlandization" of Western Europe without a shot fired. Dwells on Soviet encouragement of the antinuclear movement and charges, incredibly, that opposition to Margaret Thatcher and Ronald Reagan is the first step on the path to "the disintegration of the West's system of collective security. "

564. CLARK, Jil. "No Nukes, No Queers? Lesbians, Gay Men and the Anti-Nuclear Movement. " Gay Community News 10 (Nov. 27, 1982): 8.

A good discussion of the roles gays and lesbians occupy in the antinuclear movement, including their relations with straight protestors and with the public at large. " [G]enerally cops reserve their most sadistic treatment for the dykes and fags. "

565. CONETTA, Carl. "Common Sense for a Mass Movement. " WIN 18 (Nov. 1, 1982): 15-18.

Shares some of the reservations about the Freeze movement as too shallow in its social vision, but acknowledges the rectitude of "nuclear madness" as a descriptive term for superpower strategy. Believes that the Freeze can inspire new activists toward work on fundamental issues concerning interventionism, the draft, militarization of the economy, etc.

566. Counterspy 6 (July-Aug. 1982).

This issue focuses on nuclear topics, including coverage of
protests against the weapons in the Pacific island of Belau,
a "Documentary History" of U.S. nuclear threats in Eastern
Europe, Korea, Vietnam, Berlin, Cuba, Laos, etc.; also
looks at the first-strike utility of the Navy's ELF communications system, and nuclear research at Princeton University.

567.   "Creating a Nuclear Free Pacific." WIN 18 (Aug. 1,
       1982).

A 23-page special feature, with articles on nuclear waste
dumping in the Pacific, grassroots opposition to nuclear power
in the Philippines, French bomb tests in Polynesia, U.S. nuclear buildup in the region, the Japanese antinuclear movement,
victims of fallout in the Marshall Islands.

568.   "The Cry for Peace." New Age 7 (June 1982).

An issue devoted to the peace movement, articles treating
the movement's standing, American atomic-test casualties,
peace through personal action and "positive thinking," Chicago's Peace Museum, etc.

569.   CUNNINGHAM, Ann Marie.   "Preventive Medicine."
       Working Papers Magazine 10 (Jan.-Feb. 1983): 28-
       33.

Profiles Howard H. Hiatt, Dean of the Harvard School of
Public Health and a prominent antinuclear voice. Dr. Hiatt
has done much to broaden the base of the peace movement
"by describing nuclear war as a public health problem."
Describes Hiatt's conversion to the antinuclear view (spurred
by Vice President George Bush's remarks about the U.S.
"winning" a nuclear war.) Attention to problems associated
with the antinuclear movement's growing institutional respec-
tability.

570.   DARNOVSKY, Marcy.   "Smile and Say Freeze." Radi-
       cal America 16 (July-Oct. 1982): 7-9.

Friendly criticism of the Freeze movement as too concerned
with its immediate objective and not attentive to underlying
causes of the arms race or the problems (thousands of warheads) still to be dealt with even if a Freeze succeeds. Cites
the 1963 Test Ban as historical precedent for partial success
leaving the door open for further trouble--since the atmospheric ban did nothing to keep weapons from being tested underground.

571. DAY, Samuel H. 'The New Resistance: Confronting the Nuclear War Machine." Progressive 47 (April 1983): 22-30.

The author, a former editor of the Bulletin of the Atomic Scientists, covers the growth of peaceful antinuclear civil disobedience, reporting that at least 4,000 persons were arrested in the U.S. in 1982 for acts of civil disobedience against nuclear facilities. Includes a profile of Jack and Felice Cohen-Joppa, publishers of the newspaper The Nuclear Resister, among other sketches of those active in the movement.

572. _____. 'The Restless Ranchers of Missile Country." Progressive 47 (Oct. 1983): 22-25.

An account of the developing grass roots movement among Montana ranchers and other residents toward removal of ICBMs from the 200 silos which pepper the north central part of the state. Focus on the "Silence One Silo" campaign, aimed at "decommissioning" one ICBM launch site. Includes report of the author's arrest and jail sentence for coming within 25 feet of the fence surrounding a silo site.

573. FERRY, W.H. 'What Was I Doing with Such Dreams?" Monthly Review 34 (Jan. 1983): 43+

The elderly U.S. organizer for European Nuclear Disarmament speaks of how he has shelved plans for a genteel retirement of travel, reading, and piano study for dedication of the remainder of his life to the antinuclear movement.

• ◦ •

'The Air Force treats us like a bunch of Vietnam peasants. As far as the Air Force is concerned, there is nothing out here but missile silos. That's all they care about."
                    --Montana rancher David
                      Hastings, in whose former
                      land the Air Force main-
                      tains ICBMs. Item 572,
                      p. 22.

• ◦ •

574. FLICKINGER, Richard. "Public Opinion, The Peace Movement and NATO Missile Deployment." Peace and Change 9 (Spring 1983): 17-30.

Investigates the question of how, if at all, public opinion and
the peace movement affected the nuclear buildup in the Nether-
lands, West Germany, and Great Britain. Concludes that all
three governments have responded to movement pressure
through buying time (hoping the deployment issue would go
away), supporting arms control negotiations, and propagandi-
zing in behalf of official nuclear policy.

575. FOOTE, Frederick C. "No Nukes, No Consistency. "
      The Freeman 33 (August 1983): 460-461.

Those who protest nuclear weapons are "peaceniks" who re-
fuse to admit the true origin of the arms race: socialism.
Why, if it weren't for socialism, we would be living in a
world at peace in the glories of laissez-faire capitalism, "the
only social system fundamentally opposed to war. " Assumes,
for no discernible reason, that nuclear protestors have in
mind only U.S. weapons. Textbook right-wing hyperventila-
tion.

576. GORDON, Suzanne. "The Ultimate Single Issue: How
      Middle America Learned to Stop Loving the Bomb and
      Start Worrying. " Working Papers Magazine 9 (May-
      June 1982): 20-25.

An account of the antinuclear weapons and Freeze movement's
development in the U.S. , with attention focused on the Freeze
referendum on the November, 1982 California ballot.

577. "The Great Debate: To Freeze or Not to Freeze?"
      New Age 8 (January 1983): 32 +

A generally acrimonious debate among Phyllis Schlafly, John
Anderson, Helen Caldicott, Michio Kaku and other pro- and
anti-nuclear Freeze spokespersons. The debate generates far
more heat than light, turns (in many cases) on simplistic
slogans and trite characterizations, and in its depressing
head-butting typifies the usual feeble level at which public
debate of emotional issues takes place.

578. HARRIS, Martyn. "Where the Disarmers Stand Now. "
      New Society 65 (Sept. 8, 1983): 353-355.

A human-interest portrayal of England's present Campaign for
Nuclear Disarmament on the eve of Cruise missile shipment
to Great Britain. The author considers the movement's factional differences "problems of growth rather than morbidity. "

579. HOLSWORTH, Robert D. "A World Worth Living In: The Making of a Counter-Culture in the New Peace Movement. " The Massachusetts Review 23 (Winter 1982): 573-592.

An effort "to explain the criticisms which the new peace activists make of American society, " and to evaluate their preferred culture. The author spent a year studying local peace activism in Richmond, Virginia. Part of the essay concerns the way activists connect their perceptions of the nuclear threat to broad aspects of U.S. life; part concerns their work to spread their beliefs among their fellow citizens.

580. JUDIS, John B. "Freeze Movement is Snowballing ... " In These Times 7 (March 23-29, 1983): 6-8.

On the growing public sympathy--and action in behalf of--the Freeze. Cites arguments of such authorities as Paul Warnke in response to criticism of the Freeze. Discusses organizational difficulties of Freeze movement and Freeze fortunes connected with the 1984 Presidential campaign.

581. KEELEY, James. "Myth and Magic in Disarmament. " International Perspectives: The Canadian Journal on World Affairs (Sept. -Oct. 1983): 11-15.

Considers the disarmament movement politically naïve and so-far uninterested in the international complexities of disarmament, though does not dismiss disarmament as a rational goal.

582. KEYES, Ken. "You Could be the Hundredth Monkey. " New Age 7 (March 1982): 46-49.

Combines a personality profile of Keyes [see also item 529] with excerpts from his book The Hundredth Monkey. Keyes is a powerful believer in the ability of grass roots activism to reverse the arms race and the threat of nuclear war.

583. KLARE, Michael T. "Inescapable Links: Interventionism and Nuclear War. " Our Generation 15 (Fall 1982): 7-10.

Points out the antinuclear movement's failure to adequately address the threat of nuclear war posed by conventional military action of nuclear powers, e.g., Great Britain in the Falklands. Lists and describes a number of considerations which should enlighten the reader on this issue, such as the increasing ferocity of conventional war, the inclination of superpowers to meddle in Third World conflicts, and the proliferation of "hot spots" and war zones on a global basis.

584. LEONARD, Jonathan A. "Danger--Nuclear War." Monthly Review 32 (Feb. 1981): 23-34.

Discusses the new vitality of the antinuclear group Physicians for Social Responsibility. Focus on the issues provoking the group to intensified action and on some of the individuals involved. (The same article appears in the Nov. -Dec. 1980 Harvard Magazine.)

585. LIFTON, Robert J. "Beyond Psychic Numbing: A Call to Awareness." American Journal of Orthopsychiatry 52 (Oct. 1982): 619-629.

Lifton turns to the theme he has dealt with often: the self-defeating defenses we raise against the nuclear threat, the "numbing" we employ to avert the distress of nuclear consciousness. Lifton is not hopeless in spite of a grim assessment; he believes that the growing public recognition of the nuclear war threat is grounds for change.

586. _____. "The Prevention of Nuclear War." Bulletin of the Atomic Scientists 36 (Oct. 1980): 38-43.

Adapted from a speech at a conference on nuclear war's medical consequences. "A potential change of consciousness is held out before us.... Certainly, we have to agree that however things go, we are all involved in the process."

587. LIPSEY, David. "What Do We Think about the Nuclear Threat?" New Society 53 (Sept. 25, 1980): 603-606.

Reports results of 1980 Gallup opinion survey of a sample of British adults concerning nuclear war-related issues. Findings include a high degree of concern, low faith in the power of antinuclear activism to reduce the threat.

588. LIVINGSTON, Robert G. "Anti-Nuclear Protest and the Alliance." Atlantic Community Quarterly 21 (Spring 1983): 63-70.

Calls the anti-nuclear movement a "problem of the first magnitude" because it interferes with U. S. -European freedom of nuclear policy. Refers to nuclear opponents as "peaceniks."

This generally hostile-to-disarmament advocates article never-theless concludes that "sustained effort at nuclear arms limitation" must be a keystone "of any Western policy toward the Soviet Union that is to retain public support. "

589. LOWN, Bernard. "Nuclear War and the Public Health." Journal of Public Health Policy 3 (March 1982): 12-21.

States that 400 megatons dropped on either the U. S. or the U. S. S. R. could immediately destroy 30 percent of their populations and 75 percent of either's industrial capacity. Each nation possesses over 13, 000 megatons. Discusses the international movement of physicians against nuclear war; "we must break out of the intellectual stranglehold of conditioned responses and habitual modes of thinking" to deal effectively with the nuclear threat.

590. McFADDEN, Dave, et al. "The Freeze Economy: The Economic Impact of a Bilateral Nuclear Weapons Freeze. " Socialist Review 13 (July-Aug. 1983): 35-65.

Calls the Reagan military buildup a drain on the economy as well as a hindrance to national security; holds that over $200 billion in national budget savings as a result of a Freeze could be invested in creative projects beneficial to the economy. (Many mainstream economists, including Murray Weidenbaum, former chairman of the Council of Economic Advisers under Reagan, have decamped from the old platitude that "war is good business. " War has never been good business for more than a very few, and nuclear war would be bad for everyone's business.)

591. MARTIN, Brian. "How the Peace Movement Should be Preparing for Nuclear War. " Bulletin of Peace Proposals 13 (Nov. 2, 1982): 149-159.

A thought-provoking if sobering examination of the need for the peace activist to prepare psychologically for a nuclear war. Protest is the best form of civil defense, but if such war occurs--as it probably will, in Martin's estimation--one must be ready to apply whatever constructive energy is possible toward a re-ordered society. Counsels resistance against state oppression, anticipation of moral dullness, attention to the terminally injured, etc. Short but useful looking bibliography.

592. MEWES, Horst. "The West German Green Party."
      New German Critique (Winter 1983): 51-85.

The Green Party, which originated as a radical ecology party,
won over 5 percent of the popular vote in the March, 1983
German federal election, good for 27 seats in the Bundestag.
This article examines the history and current role of the
Greens, who have become among the most vocal opponents of
the nuclear arms race. Mewes finds the Greens' historical
roots not in Romanticism, as is often believed, but in socialism.

593. MOJTABAI, A. G. "Amarillo: The End of the Line."
      Working Papers Magazine 9 (July-Aug. 1982): 26-35.

Amarillo, Texas, is the site of final U. S. nuclear weapons
construction at the Pantex Plant. The author discusses the
plant and its employees, local religious leaders' accommodation of the place (they defend it with Biblical quotations), and
profiles Bishop Leroy Matthiesen, who has called upon Pantex
workers to turn to more peacefully-oriented labor. [See also
item 610.]

594. MURAVCHIK, Joshua. "The Perils of a Nuclear Freeze."
      World Affairs 145 (Fall 1982): 203-207.

The author argues, in this journal published by the ironically-
named "American Peace Society," that the "genuinely peace-
seeking" U. S. must not be blinded by the attractions of the
Freeze, for a freeze on nuclear weapons would merely encourage Soviet aggression. Only by rearming and practicing
deterrence, including the specific threat of nuclear weapons
use, can true peace be maintained in these nuclear times.

595. NELSON, Bob. "News Media Miss the Point." Gay
      Community News 9 (June 26, 1982): 1.

Critical analysis of mainstream media coverage of the June
12, 1982 antinuclear demonstration in Manhattan. Accuses
the New York Times and Wall Street Journal of a failure of
seriousness, red-baiting, and, in the case of the Daily News
treatment, suggests journalistic incompetence. A particular
sticking point: refusal of mainstream papers to acknowledge
gay and lesbian components of the antinuclear crowd.

596. "Nuke Plant Blast." Overthrow 4 (No. 3, 1982): 8-9.

This is a statement from Direct Action, the group which

claimed responsibility for the Oct. 14, 1982 bomb attack on the Litton plant--home of the Cruise missile guidance system --near Toronto. Admits that mistakes resulted in injuries, but emphasizes the group's belief that "widely practiced militant resistance and sabotage will become effective ... " in combatting the global rush to nuclear oblivion.

597. PALMER, Bryan. "Rearming the Peace Movement." Canadian Dimension 16 (July 1982): 3-6.

An overview in one of Canada's best alternative magazines of the peace and antinuclear movement as response to reckless strategic policies and weapons developments of the 1980s. Includes discussion of the peace movement's Canadian potential, and a statement in behalf of the Canadian group Academics for Nuclear Disarmament.

598. PETERS, Paul. "The Triumph of Angst: The Green and the Black in Germany." Canadian Forum, (June 1983): p. 14-17.

Reviews the Greens' rise in West Germany and their antagonistic relationship with the Christian Democrats (their party color is black), who support the deployment of the Euromissiles. The author looks forward to a long season of civil disobedience and demonstration against the missiles.

599. "The Race Against Death." Mother Jones 7 (Sept. - Oct. 1982).

A "Special Disarmament Issue," with articles on the Freeze, the arms race, the European disarmament movement, a current profile of Daniel Ellsberg, the "Holocaust Lobby" (advocates of "winning" nuclear war), and an excellent parody of Ripley's "Believe it or Not" on nuclear weapons madness.

• • •

On Genocide: "The Contracting Parties confirm that genocide, whether committed in time of peace or war, is a crime under international law which they undertake to prevent or punish."
--The Geneva Convention, Article I.

• • •

600. RENSENBRINK, John. "The Anti-Nuclear Phenomenon: A New Look at Fundamental Human Interests." New Political Science 7 (Fall 1981): 75-89.

Makes seven "observations" not only on the antinuclear movement but on environmentalism in general.   These include the
movements' bases in perceived threat to physical security and
biological continuity, the threat of nuclear pollution to civilization's survival capacity, the threat to land and livelihood
not only of whole communities and regions but to the planet
itself; the author's belief that the immense destructive potential of nuclear arsenals may point toward survival through
"real communication" suggests that Einstein's call for a new
way of thinking is alive and well.

601.   RIORDAN, Michael.   "Cruising for Peace." Body
        Politic 91 (March 1983):   33-35.

An account of the Canadian group Gay-Lesbian Action for
Disarmament (GLAD) and its opposition to Litton and the
Cruise missile it helps manufacture.

602.   "Robert Jay Lifton: Art and the Imagery of Extinc-
        tion."   Performing Arts Journal 6 (No. 3, 1982):
        51-66.

An interview with Lifton in which he speaks of "nuclear fundamentalism," the effort in the U.S. to deny death's reality
and other topics; Lifton thinks that the growing number of
people making the imaginative effort to deal with the threat
of nuclear war "means more and more people are open to
art in the best sense," an openness that concerned and alert
people in the theater can turn to their and the public's advantage.   (Performing Arts Journal has published several
articles and features in the last few years on the theater's
connection with the antinuclear movement.)

603.   SAGAN, Carl.   "Planet Earth: A Universal Anomaly."
        Gray Panther Network, Jan.-Feb. 1982, p. 4+

Declaring "no issue more important than nuclear war," as-
tronomer Sagan describes the consequences of nuclear war,
and urges attention to the need for disarmament.   "[T]hrough
the courageous examination of these deep and painful issues
... we can make an important contribution towards preserving
and enhancing the life that has graced our small world."

604.   SCHOFIELD, Rosalie F.   "Beyond the Freeze Campaign."
        Gray Panther Network, July-Aug. 1982, p. 3+

On direct action against a Trident submarine in Groton, Conn., by the "Trident Nein"; ties the action to traditions of protest carried on by members of Jonah House, a Baltimore group which enacts die-ins and spreads ashes and human blood on the pillars of the Defense Department and the Pentagon. Jonah House members call for not just a nuclear freeze, but for a freeze on violence.

605. SMITH, Damu. "The U.S. Peace Movement and the Middle East." Freedomways 23 (No. 2, 1983): 70-80.

Smith thinks that the U.S. peace movement is too single-minded in its devotion to nuclear disarmament, that it does not carefully or thoughtfully examine regional conflict sites capable of leading to superpower confrontation, nor does it pay sufficient attention to the conventional armaments race.

606. "Special Section on the German Peace Movement." Telos: A Quarterly Journal of Critical Thought No. 56 (Summer 1983): 119-192.

Eight articles on the movement by writers both hostile and friendly toward it. Attention to politics, motivations, historical origins, and future directions of the Greens and their sympathizers. Excellent source for a variety of clashing views.

607. STEINKE, Rudolf and Vale, Michel, eds. "Germany Debates Defense: The NATO Alliance at the Crossroads." International Journal of Politics 13 (Spring-Summer 1983): 208 p.

A special issue published in collaboration with the Committee for a Nuclear-Free Europe. Analysis of "the Soviet threat," relevance of the German peace movement to Europe at large, alternatives to nuclear deterrence as defense policy. See especially Christian Krause's "What Is a Military Threat: An Analysis of an Ambiguous Concept," p. 5-15, for an interesting departure from "the threat to the West" routinely trumpeted by the popular media.

608. SWEET, William. "Can Green Grow?" Progressive 47 (May 1983): 28-33.

On the accession of the radically antinuclear and anti-industrial West German Green Party; covers some establishment and leftist criticism of the Greens, speculation on ability of Greens to grow through their uncompromising devotion to the ideas that matter to them.

609. _____ . "Europe's Peace Movement: Topic or Target?" Columbia Journalism Review 22 (Sept. -Oct. 1983): 46-50.

Brief but worthwhile criticism of the frequently shallow and distorted coverage of the European antinuclear movement in the U.S. press.

610. TOTTEN, Sam and Totten, Martha W. "An Act of Faith." Southern Exposure 11 (March-April 1983): 46-50.

The Tottens interview Bishop Leroy Matthiesen, who has urged workers at Amarillo's Pantex Plant (final assembly point for U.S. nuclear weapons) to "consider the moral implications of their work." Discusses his relations with Pantex workers, the community, and the religious grounds for his anti-nuclearism.

611. _____ . "You Don't Have to be Grim to be Serious." Southern Exposure 11 (Jan. -Feb. 1983): 29-33.

An interview with Mavis Belisle, Dallas antinuclear activist, both weapons and power. Ms. Belisle talks about her motivations, her protest and arrest over a nuclear plant, and her view of her work.

612. "Unions Can Build Peace." Industrial Worker 79 (June 1982): 1.

Cites various authorities on the nature of nuclear devastation, posits the international union movement as one antidote to the nuclear disease.

613. VON BREDOW, Wilfried. "The Peace Movement in the Federal Republic of Germany: Composition and Objectives." Armed Forces and Society 9 (Fall 1982): 33-48.

Locates the intellectual and political streams of the movement as flowing from a German tradition of Christian and humanist pacifism antedating WW I; the ecological movement; "undogmatic" socialism; and communism. Believes that the possibility of a "unite Germany" movement is not to be discounted but doubts that the movement "will generate a serious strategic debate" about Western Europe's defense, though such debate is desirable.

614. "Waging Peace." Southern Exposure 10 (Nov. -Dec. 1982): 120 p.

A special issue on the peace movement. Although the general focus is on the South, the ideas and insights are broadly applicable. Features on anti-nuclearism, the draft, economic consequences of military spending, civil defense, much more.

615. WAGONER, David. "In Distress." Bulletin of the Atomic Scientists 39 (Jan. 1983): 4-5.

A breathtaking poem on nuclear fear and disaster "selected entirely from the International Code of Signals, U. S. edition." Worth tracking down.

616. WHEELER, Tim. "Growing Challenge to Nuclear Peril." Political Affairs 61 (May 1982): 9+

An overview of the growth of the antinuclear and Freeze movements in the U. S. in both public and elected official circles, in spite of the Reaganites' efforts to portray the Soviet Union as the locus of everything wrong and evil in the world. Considerable emphasis on the criticism by McGeorge Bundy, Robert S. McNamara, et al., of the nuclear "first use option." Calls this criticism representative of a "deep split in the U. S. ruling class."

617. "Women in Italy Protest Missiles Genocide." Big Mama Rag 11 (July 1983): 13+

Reports violence against women peacefully protesting at the Comiso, Italy site in preparation for Cruise missiles. Eleven women were deported for their part in the protest.

618. WOODSON, Helen. "Harvest of Justice Editor Sentenced." Harvest of Justice: Newsletter of the Gaudete Peace and Justice Center Sept. 1983, p. 1.

Reports the arrest, trial and jail sentencing of this newsletter's editor. Ms. Woodson received a 6-month term for pouring blood on a Minuteman missile in the Smithsonian Institution's Air and Space Museum in the summer of 1983. Harvest of Justice (Gaudete Peace & Justice Center, 634 Spruce St., Madison, WI 53715) is one of a number of newsletters published on a shoestring which report antinuclear activities and civil disobedience around the country and the world. Another is The Nuclear Resister (NNNPSC, Box 37, Tempe, AZ 85281), published by the National No-Nukes Prison Support Collective.

619. WRONG, Dennis. "Avoiding Nuclear War. " <u>Partisan</u>
     <u>Review</u> 50 (No. 2, 1983): 282-290.

Characterizes antinuclear protests as "not only inevitable, "
but "also desirable as a reminder to our leaders that their
fellow citizens ... give top priority to the avoidance of nuclear war. " Believes, however, that such protest is often
shallowly informed about nuclear strategy.   Gives considerable space to critical dissection of J. Schell's <u>Fate of the</u>
<u>Earth</u> (item 542).

620. YOUNG, Nigel.   "The Contemporary European Anti-
     Nuclear Movement: Experiments in the Mobilization
     of Public Power. "   <u>Peace and Change</u> 9 (Spring
     1983):   1-16.

Traces the history and issues of the movement from Dutch
opposition to the neutron bomb in 1976 to END (the European
Nuclear Disarmament movement, originating in Britain in
1980.)   END advocates a nuclear free Europe, or, at least,
nuclear-free zones.   Analysis of program differences among
various groups; argues that the U. S. movement should not allow tactical differences to "disguise the fundamental solidari-
ty of the long-term vision. "

● ● ●

"Over the bleached bones and jumbled residue of numerous
civilizations are written the pathetic words: 'Too late.' ...
We still have a choice today: non-violent co-existence or
violent co-annihilation. "

> --Rev. Martin Luther King,
> Jr. , from his speech
> "Beyond Vietnam, " de-
> livered at Riverside
> Church, New York City,
> April 4, 1967.

● ● ●

Nuclear Power: The Establishment's Case

"The least constrained practical source of energy on a large
scale remains nuclear energy.   Not all the cries of the war-
riors against the atom can efface that fact, and if we are
very fortunate we will come to our senses on the matter,
and quickly. "

> --Samuel McCracken, Item
> 663, p. 184.

621. ADDINALL, Eric and Ellington, Henry. Nuclear Power in Perspective. Nichols Pub., 1982. 214 p.

Written in the belief that reliance on nuclear power is necessary unless we "adopt a radically different economic and industrial policy, together with a drastic change in lifestyle ... totally unacceptable to the great majority of the public." This is an attempt to correct what the authors see as the consistent "bad press" given nuclear power. Gives the basics of nuclear reactors, radioactivity, suggests long-term nuclear energy strategy. Focus is on the situation in Great Britain.

622. AVIEL, S. David. The Politics of Nuclear Energy. University Press of America, 1982. 263 p.

Investigates attitudes of Congressional members and State governors toward nuclear power. Employs the questionnaire method to determine such attitudes.

623. BECKMANN, Petr. The Health Hazards of NOT Going Nuclear. Golem, 1976. 190 p.

Dedicated "To Ralph Nader and all who worship the water he walks on," this is a pro-nuclear polemic in one sense, but in a broader sense is a tirade against what the author regards the typically know-nothing criticism of nuclear power. No trace of restraint or any notion that opposing arguments bear even a shred of substance. Does reveal some casual idiocies in the antinuclear arguments some prominent figures have made, and is therefore of interest to the antinuclear activist.

624. BISHOP, Amasa S. Project Sherwood: The U.S. Program in Controlled Fusion. Addison-Wesley, 1958. 216 p.

Bishop was head of the Atomic Energy Commission's Controlled Thermonuclear Branch; this is a study of the A.E.C. fusion program in the 1950s. Strictly a technical approach.

625. BUPP, Irvin C. and Derian, Jean-Claude. Light Water: How the Nuclear Dream Dissolved. Basic Books, 1978. 241 p.

Focus on the failure of American-built light-water reactors. Much concerned with influence of U.S. nuclear program on Europe.

626. BURN, Duncan L. Nuclear Power and the Energy Crisis:

Politics and the Atomic Industry. New York University Press, 1978. 348 p.

A complex presentation by a British economist covering European and U.S. decision-making in nuclear power.

627. CADWELL, Jerry J. Nuclear Facility Threat Analysis and Tactical Response Procedures. C.C. Thomas, 1983. 101 p.

Is the government worried about terrorist action at nuclear plants? Yes. The U.S. Code of Federal Regulations requires security plans for such facilities; Cadwell, a lawyer associated with the Department of Nuclear Energy at the Brookhaven National Laboratory, outlines measures for handling nuclear plant alarms, including intruders, bomb threats, kidnappers, radiation and fire.

628. CHICKEN, John C. Nuclear Power Hazard Control Policy. Pergamon, 1982. 272 p.

"An analysis of the factors that appear to have influenced the formation and form of nuclear power hazard control policy in Britain, " says the preface. Discussion of economic, political, and administrative factors, from 1939 on, including attention to the British A-bomb. Fairly long and up-to-date bibliography will aid further inquiry into the British nuclear situation.

629. COHEN, Bernard L. Before It's Too Late: A Scientist's Case for Nuclear Energy. Plenum Press, 1983. 302 p.

What the author considers the nuclear facts and popular antinuclear fantasy. Covers radiation, waste management, the Three Mile Island accident, etc.

630. COTTRELL, Alan. How Safe is Nuclear Energy? Heinemann, 1981. 124 p.

Safe enough, he thinks. An introduction for the layman by a pro-nuclear authority.

631. DEESE, David A. Nuclear Power & Radioactive Waste: A Sub-Seabed Disposal Option? Lexington Books, 1978. 206 p.

Argues that advances in geological oceanography and ocean engineering augur well for the possibility of radioactive waste isolation in deep seabed or sub-seabed sites. Urges further attention to all aspects of the issue--social, political, legal, economic. Selected bibliography.

632. DeLEON, Peter. Development and Diffusion of the Nuclear Reactor: A Comparative Analysis. Ballinger, 1979. 325 p.

Uses case studies from England, the U.S.S.R., France, Canada, and West Germany to illustrate the dynamics of nuclear development. Covers issues of technology and public policy, comparative analyses of national reactor programs. Originated as a Ph.D. thesis, and reads like it.

633. DEL SESTO, Steven L. Science, Politics, and Controversy: Civilian Nuclear Power in the United States, 1946-1974. Westview Press, 1979. 259 p.

A good scholarly study. On government control, the government-industry partnership, evolution of anti-nuclear movement in the U.S. Long bibliography.

634. DOERN, G. Bruce. Government Intervention in the Canadian Nuclear Industry. Institute for Research on Public Policy, 1980. 208 p.

Historical analysis of the industry's development and the effects of government regulation.

635. DUDERSTADT, James and Kikuchi, Chihiro. Nuclear Power: Technology on Trial. University of Michigan Press, 1979. 228 p.

Although the authors express approbation over development of such alternative energy sources as solar and geothermal, they consider nuclear power "a proven technology, characterized by significant advantages over alternative energy technologies in minimizing public risks, environmental impact, and costs of generating electricity." Historical overview of nuclear power, discussion of the fuel cycle, international aspects, and more.

636. FAIRCHILD, Johnson E. and Landman, David, eds. America Faces the Nuclear Future. Sheridan House, 1961. 156 p.

Nine articles by a diverse set of writers--scientists, engineers, educators, a physician--on aspects of nuclear power. The

passage of over twenty years makes hindsight easy, but even
so, the innocence of this book suggests that we had rather
little idea, in spite of claims to the contrary, of what we
were getting into when we cracked the atom for peaceful purposes.

637. FERMI, Laura. Atoms for the World: United States
Participation in the Conference on the Peaceful Uses
of Atomic Energy. University of Chicago Press,
1957. 227 p.

The author attended the international conference held at Geneva
in 1955 as historian for the U.S. delegation. The conference
may well have been the high point of the movement--such as
it was--marked by the sentiments of Eisenhower's "Atoms for
Peace" program. (Though some do argue that it was not
sentiment but political calculation which motivated this program.) Fermi's is a prosaic, chronological account of the
conference.

638. FERRARA, Grace M., ed. Atomic Energy & the Safety
Controversy. Facts on File, 1978. 167 p.

A handy factual overview of the issue in the U.S. and abroad
through the 1970s. Material is presented in a concise fashion,
and covers the safety controversy in general, the threat of
sabotage, accidents, waste management, non-proliferation,
and so on. Good index.

639. FOREMAN, Harry, ed. Nuclear Power and the Public.
University of Minnesota Press, 1971. 273 p.

Pro and con arguments on various aspects of nuclear power.

640. GARVEY, Gerald. Nuclear Power and Social Planning:
The City of the Second Sun. Lexington Books, 1977.
159 p.

Although approving of work on solar energy technology, Garvey believes that energy requirements, coupled with the inevitable exploitations of nuclear power by foreign nations,
compel the U.S. to stay in the forefront of civilian nuclear
development. One of the best pro-nuclear books, by an author who is not afraid to direct the reader to explicitly antinuclear sources.

641. GLASSTONE, Samuel and Jordan, Walter H. Nuclear
Power and Its Environmental Effects. American Nuclear Society, 1980. 395 p.

A pro-nuclear orientation does not get in the way of a comprehensive examination of nuclear power issues: reactor function, radiation hazards, radioactive and heat waste management, etc.

642. GLASSTONE, Samuel. Sourcebook on Atomic Energy. Krieger, 1979. 892 p. 3d ed.

This is a reprint of the 1967 edition; a basic textbook on atomic energy, first published in 1950 under sponsorship of the Atomic Energy Commission.

643. GOLDSCHMIDT, Bertrand. The Atomic Complex: A Worldwide Political History of Nuclear Energy. American Nuclear Society, 1982. 479 p.

Translated from the French, this is one of the most comprehensive studies of its kind. Covers both peaceful and military applications and developments of nuclear power; especially valuable to U.S. readers because of its foreign perspective. The author, a former personal assistant to Marie Curie, has a broad background in nuclear matters, including work in behalf of the U.S. and British governments and as a board member of the International Atomic Energy Agency. He insists on the importance of pursuing both nuclear power and nuclear disarmament.

644. GREENHALGH, Geoffrey. The Necessity for Nuclear Power. Graham & Trotman, 1980. 250 p.

Regards nuclear power as vital in meeting world energy demands and in averting dangerous political tensions arising from energy shortages. ''The consequence of a world plunged into severe and widespread energy shortages would be catastrophic.... Nuclear power is no longer an option, it is a necessity that the world cannot forego.'' Addresses such issues as safeguards and non-proliferation, waste disposal, TMI, carbon dioxide and the greenhouse effect.

645. GRENON, Michel. The Nuclear Apple & the Solar Orange: Alternatives in World Energy. Pergamon, 1981. 155 p.

A generally pro-nuclear discourse on the global energy picture; surveys fossil fuels, geothermal, coal, solar and nuclear. Chief concern about nuclear power is the difficulty posed by its fuel cycle, from mine to waste storage. The author is a former executive at the French Institute of Petroleum and the Atomic Energy Commissariat.

646. HEPPENHEIMER, T. A. The Man-Made Sun: The Quest for Fusion Power. Little, Brown, 1983. 320 p.

A portrayal, with emphasis on political considerations and academic competition, of the pursuit by atomic scientists of fusion power.

647. HOYLE, Fred. Energy or Extinction? The Case for Nuclear Energy. Heinemann, 1977. 81 p.

Environmentalists are ignorant, coal is running out, solar and other alternative energy sources won't work; nuclear power is our only choice.

648. _____ and Hoyle, Geoffrey. Commonsense in Nuclear Energy. W. H. Freeman, 1980. 88 p.

A once-over quickly rationale for nuclear power, citing the usual arguments.

649. HUGHES, Donald J. On Nuclear Energy: Its Potential for Peacetime Uses. Harvard University Press, 1957. 263 p.

A highly optimistic look at nuclear power's applications to medicine, industry, agriculture and other peaceful enterprise.

650. HUNT, Stanley E. Fission, Fusion & the Energy Crisis. Pergamon, 1980. 2d ed., 164 p.

Intended primarily for undergraduates, seeks to emphasize the relationships of the scientific, technological, economic and ecological facets of nuclear power. Will require some familiarity with physics for complete comprehension. Pro-nuclear, but does not hail nuclear as a panacea.

651. INTERNATIONAL Atomic Energy Agency. Factors Relevant to the Decommissioning of Land-Based Nuclear Reactor Plants. IAEA, 1980. 28 p.

A booklet in the IAEA safety series. "Decommissioning" refers to actions involved in retiring a nuclear plant from service at the end of its useful life. Discusses plans, radiation protection, etc. Bibliography.

652. _____. Planning for Off-Site Response to Radiation Accidents in Nuclear Facilities. IAEA, 1981. 99 p.

Covers accident analysis, protective measures and associated risks, pre-accident planning, on and off-site organizational considerations. In an accident which releases a continuous flow of airborne radioactive material, the hot debris disperses downwind in a plume; "A person immersed in the plume would inhale an amount of radioactive material proportional to the time of passage of the plume, the person's respiration rate, and the concentration of radioactive material at the person's location."

653. _____ . Safety in Nuclear Power Plant Siting: A Code of Practice. IAEA, 1978. 37 p.

Identifies a number of phenomena to be considered during plant siting, such as floods, surface faults, earthquakes, soil liquefaction, storms, aircraft crashes, population distribution and others.

654. _____ . Steps to Nuclear Power: A Guidebook. IAEA, 1975. 106 p.

A summary "of the work that has to be undertaken in the preparation for and introduction of nuclear power in a country." Deals with studies, organization and manpower requirements. (Note: the IAEA has produced a large number of books and technical manuals on nuclear power plants; the four immediately above are a small sample.)

655. JOHANSSON, Thomas B. and Steen, Peter. Radioactive Waste from Nuclear Power Plants. University of California Press, 1981. 197 p.

Sweden has decided, through a Parliamentary decision, to close all its nuclear plants by the year 2010. Meanwhile, the waste problems remain, as they will for several thousand years. This book is a technical but relatively comprehensible essay on what to do with the stuff. A model for investigators of the problem.

656. KAKU, Michio and Trainer, Jennifer, eds. Nuclear Power, Both Sides: The Best Arguments for and Against the Most Controversial Technology. Norton, 1982. 279 p.

Nuclear weapons technology is rather more controversial than that for nuclear power, but, title slips aside, this is a good one-source handbook for anyone who wants to get a grip on the power issue without reading dozens of books and articles.

The topics of radiation, reactor safety, waste disposal, economics, and the future of nuclear power all come into discussion here by both pro- and anti-nuclear authorities. Footnotes and index.

657. KLEMA, Ernest D. and West, Robert L. Public Regulation of Site Selection for Nuclear Power Plants: Present Procedures and Reform Proposals--An Annotated Bibliography. Resources for the Future, 1977. 129 p.

Lengthy annotations of selected items and unannotated citations to other material (books, reports, periodical articles) on the siting process, public regulation, criticism of the nuclear regulatory experience, and reform ideas.

658. KLINEBERG, Otto, ed. Social Implications of the Peaceful Uses of Nuclear Energy. Unesco, 1964. 169 p.

Eight articles on the topic, touching on social, moral, educational and other considerations in the nuclear world. Johan Galtung's "Atoms for Peace: Student Attitudes," is probably the most interesting selection; it reports the results of an international poll of student attitudes on nuclear power, partially reduced at one point to a device labeled the "Atom Happiness" scale. At the time, students in France, the U.S. and Japan had the greatest enthusiasm for nuclear power of the groups surveyed.

659. KRAMISH, Arnold. Atomic Energy in the Soviet Union. Stanford University Press, 1960. 232 p.

A study of Soviet atomic achievements and aims up to the publication date; makes clear, based on examination of Soviet scientific literature, that Soviet nuclear physicists were running apace with their Western counterparts at the beginning of WW II.

660. _____. The Peaceful Atom in Foreign Policy. Harper, 1963. 276 p.

Discusses the potential of peaceful uses, the difficulty in separating peaceful intentions from military exploitation, and makes a case for improved international cooperation to insure this separation.

661. LATHROP, J.W., ed. Planning for Rare Events:

Nuclear Accident Preparedness & Management Proceedings. Pergamon Press, 1981. 268 p.

Proceedings of an international workshop attended in 1980 by
representatives from 17 countries, including the U. S. and the
Soviet Union. Addresses preparation for reactor accidents.

662. LILIENTHAL, David E. Atomic Energy: A New Start.
Harper & Row, 1980. 124 p.

Advocates continued peaceful development of nuclear power,
with work toward the control--or abolition--of nuclear weapons.

663. McCRACKEN, Samuel. The War Against the Atom.
Basic Books, 1982. 206 p.

Joins Petr Beckmann (item 623) in the rather short parade of
anti anti-nuclear polemics. McCracken insists that "nuclear
energy is environmentally the most benign of major energy
sources except natural gas, the most benign in terms of public health, the safest in terms of major accidents, and the
only major source able, over a long period of time, to give
us large amounts of flexible energy. " He ridicules what he
considers the technological ignorance of nuclear critics, flays
those he calls the "Commanders" of the anti-nuclear power
movement (the Union of Concerned Scientists, Ralph Nader,
Helen Caldicott, John Gofman, inter alia), identifies those
who oppose nuclear power as habitual whiners without a suitable target since the U. S. pulled out of Vietnam--until the
atom reared its head.

664. McCULLOUGH, Campbell R. , ed. The Safety Aspects
of Nuclear Reactors. Van Nostrand, 1957. 237 p.

Several books came out of the 1955 International Conference on
the Peaceful Uses of Atomic Energy held in Geneva. This is
one; it discusses normal reactor operations, radiation safety
criteria, reactor accidents and their consequences.

665. MANN, Martin. Peacetime Uses of Atomic Energy.
Viking Press, 1961. 191 p.

If we can believe the author, atomic power will feed the
world, regenerate industry, and, in general, make the world
a wonderful place. Full of pictures showing nature aglow with
life, including a handsome couple romping on a beach above
the caption "The atomic age already promises better health

and a longer life span for the average man and woman. "
At best naïve, at worst a calculated effort to pacify the ap-
prehensive.

666. MODELSKI, George A. Atomic Energy in the Com-
     munist Bloc. Melbourne University Press, 1959.
     226 p.

A summary of what was known at the time about nuclear
power endeavors in the Soviet Union, Eastern Europe and
China. The author points out the already-existing military
stalemate in place through something like nuclear parity and
characterizes nuclear power development by the communist
nations as representing desire to excel in economic competition
with the West.

667. MUELLER, Kimberly J. The Nuclear Power Issue:
     A Guide to Who's Doing What in the U.S. and Abroad.
     California Institute of Public Affairs, 1981. 106 p.

A directory to "organizations representing the whole spectrum
of opinion on the issue, as well as neutral scientific bodies. "
Annotated entries cover U.S. federal and state agencies, citizens', professional, research and other organizations, nuclear power plants in the U.S., international organizations;
a good source, though already dating.

668. MULLENBACH, Philip. Civilian Nuclear Power: Eco-
     nomic Issues and Policy Formation. Twentieth Cen-
     tury Fund, 1963. 406 p.

Covers both U.S. and foreign issues, chiefly concerned with
economics. Argues that the role of nuclear power will be
in large part to prevent great increases in conventional fuel
prices, rather than portraying nuclear power as itself a form
bound to be inexpensive.

669. MUNTZING, L. Manning, ed. International Instruments
     of Nuclear Technology Transfer. American Nuclear
     Society, 1978. 639 p.

Composed principally of treaties and other international agreements governing trade in nuclear commodities. Nations whose
treaties receive extensive coverage: Canada, the Federal Republic of Germany, France, the U.S.S.R., the United Kingdom
and the United States.

670. MYERS, Desaix. The Nuclear Power Debate: Moral,

Economic, Technical & Political Issues. Praeger, 1977. 153 p.

Based on a 1974-76 study of issues involved in the title debate, conducted by the Investor Responsibility Research Center. The study entailed a survey of published materials, analysis of a questionnaire sent to 82 nuclear utility companies, and interviews with both nuclear advocates and opponents. Among the specific issues: the federal role in nuclear power, growth of the nuclear industry, potential and probability of accidents.

671. NAU, Henry R. National Politics and International Technology: Nuclear Reactor Development in Western Europe. Johns Hopkins University Press, 1974. 287 p.

Especially useful for insights into political (both domestic and international) influences on nuclear power programs. Considers the U.S., France, Germany, Belgium, and other nations regarding technological cooperation, rivalry, interdependence.

672. OAK Ridge Associated Universities. Institute for Energy Analysis. Economic and Environmental Impacts of a U.S. Nuclear Moratorium, 1985-2010. MIT Press, 1979. 381 p.

The work of a study team coordinated by Charles E. Whittle, reviewed in progress by both pro- and anti-nuclear consultants. The authors conclude that, if the nation is to exercise the nuclear option for energy sufficiency, all nuclear facilities in the U.S., including waste disposal sites, should be confined to approximately 100 sites of 50 square miles each, with responsibility for operation in the hands "of a highly trained, specialized cadre." Regards effects of national nuclear moratorium as ranging from severe in the Northeast to almost nil in the Northern Plains; increase in coal use would not necessarily lead to greater pollution than now present, except for particulate matter and atmospheric carbon dioxide levels. Suggests that total U.S. energy demand will not grow nearly as fast as many other studies indicate.

673. OKRENT, David. Nuclear Reactor Safety: On the History of the Regulatory Process. University of Wisconsin Press, 1981. 370 p.

An official history of the Atomic Energy Commission's Advisory Committee on Reactor Safeguards. Jargon is too plentiful, the prose is colorless, but not technically incomprehensible.

674. OSTERHOUT, Marilyn, M., ed. Decontamination & Decommissioning of Nuclear Facilities. Plenum Press, 1980. 803 p.

Proceedings of the American Nuclear Society topical meeting, September, 1979. Numerous articles on measures regarding specific facilities, e.g., Chalk River, Hanford, Dresden, Rocky Flats, Vermont Yankee, etc. Those without technical background may find this confusing.

675. PENTREATH, R.J. Nuclear Power, Man & the Environment. Taylor & Francis, 1980. 255 p.

The author assumes nuclear power as a given which is here to stay, and proceeds from there to a discussion of radiation in general, its effects on human beings, and the various issues connected with nuclear reactors, such as siting, the fuel cycle, wastes, effects on terrestrial and aquatic systems, etc. Considerable technical data.

676. RAMBERG, Bennett. Destruction of Nuclear Energy Facilities in War: The Problem and the Implications. Lexington Books, 1980. 203 p.

Investigates the likelihood that reactors pose an inviting target in war, and maintains that reactor vulnerability to acts of war must be foreseen in the planning stage.

677. REINIG, William C., ed. Environmental Surveillance in the Vicinity of Nuclear Facilities. C.C. Thomas, 1970. 465 p.

An indexed (fortunately) compilation of the proceedings of a 1968 symposium sponsored by the Health Physics Society. The preface informs us that "the 46 papers ... indicate an international viewpoint diverse in substance, but uniformly confident that present technical competence permits accurate measurement and control of environmental radioactivity."

678. ROLPH, Elizabeth S. Nuclear Power and the Public Safety: A Study in Regulation. Lexington Books, 1979. 213 p.

A study of the Atomic Energy Commission's regulation of commercial nuclear power plants. Reviews historical develop-

ments, early standards for siting, licensing, emergence of
safety problem awareness, economic costs, etc. Suggests
that the quality of AEC regulatory decisions and the agency's
credibility both suffered from over-reliance on industrial
safety research results and subjective judgment.

679. SAGAN, Leonard A., ed. Human & Ecologic Effects
     of Nuclear Power Plants. C. C. Thomas, 1974.
     536 p.

Fourteen papers on such topics as reactor design, accidental
release of radioactivity, shipment of radioactive materials,
effects of thermal discharge into surface waters, genetic radiation damage. The editor concludes that the risk associated
with radiation exposure from nuclear power is small "and
does not represent a significant public health hazard."

680. SCHMIDT, Fred H. and Bodansky, David. The Fight
     Over Nuclear Power: The Energy Controversy.
     Albion, 1976. 154 p.

A calm rationale for nuclear power and a defense of its safety record.

681. SCHURR, Sam H. and Marschak, Jakob, eds. Economic
     Aspects of Atomic Power: An Exploratory Study.
     Princeton University Press, 1950. 289 p.

A study pre-dating the industry it analyzes; the authors hedge
their bets on the economic promises of nuclear power, but
do a good job of managing information publicly available at
the time.

682. SHRADER-FRECHETTE, K. S. Nuclear Power & Public
     Policy: The Social & Ethical Problems of Fission
     Technology. Reidel, 1980. 176 p.

An attempt to place the issues of nuclear power under the
lens of a philosophical examination of the involved ethics.
The author wants to avoid the "overly emotive and question-
begging" assessments of nuclear power produced by environmentalists, as well as the pro-nuclear discourse "which almost always ignore[s] the social and ethical aspects of energy
decision making." Clearly written; an unusual set of arguments which lead the reader to a skeptical view of the public
policy process as it involves nuclear power.

683. SKOUSEN, Eric N. The War Against Nuclear Power.
     Freemen Institute, 1981. 211 p.

If one is in the mood, this book could come across as un-
intentionally humorous; if not, merely obtuse. The pro-
nuclear flip-side of the most intellectually shallow antinuclear
power position; the author believes that those who oppose nuclear power development are dupes of Soviet propaganda, or,
like the American Friends Service Committee are supposedly
knowing collaborators with the U. S. S. R.; anti-nuclear leaders
"share a more disturbing and aberrant mindset. Having come
up through the ranks of lawlessness, they seemingly cannot
anymore distinguish right from wrong. Their writings are
filled with meaningless philosophies.... " Furthermore, they
don't believe in God. Better arguments in behalf of nuclear
power are available from many books in this bibliography,
but few can approach Skousen's screed as a repository of
right-wing fear and hatred "of individuals who are loath to be
responsible for anything but their purely selfish interests."
(He is talking not about utility executives here, but about
their critics.) A gem of its kind.

684. SMART, Ian, ed. World Nuclear Energy: Toward a
     Bargain of Confidence. Johns Hopkins University
     Press, 1982. 394 p.

A scholarly treatment dividing its attention between the proliferation problem and the outlook for the nuclear industry.
The penultimate chapter, "World Nuclear Energy Paths, "
written on the assumption that nuclear power will proceed
steadily, is itself at 128 pages almost a book within a book;
the authors try to forecast the nuclear power world situation
to the year 2020.

685. SROUJI, Jacque. Critical Mass: Nuclear Power, the
     Alternative to Energy Famine. Aurora Publications,
     1977. 409 p.

An anecdotal defense of nuclear power by a journalist who
originally began researching the topic with an anti-nuclear
bias. For a writer who pretends to objectivity, Srouji's effort to allegedly set the record straight on the death of Karen
Silkwood must make the reader wonder when Srouji begins
quoting from an astrological guide on the supposed characteristics of people born under Silkwood's Zodiacal sign. You
can't have it both ways, relying on "hard-headed" observation
to reach your conclusions while simultaneously propping them
up with soft-headed quasi-mystical mush as to "how personality traits often seem to follow a pattern tied to the infinite
universe."

686.   STEVER, Donald W., Jr.   Seabrook and the Nuclear
       Regulatory Commission: The Licensing of a Nuclear
       Power Plant.   University Press of New England,
       1980.   248 p.

The Seabrook, New Hampshire nuclear plant has received a
lot of public opposition, especially because of its siting
Stever covers the five-year period of legal challenges to the
plant, civil disobedience, inadequacies of nuclear siting criteria, financing, etc.   Argues that economic investment in a
nuclear plant of even marginal merit is so great that it over-
whelms consideration of environmental and health issues during
the licensing process.

687.   STEWART, Hugh B.   Transitional Energy Policy, 1980-
       2030:   Alternative Nuclear Technologies.   Pergamon
       Press, 1981.   266 p.

Tells us that "at best, the impact of the energy supply/demand
crisis in the 1980s and 1990s will be measured by economic
disruptions in world societies; at worst, by a disastrous nuclear holocaust."   Regards nuclear power not as a threat of
war given weapons proliferation, but as a tool of peace in its
potential for meeting world energy demand.   His big reservation is that nuclear power may not be susceptible to the rapid
deployment he would like to see.

688.   THOMAS, Morgan.   Atomic Energy and Congress.
       University of Michigan Press, 1956.   301 p.

A study aiming "to give a clear analysis of decisionmaking,
and to relate this analysis to certain broader theories of
government in the United States."   Much attention focuses on
the Joint Committee on Atomic Energy.

689.   U.S. Nuclear Regulatory Commission.   Reactor Safety
       Study: An Assessment of Accident Risks in U.S.
       Commercial Nuclear Power Plants.   Nuclear Regula-
       tory Commission, 1975.   221 p.

Often referred to as "The Rasmussen Report," after study
director Norman C. Rasmussen, this document intends to
place the risks of nuclear power in perspective, especially
through comparing them with risks in other, non-nuclear
areas.   Conclusions are that nuclear power is as safe, or
safer than, non-nuclear endeavors.   Aside from other criticisms to which the study may be liable, the major issue of
its objectivity must be raised.   The work was originally spon-

sored by the Atomic Energy Commission, not only the regula-
tor but a major promoter of nuclear power, and was then
picked up by the N. R. C. when it supplanted the A. E. C. in
1975. The study was conducted chiefly at A. E. C. headquarters; 10 of the 60 people involved in the study were A. E. C.
employees. The vested interest of the A. E. C., N. R. C. and
of a substantial number of the study operatives in concluding
that nuclear power is "safe" forces an a priori skepticism
about the project's overall commitment to an unbiased inquiry
and presentation.

690. WEBB, Richard E. The Accident Hazards of Nuclear
      Power Plants. University of Massachusetts Press,
      1976. 228 p.

Possible reactor accidents and subsequent disasters considered
by an advocate of nuclear power.

691. WOODBURY, David O. Atoms for Peace. Dodd, 1955.
      259 p.

An uncritical survey of the potentials for peaceful use of nuclear power.

692. World Energy Resources, 1985-2020. IPC Science
      and Technology Press, 1978. 203 p.

One of a series of reports prepared for the Conservation Commission of the World Energy Conference, chaired at the time
of this book's publication by John R. Kiley of the Bechtel
Corporation, which has large interests in nuclear power. The
book assesses the prospects for nuclear power growth, uranium resources, technological resources (reactors, fuel fabrication & reprocessing, etc.), and other topics.

• Periodical Articles •

693. "Assessing the Environmental Impacts of the Nuclear
      Fuel Cycle. " Environmental Impact Assessment Re-
      view 3 (June-Sept. 1982).

A special issue on the title topic, presenting strongly opposed
views on the safety of nuclear power, together with nine sum-
maries of Environmental Impact Statements on uranium milling,
handling and storage of spent reactor fuel, transport of radioactive material, decommissioning of nuclear facilities, etc.
Also includes reports on the French, German and Japanese
environmental accommodation of nuclear facilities.

694.   BAKER, Earl J., et al. "Impact of Offshore Nuclear-
       Power Plants: Forecasting Visits to Nearby Beaches."
       Environment and Behavior 12 (Sept. 1980): 367-407.

"Attempts to forecast ... behavioral effects of a proposed
technological innovation of the 1980s, the offshore floating nuclear plant." Reviews literature on subject, concentrates on
surveys regarding attendance at beaches in vicinity of hypothetical offshore nuclear plants in Florida, New Jersey, and
Massachusetts. A straight sociological work, supported by
chi-square significance tables and other data.

695.   BENEDICT, Robert, et al. "The Voters and Attitudes
       toward Nuclear Power: A Comparative Study of 'Nu-
       clear Moratorium' Initiatives." Western Political Quar-
       terly No. 1 (March 1980): 7-23.

Examines 1976 ballot propositions in Washington, Oregon,
Colorado, and Arizona aimed at additional regulation of nuclear plants. Voter survey indicates that only token represen-
tation of the public in energy decisions is likely to engender
hostility toward policy-makers. Discusses voting behavior according to such values as perception of energy need, concern
for environment, etc.

696.   BERGMAN, Lars. "The Impact of Nuclear Power Dis-
       continuation in Sweden: A General Equilibrium Analy-
       sis." Regional Science and Urban Economics 11
       (Aug. 1981): 269-286.

"Reports on methodology and results of a study of the economic consequences of a discontinuation of the Swedish nuclear
program.... [A] proposed nuclear discontinuation strategy
does not significantly affect the investigated macroeconomic
indicators."--Journal abstract.

697.   BICKERSTAFFE, Julia and Pearce, David. "Can There
       be a Consensus on Nuclear Power?" Social Studies
       of Science 10 (Aug. 1980): 309-344.

Examines the specific worries connected with nuclear power
(proliferation, terrorism, repression of civil liberties, health
risks, and radioactive waste) and finds objections to nuclear
power "rational." Argues that a consensus on nuclear power
depending "not only on whether nuclear power presents the
best way to achieve social goals, but also about the nature of
those goals themselves," is unlikely. Critical of nuclear decision making and the public information process; suggests that

greater involvement of legislatures is advisable in nuclear power matters.

698. BURNESS, H. S. , et. al. "The Turnkey Era in Nuclear Power. " Land Economics No. 2 (May 1980):
188-202.

Economic analysis of the reactor business between late 1962 and mid-1966, when the leading U. S. manufacturers sold 13 reactors to public utilities on "turnkey" terms, i. e. , the seller took all responsibility for design, construction and testing, then "turned the key over" to the utilities when the reactors were operational.

699. COCHRAN, Thomas B. "Secrecy and Nuclear Power."
Bulletin of the Atomic Scientists 37 (Aug. -Sept. 1981):
37-41.

Criticizes official policy of withholding information on nuclear power matters, contending that public cannot accurately assess nuclear risks without such knowledge. Describes several cases whose details were kept from public circulation.

700. COHEN, Bernard L. "Nuclear Journalism. " Policy
Review No. 26 (Fall, 1983): 70-74.

Policy Review is the journal of the right-wing Heritage Foundation. Cohen recites the familiar litany of pro-nuclear com-
plaints about the media treatment of the nuclear power issue: they pay too much attention to it, they're sensationalistic, in-
accurate, and worst of all, they don't put radiation risks in the right perspective (e. g. , it's more dangerous to be over-
weight than to live next door to a reactor.)

701. COOK, Earl. "The Role of History in the Acceptance
of Nuclear Power. " Social Science Quarterly 63
(March 1982): 3-15.

Reviews nuclear power programs in the U. S. and Canada; suggests that different historical experience (such as no Canadian nuclear accident which led to radioactive contamination outside the reactor building) and level of confidence in government have led to a viable Canadian program and the nearly moribund U. S. program.

702. CORDES, Colleen. "Human Factors and Nuclear Safety:
Grudging Respect for a Growing Field. " APA Monitor
14 (May 1983): 1+

A report on the Nuclear Regulatory Commission's and the industry's belated awakening to the necessity of carefully relating nuclear reactor control facilities to human needs and abilities. (Of the 1,900 displays on TMI vertical panels, more than a quarter were so ill-positioned that some operators could not see them.) The NRC has hired 30 psychologists since the TMI accident in an attempt to redress such oversights, though suspicions of the "soft sciences" persist in the industry.

703. _____. "Human Factors and Nuclear Power: Nose to Grindstone or Lip Service?" APA Monitor 14 (June 1983): 3+

Further discussion of the difficulties advocates of human factors engineering have faced in persuading the nuclear industry to recognize the importance of their insights.

704. DAVIS, W. Kenneth. "Nuclear Power: Problems and Prospects." Nuclear Energy: Journal of the British Nuclear Energy Society 19 (April 1980): 79-92.

Nuclear power is safe, economical, and able to contribute to the resolution of the energy crisis, but antinuclear activists have swayed public opinion deleteriously against it. Still, "the basic logic of nuclear power appears unassailable," and the growing demand for electric power "shows no sign of abating."

705. "Energy Politics: USA-USSR." Society 18 (July-Aug. 1981): 5-84.

A good section featuring articles by writers with diverse political opinions. Covered are communist nuclear practice, nuclear protest and national policy, waste management, Soviet nuclear setbacks, destruction of nature in the U.S.S.R. and other topics.

706. ENSTROM, James E. "Cancer Mortality Patterns Around the San Onofre Nuclear Power Plant, 1960-1978." American Journal of Public Health 73 (Jan. 1983): 83-92.

The San Onofre plant, surrounded by major population areas in Southern California, began operation in 1968. This study compares mortality rates for leukemia, lung cancers, and other factors between those in the San Onofre area and for California and the entire U.S., 1960-1978. Findings indicate that cancer and total mortality rates near San Onofre have remained similar to corresponding rates in other locations.

707. FIREBAUGH, M.W. "Public Attitudes and Information on the Nuclear Option." Nuclear Safety 22 (March-April 1981): 147-156.

Summarizes results of public opinion polls concerning plant construction, safety, moratoria, etc. Support of nuclear power appears stronger in communities that already have it than in the public at large.

708. FREEMAN, S. David. "Reinventing the Nuclear Wheel." Across the Board 20 (Oct. 1983): 31-34.

Claims that the nuclear industry is fueling its own demise through escapist public relations campaigns and attacks on regulation, a phenomenon that reflects real technological problems. Discusses absence of design standards among U.S. reactors; suggests some new, standardized designs to supplant current U.S. models, "which are so unforgiving of human and mechanical errors."

709. GAMBLE, Hays B. and Downing, Roger H. "Effects of Nuclear Power Plants on Residential Property Values." Journal of Regional Science 22 (Nov. 1982): 457-478.

Presents results of studies conducted before and after the TMI accident. Findings show no significant difference in TMI-area property values after the accident; analysis of property values around four other nuclear plants before the TMI problems showed no evidence that the plants affected values in any way.

710. GREEN, Harold P. "The Peculiar Politics of Nuclear Power." Bulletin of the Atomic Scientists 38 (Dec. 1982): 59-65.

Argues for a new approach to nuclear power regulation which would simplify the licensing process, "eliminate opportunities for opponents of nuclear power to delay or obstruct licensing proceedings," improve public confidence in nuclear regulation. Opponents of nuclear power are "know-nothings."

711. HAHN, R.W. "An Assessment of the Determination of Energy Needs: The Case of Nuclear Power." Policy Sciences 13 (Feb. 1981): 9-24.

Examines the response of the Atomic Energy Commission
(and then the Nuclear Regulatory Commission) to the National
Environmental Policy Act's requirement that the agency make
a cost-benefit analysis of proposed nuclear plants.

712. HENDERSON, Robert D'A. "Nigeria: Future Nuclear
     Power." Orbis 25 (Summer 1981): 409-423.

Nigeria has been a "major promoter of the view that Third
World countries have an inalienable right to develop nuclear
power programs" as they see fit. The country will probably
pursue in the near future a program emphasizing a pool of
trained scientists and technicians "for a small-scale nuclear
research center. " The essay covers political, technical, and
mineral considerations.

713. HODGSON, P. E. "The Future of Nuclear Power. "
     SPP: Science and Public Policy 10 (Feb. 1983):
     2-9.

Concludes that nuclear power alone can allow sufficient access
to energy in both "developed" and "developing" countries.
Makes the usual pro-nuclear assessment of risks and benefits
of nuclear, conventional, and alternative technologies, finding
nuclear out front in all respects.

714. KELLY, William J. , et al. "The Economics of Nu-
     clear Power in the Soviet Union. " Soviet Studies 34
     (Jan 1982): 43-68.

The authors conclude that "nuclear power is economically rational in the European U. S. S. R. , " but not in Siberia, where
other conventional energy sources are plentiful.

715. LEVI, Isaac. "Assessing Accident Risks in United
     States Commercial Nuclear Power Plants: Scientific
     Method and the Rasmussen Report. " Social Research
     48 (Summer 1981): 395-408.

Attacks the scientific methodology used (or abused) in the
"Rasmussen Report" (item 689), claiming that its authors
have produced a variety of "bizarre arguments. "

716. LIHACH, Nadine. "Keeping Cool in a Nuclear Plant. "
     Across the Board 20 (Jan. 1983): 60-63.

What the well-dressed nuclear power worker wears on the job.
Features photos of one climbing into his radiation suit.

717. LUDDEMANN, Margarete K. "Nuclear Power in Latin
      America: An Overview of Its Present Status." Jour-
      nal of Interamerican Studies and World Affairs 25
      (Aug. 1983): 377-415.

A handy country-by-country survey; for each nation discusses
nuclear policy, present nuclear power situation and forecast,
international cooperation, and approach to nonproliferation.

718. MATHIESON, R. S. "Nuclear Power in the Soviet Bloc."
      Association of American Geographers. Annals. 70
      (March 1980): 271-279.

Estimates that by the year 2000, the Soviet Union and its
Eastern Europe dependents will obtain 60 percent of their
electricity from nuclear sources. Asserts that lack of "democratic constraints on nuclear plant expansion" promises an
energy-rich future for these states, and that the West should
"reappraise its future energy policies in this light."

719. MILLS, Mark P. and Starr, Roger. "France Declares
      Energy Independence." Across the Board 20 (March
      1983): 12-21.

On France's flourishing nuclear power program, fueled by
national pride, effective centralization, and the country's total
lack of petroleum resources. French plants "have operated
somewhat better than the U. S. average."

720. NELKIN, Dorothy and Pollak, Michael. "French and
      German Courts on Nuclear Power." Bulletin of the
      Atomic Scientists 36 (May 1980): 36-42.

The court systems have a growing involvement in mediating
citizen-government nuclear power disputes. The authors examine the practices of the two nations. Under both French
and German civil codes, "nuclear energy is subject to strict
liability, and the courts may compensate for personal injury
or loss of property due to radiation."

721. PEREZ-LOPEZ, Jorge F. "Nuclear Power in Cuba:
      Opportunities and Challenges." Orbis 26 (Summer
      1982): 495-516.

Looks at the nuclear program in Cuba, in the development
stages for close to a decade. Use of Soviet-built reactors,
with weaker safety standards than enforced in the U. S., poses
a small but real threat of radioactive contamination, which

could reach the U.S. Cuba has placed its reactors under International Atomic Energy Agency safeguards, but the proliferation issue still remains.

722. PERRY, Ronald W. "Population Evacuation in Volcanic Eruptions, Floods, and Nuclear Power Plant Accidents: Some Elementary Comparisons." Journal of Community Psychology 11 (Jan. 1983): 36-47.

Approximately 144,000 people within a 15-mile radius of TMI evacuated their homes at some point during the emergency. The author states that the high evacuation level "appears to be related to the public's perception of high personal risk." The rest of the article is, fortunately, not as self-evident, and has some interesting things to say about why people leave disaster scenes--and why they stay.

723. POWELL, John W. "Nuclear Power in Japan." Bulletin of the Atomic Scientists 39 (May 1983): 33-39.

Japan has proceeded full speed ahead with its nuclear power program because of its rapid increase in energy consumption; the government hopes to raise its nuclear-fueled electrical output more than 500 percent by the end of the century. Waste disposal is a serious problem, as is the pool of "nuclear gypsies" hired by contractors for dangerous repair and cleanup work.

724. SABATO, Jorge A. and Ramesh, Jairam. "Atoms for the Third World." Bulletin of the Atomic Scientists 36 (March 1980): 36-43.

Surveys the nuclear scene in a variety of industrially-developing nations, including Argentina, Mexico, Spain, Egypt, etc. "It would be politically naïve," state the authors, "to think that the industrialized countries will stop all nuclear development in the foreseeable future."

725. SILVER, Melinda. "Nuclear Power Plant Licensing: Jurisdiction to Consider Foreign Impacts." Natural Resources Journal 23 (Jan. 1983): 225-237.

Analyzes a 1981 case in which the U.S. Court of Appeals for the District of Columbia held that exporting nuclear material and a nuclear plant to the Philippines posed no threat to U.S. security or to public health, and thus required no environmental impact statement. (Because the Philippines is party to the

Non-Proliferation Treaty, it must place all nuclear facilities under International Atomic Energy Agency safeguards.)

726. TEMPLES, James R. "The Politics of Nuclear Power: A Sub-Government in Transition. " Political Science Quarterly No. 2 (Summer 1980): 239-260.

Contends that the federal government's role in the development and licensing of nuclear power plants from 1946 on should be seen as a nuclear "subgovernment" which has evolved according to the influence of public policymaking, "from a distributive to a regulatory nature. "

727. TOMAR, Ravindra. "The Indian Nuclear Power Program: Myths and Mirages. " Asian Survey 20 (May 1980): 517-531.

India began a nuclear R & D program in 1954; Tomar finds it pursued with "a near total lack of public debate on the economic, safety, and environmental effects of the development and growth of nuclear energy in the country. The little debate that did take place has been an elitist exercise among scientists.... "

728. USEEM, Bert, and Zald, Mayer N. "From Pressure Group to Social Movement: Organizational Dilemmas of the Effort to Promote Nuclear Power. " Social Problems 30 (Dec. 1982): 144-156.

Considers the pro-nuclear power movement (evidently they believe there is one) "as a case study of a pressure group [the nuclear industry] which lost power and mobilized a social movement to restore it. "--Journal abstract. Discussion of such front organizations as the Committee for Energy Awareness (founded after the TMI accident by the power industry's two major trade associations, the Atomic Industrial Forum and the Edison Electric Institute) and Nuclear Energy Women (women employed by the industry.)

729. WEBBER, David J. "Is Nuclear Power Just Another Environmental Issue ? An Analysis of California Voters. " Environment and Behavior 14 (Jan. 1982): 72-83.

Upon analyzing data from a sample of over 2, 000 voters in the 1976 California primary, the author finds that nuclear power is not "just another environmental issue, " for environmentally-concerned citizens may not support efforts toward nuclear regulation, and those who oppose environmental regulation may also oppose nuclear power.

730. WILSON, Richard. "Soviet Scientists on Nuclear Power." Bulletin of the Atomic Scientists 36 (Feb. 1980): 44-46.

During a visit to the Soviet Union, Wilson interviewed a number of scientists on nuclear power and related matters. Condenses their responses here. "All the scientists I talked to insisted that the proliferation potential demands government ownership of nuclear facilities."

731. YELLIN, Joel. "High Technology and the Courts: Nuclear Power and the Need for Institutional Reform." Harvard Law Review 94 (Jan. 1981): 489-560.

Yellin investigates a number of nuclear legal cases, and concludes that the present courts are unable to deal with the scientific and technological aspects of such cases--they cannot, to be blunt, understand them. He suggests that a review board competent in both legal and scientific areas be created to deal with cases beyond the capacity of the traditional court system.

● VIII ●

Radiation Blues: The Anti-Nuclear Power Case

"It should be noted that with the number of plants soon to be operating in the United States, a frequency of core melt of one in a thousand reactor years will correspond to one every ten years or so. "

--James J. MacKenzie,
Item 693, p. 147.

732. BERGER, John. Nuclear Power: The Unviable Option. Ramparts, 1976. 384 p.

An anti-nuclear power standard. Covers the usual objections: accidents, radioactive waste, economic costs, weapons proliferation, and presents the usual alternatives of energy conservation and solar power.

733. COOK, Constance E. Nuclear Power and Legal Advocacy: The Environmentalists and the Courts. Lexington Books, 1980. 155 p.

An academic study of what the author acknowledges as the antinuclear movement's skillful use of the law in its fight against nuclear power--though she argues that the principal cause of nuclear decline in the U.S. has been excessive governmental regulation. Much of the book concerns legal challenges to the nuclear plant under construction at Midland, Michigan.

● ● ●

"In some sort of crude sense which no vulgarity, no humor, no overstatement can quite extinguish, the physicists have known sin; and this is a knowledge which they cannot lose. "
--J. Robert Oppenheimer,
Item 797, p. 88.

● ● ●

734. CROALL, Stephen. The Anti-Nuclear Handbook. Pantheon Books, 1979. 133 p.

In adult comic-book format presents the basics of the anti-nuclear power arguments.

735. CURTIS, Richard and Hogan, Elizabeth. Nuclear Lessons: An Examination of Nuclear Power's Safety, Economic, and Political Record. Stackpole, 1980. 285 p.

A post-Three Mile Island updating of item 736, with equally pessimistic conclusions about nuclear power's advisability. A polemic with many valid points, but even some who share the authors' reservations will wish that it possessed greater qualities of deliberation and restraint of tone.

736. _____. Perils of the Peaceful Atom: The Myth of

<u>Safe Nuclear Plants</u>. Doubleday, 1969. 274 p.

Calls for a shutdown of the U.S. nuclear industry on the
grounds that mistakes, accidents, and regulatory problems
make the risks too great to bear.

737. EBBIN, Steven and Kasper, Raphael. <u>Citizen Groups</u>
     <u>& the Nuclear Power Controversy: Uses of Scientific</u>
     <u>& Technological Information</u>. MIT Press, 1974.
     307 p.

Concerned chiefly with the layman's role in nuclear plant
siting. Based on interviews with Atomic Energy Commission
officials, attorneys for citizens' groups, examination of literature, and detailed investigation of the Midland, Michigan, and
Vermont Yankee plants, including attendance at public hearings
and interviews with participants. Sympathies are with citizens
opposed to licensing: "We have found that the licensing process is one which is geared to the promotion of nuclear power plants." The authors also question the common assertion
of nuclear advocates regarding the "costly" features of licensing delays. They argue that "mis-estimates of labor
productivity, materials requirements, and delivery schedules
... and in some cases poor planning" have been more in-
strumental in delays than have citizen protests.

738. ENVIRONMENTAL Action Foundation. <u>Accidents Will</u>
     <u>Happen: The Case Against Nuclear Power</u>. Harper
     <u>& Row, 1979. 339 p.</u>

A variety of anti-nuclear essays on accidents, waste disposal
and transportation, economics, alternative energy sources.

739. FALK, Jim. <u>Global Fission: The Battle Over Nuclear</u>
     <u>Power</u>. Oxford University Press, 1982. 410 p.

An Australian nuclear physicist's history of the global movement against nuclear power, dwelling on the implications of
Three Mile Island, economics, the state-industry connection,
political influences of anti-nuclearism. One of the most
broadly-based and inclusive treatments of the anti-nuclear
power movements listed here. Index and footnotes.

740. FAULKNER, Peter T., ed. <u>The Silent Bomb: A Guide</u>
     <u>to the Nuclear Energy Controversy</u>. Vintage, 1977.
     382 p.

This is not what the subtitle implies as much as it is a tract opposing nuclear power. Includes articles and excerpts from books.

741. FULLER, John G. We Almost Lost Detroit. Reader's Digest Press, 1975. 272 p.

An antinuclear argument employing the near-meltdown at Michigan's Fermi Plant in 1966 as a catalyst. Competently written in journalistic style, based in part on the author's access to A. E. C. records, but suffers to some extent through some technical oversights and rather badly through lack of bibliographic documentation.

742. GARRISON, Jim. The Plutonium Culture: From Hiroshima to Harrisburg. Continuum, 1981. 275 p.

Researchers working on the Karen Silkwood case might be interested in the chapter "Karen Silkwood: A Life in Death"; otherwise this book is satisfactory as a general survey for the reader seeking an antinuclear argument which is both readable and careful to touch most of the issue bases.

743. GOFMAN, John W. "Irrevy": An Irreverant, Illustrated View of Nuclear Power. Committee for Nuclear Responsibility, 1979. 248 p.

A collection of talks on such topics as the radioactive waste problem, nuclear civil disobedience, public health, solar energy; a handy directory to issues serves in lieu of a detailed index. Resolutely antinuclear, lightened with cartoons.

● ● ●

"Because the means of producing this peaceful power can readily be converted into an atomic bomb for destruction, the mechanism for world peace and the mechanism for world control of atomic energy are profoundly interrelated."
                                        --Vannevar Bush, 1946.
                                        Item 10, p. 101.

● ● ●

744. _____ and Tamplin, Arthur R. Poisoned Power: The Case Against Nuclear Power Plants. Rodale, 1971. 368 p.

The authors worked at the Lawrence Radiation Laboratory in Livermore, California. Following Linus Pauling, they believe that there is no "safe" level of radiation exposure, and that the continued pursuit of nuclear power will cause a significant increase in cancer among the public. They make a similar case in their earlier book, "Population Control" Through Nuclear Pollution (Nelson Hall, 1970).

745. GROSSMAN, Karl. Cover Up: What You Are Not Supposed to Know about Nuclear Power. Permanent Press, 1980. 293 p.

Employs a large number of government and commercial documents, many reproduced in whole or in part, to present nuclear power as an adventure whose considerable dangers have been obscured by federal secrecy and utility propaganda. The last chapter, "What You Can Do about It," features statements by close to twenty prominent antinuclear activists.

746. GYORGY, Anna. No Nukes: Everyone's Guide to Nuclear Power. South End Press, 1979. 478 p.

A bit dated, but still an information-packed compendium of the anti-nuclear power persuasion. Covers the basics of atomic reactions, then moves on to health dangers, economics, the development of the antinuclear movement, alternatives to nuclear power. Lots of footnotes; cartoons and other illustrations.

747. HAYES, Dennis. Rays of Hope: The Transition to a Post-petroleum World. Norton, 1977. 240 p.

A readable case for solar power. Hayes regards the costs of nuclear power from standpoints of radioactive pollution and potential for terrorist possibilities. Originated in his paper Nuclear Power: The Fifth Horseman (Worldwatch Institute, 1976).

748. HERTSGAARD, Mark. Nuclear, Inc.: The Men and Money Behind Nuclear Energy. Pantheon, 1983. 339 p.

Hertsgaard, nuclear power opponent, interviews nuclear utility executives, engineers, and scientists, and presents a good overview of the industry's development and present doldrums. One of the best books in the antinuclear vein for its depth of research, clarity and scope.

749. INGLIS, David R. Nuclear Energy: Its Physics and Its Social Challenge. Addison-Wesley, 1973. 395 p.

The author, a nuclear physicist, examines nuclear power's interaction with the arms race and horizontal weapons proliferation. Covers reactor design, radiation, atomic theory, varieties of nuclear bombs. "The question is what is our determination in an era when unlimited war will mean the death of hundreds of millions--and the possible genetic impairment of a million generations to follow?"

750. JUNGK, Robert. The Nuclear State. John Calder,
     1979. 178 p.

"Only those who still cherish delusions about the nuclear future can deny the risk of misuse ... the consequences could be irreparable." With chapter titles like "Radiation Fodder," "The Gamblers," "Atomic Terrorists" and "The Intimidated," this is a throughgoing antinuclear polemic with a focus on Europe. (Published in the U.S. as The New Tyranny by Fred Jordan Books.) Jungk believes that efforts to protect nuclear plants form a basis for an authoritarian state.

751. Labor Outreach Guide. Abalone Alliance, San Fran-
     cisco, 1983. 22 p.

Explores the outlook for a labor-antinuclear coalition, one usually not regarded as easy to achieve (or even worth pursuing). Discusses local union action against nuclear power.

752. LANOUE, Ron. Nuclear Plants: The More They Build,
     the More You Pay. Center for Responsive Law,
     1977. 2d ed. 93 p.

A question-and-answer brief in opposition to nuclear power because of its economic costs. References and long bibliography.

753. LEWIS, Richard S. The Nuclear-Power Rebellion:
     Citizens vs. The Atomic Industrial Establishment.
     Viking, 1972. 313 p.

A relatively early look at developing grass roots opposition to nuclear power, including objections based on safety and economy; highly critical of the Atomic Energy Commission and of what Lewis considers its vested-interest treatment of nuclear power problems.

754. LOVINS, Amory B. and Lovins, L. Hunter. Brittle
     Power: Energy Strategy for National Security. Brick
     House, 1982. 486 p.

The Lovinses, already on record with their support for "soft" energy paths through solar and other renewable forms, here portray the highly-centralized nature of the U.S. power generation system as a grave risk to national security, a risk because of its vulnerability to sabotage, acts of war, and accidents. The book, in three main sections, first surveys the general scope of the risks, then deals with specific cases; concludes with suggestions for a "resilient" energy system base on soft path technology. Excellent bibliography, and a commendable effort to approach the whole energy issue from a new direction.

755. MURPHY, Dervla. Nuclear Stakes: Race to the
      Finish. Ticknor and Fields, 1982. 264 p.

An anecdotal guide to nuclear follies, commencing with Three Mile Island.

756. NADER, Ralph and Abbotts, John. The Menace of
      Atomic Energy. Norton, 1977. 414 p.

Nader's major antinuclear offering, covers technical, political, and other objections. From the technical point of view, there are better books, e. g. , Walter C. Patterson's (item 763).

757. NELKIN, Dorothy. Nuclear Power and Its Critics:
      The Cayuga Lake Controversy. Cornell University
      Press, 1971. 128 p.

Covers the 1968-1969 conflict over the construction of a nuclear plant at the New York lake, with plans to use the lake for plant cooling. Opposing ideas--demand for power vs. environmental concern--receive equal time.

758. _____ and Pollak, Michael. The Atom Besieged:
      Extraparliamentary Dissent in France and Germany.
      MIT Press, 1981. 235 p.

How the antinuclear movements began in these two countries. Considers political and legal facets of the phenomenon; legislation has been of central importance; cites the German law of 1976 which brought the German nuclear program to a near halt.

759. NOVICK, Sheldon. The Careless Atom. Houghton,
      1969. 225 p.

One of the early major antinuclear polemics. Describes various nuclear plant accidents and argues that the enthusiasm for nuclear power is not only unwarranted but dangerous.

760. _____. The Electric War: What the Nuclear Fight is About. Sierra Club, 1976. 376 p.

Novick maintains that nuclear power is the other face of nuclear weapons; that the dangers of nuclear power have not been adequately dealt with; includes many interviews with advocates and opponents of nuclear power.

761. OLSON, McKinley C. Unacceptable Risk: The Nuclear Power Controversy. Bantam, 1976. 309 p.

An objection to nuclear power based on unresolved issues of radiation, waste disposal, sabotage, etc. Also attends to antinuclear legal campaigns.

762. OTIS, Todd H. A Review of Nuclear Energy in the United States: Hidden Power. Praeger, 1981. 175 p.

As a freshman legislator in the Minnesota House of Representatives, the author sponsored a bill which would have prohibited construction of nuclear plants in Minnesota pending development of a safe and economical means of atomic waste disposal. His bill was defeated, but Otis went on to investigate nuclear power in detail and in the process moved from a centrist position on the issue to one in firm opposition. Here he examines the hidden economic costs of nuclear power, the danger of low-level radiation, reactor accidents, and alternative power sources.

763. PATTERSON, Walter C. Nuclear Power. Penguin, 1977. 304 p.

"An attempt to describe the reactors themselves--their construction, behaviour, maintenance, offspring and relatives-- and describe too the effect they have had, and are having, on the world in which we live." A nuclear physicist's generally downbeat explication of the basics of nuclear fission, economic costs of nuclear power, the "plutonium at large" problem, and other relevant concerns. Readable; one of the best-informed arguments against nuclear power.

764. PRICE, Jerome. The Antinuclear Movement. Twayne, 1982. 207 p.

An overview and history of the antinuclear movement, with a focus on ideology and organization. Originated as a doctoral dissertation.

765. RASHKE, Richard. The Killing of Karen Silkwood: The Story Behind the Kerr-McGee Plutonium Case. Houghton Mifflin, 1981. 407 p.

Silkwood, an employee of the Kerr-McGee Nuclear Corporation, died in an automobile wreck (her car left the road) on her way to a scheduled meeting with a New York Times reporter and an Atomic Union Workers official, to whom she planned to deliver, it is said, documents demonstrating the Corporation's deliberate negligence in manufacture of plutonium fuel rods. Was she murdered? We may never know, but Rashke's presentation of the case provides insights into the nuclear power establishment.

766. READER, Mark, et al., eds. Atom's Eve: Ending the Nuclear Age, an Anthology. McGraw-Hill, 1980. 285 p.

The editor claims that "these pages make clear that humanity is putting into place an energy technology which must, but cannot, be governed without the premature forfeiture of human life, liberty, and happiness." Thirty-plus essays of an antinuclear bent touching on Three Mile Island, radiation hazards, nuclear economics, proliferation, and civil liberties, among other topics.

767. UNION of Concerned Scientists. The Nuclear Fuel Cycle: A Survey of the Public Health, Environmental, and National Security Effects of Nuclear Power. MIT Press, 1975. Revised edition. 291 p.

Presents the results of a study conducted in response to the Atomic Energy Commission's "Environmental Survey of the Nuclear Fuel Cycle," issued in 1972. An overview of nuclear power, discussion of radiation-caused lung cancer in uranium miners, hazards of uranium mill operations, reactor accidents, fuel reprocessing, waste transportation, etc. The overall posture of the book places the viability of nuclear power in serious doubt.

768. WILCOX, Fred, ed. Grass-Roots: An Anti-Nuke Sourcebook: How to Fight Nuclear Power and Win! Crossing Press, 1980. 192 p.

Citizen action--from civil disobedience to within-the-system
political activism--designed to halt nuclear power. A good
collection of its kind.

● Periodical Articles ●

769. ADLER, Carl G. "The Pro-Solar, Anti-Nuclear Movement: A Philosophical Perspective. " American
Journal of Physics 51 (June 1983): 503-510.

Argues that the anti-nuclear power movement is a manifestation of the centuries-old popular distrust of technology and
large, centralized authority, as well as one occasionally
based in sound technical objections.

770. BAGNE, Paul. "The Glow Boys: How Desperate
Workers are Mopping Up America's Nuclear Mess. "
Mother Jones 7 (Nov. 1982): 24+

How nuclear utilities hire unemployed workers--known in the
trade as "jumpers"--and use them to clean and repair damaged
nuclear facilities following short training periods.

771. CHAPMAN, Duane. "Federal Tax Incentives Affecting
Coal and Nuclear Power Economics. " Natural Resources Journal 22 (April 1982): 361-378.

Estimates the size of tax incentives in relation to utility costs,
"relative magnitudes of benefits going to coal and nuclear facilities, " and "influence which time paths of tax payments and
after-tax net income have upon possible incentives for premature construction and excess capacity. " Concludes that
sans the tax subsidies accruing to nuclear power, no utility
would choose nuclear over coal generation.

772. LIPMAN, Harvey. "The Selling of the Atom. " In These
Times 7 (March 23, 1983): 24.

On the pro-nuclear television ad campaign worked up by the
U. S. Committee for Energy Awareness, a front for a con-
sortium of nuclear utilities. $21 million of the $25 million
cost of the ads has been contributed by utilities. Includes
discussion of this campaign and the Fairness Doctrine, which
requires opposing views to be permitted air time when controversial subjects are at issue.

773. NELSON, Lin. "Atom and Eve: The Nuclear Industry

Seeks to Win the Hearts and Minds of Women. "
Progressive 47 (July 1983): 32-34.

Portrays the group Nuclear Energy Women, a public relations organization composed of women nuclear industry professionals, as a funnel of simplistic pro-nuclear propaganda, tied to claims that failure to support nuclear power threatens the energy consuming conveniences, jobs, and freedom women have come to expect and rely on.

774. NORTON, Deborah. "Women, Children and Nuclear Power. " _New Women's Times_ 8 (Oct. 1982): 5-6.

Urges more consistent feminist attention to the nuclear power issue, which is "controlled by an all-male power structure. " Reviews various hazards of nuclear power, argues that nuclear power is not required to free the U.S. from dependence on foreign oil.

775. "Nuclear Dangers in South Korea. " _Multinational Monitor_ 4 (Feb. 1983): 18+

South Korea plans to have 25 nuclear plants in place by the end of the century. The article refers to two intercepted documents revealing serious safety hazards in ten plants now operating or under construction. The U.S. is heavily involved in the S. Korean nuclear program, which the article characterizes as being pursued "without regard for safety and health. " No public discussion of nuclear hazards is permitted in the South Korean press.

776. RUDIG, Wolfgang. "Capitalism and Nuclear Power: A Reassessment. " _Capital & Class_ No. 20 (Summer 1983): 117-156.

A socialist review of nuclear power in the U.S. and Western Europe. Contends that nuclear is a " 'cul-de-sac' technology promoted by a nuclear-industrial complex entrenched in energy policy-making and dependent on state support. " Marxist socialism has compromised itself by its accommodation of pro-nuclearism in the trade unions. New "alternative" and ecological movements may expect to be weakened if they attempt to align themselves with pro-nuclear labor groups.

777. WEINGAST, Barry R. "Congress, Regulation, and the Decline of Nuclear Power. " _Public Policy_ 28 (Spring 1980): 231-255.

Argues that antinuclear environmentalists, their aims un-
checked by Congress, have been the chief source of the nuclear industry's decline in the U. S.   The former's interests
have affected the industry through political and legal means;
thus policy-making "responds to many organized interests,
at the potential expense of both producers and consumers. "

778.   WELCH, Bruce L.   "Deception on Nuclear Power Risks:
         A Call for Action. "   Bulletin of the Atomic Scientists
         36 (Sept. 1980):   50-54.

The author, an ecologist and neurobiologist, attacks the Nuclear Regulatory Commission's 1975 Reactor Safety Study
(item 689) as a prime example of pro-nuclear propaganda
employing "pseudo-quantitative statistical probabilities" and
a distortion of facts about nuclear accidents and other risks.
[See also item 715.]

● IX ●

They Built the Bomb: The Atomic Scientists

On scientific social responsibility: "The accident that we worked out this dreadful thing should not give us the responsibility of having a voice in how it is to be used. "

--Edward Teller, Item 813,
p. 87.

779. ALSOP, Joseph and Alsop, Stewart. We Accuse: The Story of the Miscarriage of American Justice in the Case of J. Robert Oppenheimer. Simon & Schuster, 1954. 88 p.

A work condemning the public humiliation of Oppenheimer, a major figure in the U.S. development of the bomb, and the mechanism by which he was declared a security risk following his public opposition to work on the hydrogen bomb.

780. BAXTER, James Phinney, 3d. Scientists Against Time. Little, Brown, 1946. 473 p.

A history of American scientists' involvement in WW II, focusing on the Office of Scientific Research and Development. Covers a wide scope of such issues as the race for superiority in new weapons, medical developments, and the bomb. Detailed index.

781. BERNSTEIN, Jeremy. Hans Bethe: Prophet of Energy. Basic Books, 1980. 212 p.

A biography of one of the atomic and H-bomb progenitors, with an emphasis on Bethe's post-war involvement in nuclear power, which he regards as essential, at the same time as he argues in favor of developing "soft path" alternatives.

782. BLUMBERG, Stanley A. and Owens, Gwinn. Energy and Conflict: The Life and Times of Edward Teller. Putnam's, 1976. 492 p.

The first biography of Teller based on his personal correspondence and interviews with the man himself. Teller, generally credited with inventing the hydrogen bomb, has been a leading proponent of the arms race since its inception. This is a detailed account of his life, with a lot of information on bomb development and on the Oppenheimer "security risk" episode.

783. BROWN, Harrison S. Must Destruction Be Our Destiny? Simon & Schuster, 1946. 158 p.

This scientist veteran of the Manhattan Project, fearful of atomic ruin, argues that war is no longer rationally pursuable. His conclusion, echoing proposals submitted by the U.S. to the United Nations Atomic Energy Commission in 1946, is that "The use and the manufacture of atomic bombs must be controlled by a world authority if the peoples of this earth are to avoid their own destruction."

784. BULLETIN of the Atomic Scientists. The Atomic Age:
      Scientists in National and World Affairs. Basic
      Books, 1963. 616 p.

Articles from the Bulletin, 1945-1962. Even at this date,
probably the place to go for a concise introduction to scientific opinion and admonition regarding nuclear war. Not much
has changed since the contributors here, among them Einstein, Leo Szilard, Edward Teller, Oppenheimer, Bertrand
Russell, and others, first wrestled with the basic issues.

785. CLARK, Ronald W. Einstein: The Life and Times.
      World Publishing, 1971. 718 p.

A major biography of Einstein, who will probably be forever
associated in the public mind with a confused blend of mushroom clouds and incomprehensible notions about time, space,
and energy. Includes a good overview of the man's relationship to the bomb and to prospects for a future. Bibliography,
copious notes, index.

786. COMPTON, Arthur Holly. Atomic Quest: A Personal
      Narrative. Oxford University Press, 1956. 370 p.

Compton was director of the metallurgical laboratory involved
in the Manhattan Project. Provides a good description of the
deliberation over dropping the bomb on Japan. Most notable
may be the last section, "Hope," where Compton deals with
questions of morality and the bomb, "freedom in the Atomic
Age," his accommodation of the bomb as a professed Christian, his views of the Soviet Union as a society in development.

787. DAVIS, Nuel P. Lawrence and Oppenheimer. Simon
      & Schuster, 1968. 384 p.

On the relationship between Oppenheimer and Ernest O. Lawrence, another collaborator on the original bomb, who believed
in the urgency of the U.S.'s atomic acquisition lest Germany
attain the weapon first.

788. DIETZ, David. Atomic Science, Bombs and Power.
      Dodd, 1955. 316 p.

A readable book by a journalist with a longstanding interest
in atomic science; concentrates on the pioneering atomic
scientists and their successors--Bohr, Einstein, Rutherford,
Fermi, Bethe, etc.

789. FERMI, Laura. Atoms in the Family: My Life with
     Enrico Fermi. University of Chicago Press, 1954.
     267 p.

An informal, anecdotal account of her life with her husband;
many details on quotidian events at Los Alamos among the
scientists and their families as work proceeded on the bomb.

790. GILPIN, Robert G. American Scientists and Nuclear
     Weapons Policy. Princeton University Press, 1962.
     352 p.

Thanks in large part to its very complete index, this book is
a good source for ascertaining the positions and contributions
of a large number of atomic scientists on a wide range of
nuclear issues, such as testing, fallout, strategy, disarmament, and so on.

791. JUNGK, Robert. Brighter than a Thousand Suns: A
     Personal History of the Atomic Scientists. Harcourt,
     Brace, 1958. 369 p.

Covers atomic developments and scientists from 1918 through
1955. Includes the "Franck Report" (after James Franck) to
the Secretary of War in June, 1945, which contains revealing
speculations on the advisability and consequences of using
atomic bombs on Japan, among them the belief that such use
"will mean a flying start towards an unlimited armaments
race. " (Franck was one of the Manhattan Project scientists.)

• • •

"I am sorry for you ... just as I'm sorry for the millions
of others like you. You let yourselves be persuaded that
wars must be waged to preserve peace. Of all the clichés
that echo through the world, that is the most abominable.
You declare that you hate war--but you help to carry it on."
                              --A character in Kirst's
                              The Seventh Day, Item
                              1069, p. 421-422.

• • •

792. LANG, Daniel. From Hiroshima to the Moon: Chroni-
     cles of Life in the Atomic Age. Simon & Schuster,
     1959. 496 p.

Articles from The New Yorker, 1945-1958, with an emphasis

on the lives of atomic scientists. Not anti-bomb or pro-
defense writing, but a portrait through interviews of people
involved in atomic applications and research.

793. LATIL, Pierre de. Enrico Fermi: The Man and His
Theories. Eriksson, 1967. 178 p.

A biography of this important contributor to the development
of the bomb. Fermi achieved a self-sustained atomic chain
reaction in late 1942, thus bringing nuclear weapons a step
closer to reality.

794. LIBBY, Leona M. The Uranium People. Crane, Rus-
sak, 1979. 342 p.

As a young scientist, Libby participated in the development
of the bomb; she was the only woman member of the group
which built the first nuclear reactor. This is a fond, anecdotal reminiscence of those years with many details on other
scientists, some of less than overwhelming interest. Does
anyone really care that Edward Teller's daughter Wendy "was
teaching a grammar school class in the countryside south of
Washington, D.C., during the years when the astronauts were
landing on the moon"? Material of note here, but also too
much folksy pointlessness.

795. MICHELMORE, Peter. The Swift Years: The Robert
Oppenheimer Story. Dodd, 1969. 273 p.

A swift-reading biography with many details on Oppenheimer's
early career and acquaintances.

796. MOORE, Ruth. Niels Bohr: The Man, His Science,
and the World They Changed. Knopf, 1967. 436 p.

An interweaving of biographical data on Bohr, who won the
Nobel Prize for describing the atom's structure in 1913, with
explanations of atomic physics and the origins of the bomb.

797. OPPENHEIMER, J. Robert. Open Mind. Simon &
Schuster, 1956. 146 p.

Eight lectures delivered from 1946 through 1954, on weapons
and policy, science and its place in contemporary life. Speaks
of the need for international atomic controls, the roles of
physicists, the necessity to maintain "open minds" for possibilities of peaceful cooperation among men and nations.

798. ROTBLAT, Joseph, ed. Scientists, the Arms Race
and Disarmament: A Unesco/Pugwash Symposium.
Taylor & Francis, 1982. 323 p.

A good place to begin an inquiry into the relationship of so-
called "pure" scientific work to its applications, and the consequent moral responsibility of scientists. Individual sections
cover the roles of science and technology in the arms race,
the movements of scientists against that race, peace and disarmament research and education, and the pertinent function
of the United Nations.

799. SAKHAROV, Andrei D. My Country and the World.
Knopf, 1975. 109 p.

The Soviet dissident physicist admonishes the West on the
deceptive lure of détente, but stresses the need to avoid nuclear war, a priority of supreme importance. Suggests a
variety of ways to reduce the war threat, including arms reduction, better verification, and other measures to lessen
instability.

800. _____. Sakharov Speaks. Knopf, 1974. 245 p.

Essays and interviews, 1968-1974, include criticism of nuclear testing and admonitions regarding the necessity of political compromise to avoid nuclear war.

801. SEABORG, Glenn T. Nuclear Milestones: A Collection of Speeches. W.H. Freeman, 1972. 390 p.

The first part of the book, "Builders and Discoverers," concerns the early scientific architects of the atomic era; the
second, "Historic Landmarks," places emphasis on the institutions where nuclear research took place, e.g., Hanford,
Washington, Los Alamos, Livermore, the Brookhaven National Laboratory. Many historically significant black &
white photos are a plus.

802. SMITH, Alice K. A Peril and a Hope: The Scientists' Movement in America, 1945-47. University of
Chicago Press, 1965. 591 p.

The geographical heart of the scientific revolt against the
arms race that would result from use of the bomb on Japan,
and the Anglo-American brandishing of an impossible-to-retain
monopoly over the bomb, was the Chicago branch of the Manhattan Project, where scientists like Leo Szilard and James

Franck attempted to call official attention to the long-term international consequences of the bomb. This book is a good account of the movement by these scientists to take responsibility for their work.

803. STERN, Philip M. The Oppenheimer Case: Security on Trial. Harper & Row, 1969. 591 p.

Essentially "a book about the security system" rather than a book about Oppenheimer, though it is also the latter to a considerable extent. Concludes that, although a number of politically influential scientists opposed development of the hydrogen bomb, Oppenheimer attracted the fire of the security watchdogs because of "two wholly contradictory qualities: his remarkable persuasive powers and his equally extraordinary capacity to antagonize and injure."

804. STRICKLAND, Donald A. Scientists in Politics: The Atomic Scientists Movement, 1945-46. Purdue University Studies, 1968. 149 p.

Many of the scientists who developed the bomb argued vigorously in favor of civilian, international control of atomic energy and against military control. The Federation of American Scientists was an early leader in the movement, and still endures. This is another analysis of the first major involvement of scientists in American politics.

805. SZILARD, Gertrud and Weart, Spencer R., eds. Leo Szilard: His Version of the Facts. MIT Press, 1978. 244 p.

Selected recollections and correspondence edited by a science historian and by Szilard's wife, Gertrud. Szilard turned early from his involvement in the U.S. bomb program to calls for international control of the atom. [See also item 1117.]

806. U.S. Atomic Energy Commission. In the Matter of J. Robert Oppenheimer, Transcript of a Hearing Before the Personnel Security Board, 12 April- 6 May, 1954. U.S. Government Printing Office, 1954. 993 p.

Testimony from witnesses, cross-examinations, attacks and defenses; nearly 1,000 pages of closely-printed discourse all of which led to Oppenheimer's branding as a security risk.

807. WEART, Spencer R. Scientists in Power. Harvard University Press, 1979. 343 p.

198 ● The Atomic Papers

Focuses on the French involvement in nuclear development in
the 1930s and 1940s. Especially interested in political influence exercised by scientists.

808. WILSON, Jane, ed. All in Our Time: The Reminiscences of Twelve Nuclear Pioneers. Bulletin of the
  Atomic Scientists, 1975. 236 p.

A dozen then-junior scientists who worked on the bomb remember how it was. Useful insights into the scientific mind.

809. YORK, Herbert F. The Advisors: Oppenheimer,
  Teller, and the Superbomb. W. H. Freeman, 1976.
  175 p.

York, first director of the nuclear weapons laboratory at
Livermore, California, has since been a consistent critic of
U. S. conduct in the arms race, arguing that it has contributed
to a swifter race and to more severe U.S. -Soviet tensions.
Here he analyzes the debate over development of the hydrogen
bomb and Oppenheimer's security clearance revocation by the
Atomic Energy Commission. The A. E. C. 's General Advisory
Committee, chaired by Oppenheimer, recommended against
building the H-bomb on both moral and military grounds, but
its advice went against the flow of short-term political interests, Cold War hysteria--and the 'We want the Bomb and
we want it now!" cheerleading of Teller and other nuclear
hawks. The General Advisory Committee Report of October
30, 1949, urging abstention from H-bomb development, is
included here as an appendix. York concurs with the G. A. C. 's
wisdom, and confirms the short-sightedness of Truman's decision to proceed with the "superbomb. "

● Periodical Articles ●

810. BETHE, Hans. 'The Ethical Responsibilities of Scientists. " Center Magazine 16 (Sept. -Oct. 1983): 2-5.

Bethe, who participated in the development of the hydrogen
bomb, portrays weapons development in part as work that is
naturally performed to the limits of technological ability. His
remarks that "scientists face a terrible dilemma" over their
role in such development may not quite square with the technological determinism he alludes to.

811. DRUMMOND, Hugh. 'The Bomb and I. " Mother Jones
  (June 1982): 13-15.

A meditation on Japanese monster movies (obvious relivings of the bomb), the short-sightedness of the early atomic scientists, the narcissism of J. Robert Oppenheimer, all of which seems to point to our ability to forget the consequences of our actions in the light of the temporary interest those actions provide. The fact that a number of the atomic scientists thought that there was a real chance of the first atomic explosion setting off a chain reaction which would destroy the earth's entire atmosphere--yet tested the bomb anyway--lends credence to this idea.

812. EDWARDS, Rob. "A New Kind of Nuclear Victim."
New Statesman 106 (July 22, 1983): 8-10.

A report on British "nuclear dissidents," atomic scientists fired or forced to resign from their jobs for questioning and criticizing nuclear safety standards. Includes profiles of four such scientists with chronologies of their confrontations with official policy.

813. GRUBER, Carol S. "Manhattan Project Maverick:
The Case of Leo Szilard." Prologue: Journal of
the National Archives 15 (Summer 1983): 72-87.

A fine scholarly essay on atomic scientist Szilard, who, though he helped build the bomb, argued strongly against using it on Japanese civilians, and, following its use, dedicated himself to action against the U.S. -Soviet nuclear arms race. Emphasis here on Manhattan Project officer-in-charge General Leslie Groves and his relations with Szilard. Groves regarded the scientist "a dangerous threat to project security."

814. SCHNEIR, Walter and Schneir, Miriam. "The G-Men
and the H-Bomb: How the FBI Silenced the Atomic
Scientists." Progressive 47 (Sept. 1983): 28-30.

Reviews information the authors obtained through the Freedom of Information Act during research on their Rosenberg book (item 835) showing how the U.S. acted to quell scientific dissent against Truman's decision to pursue a crash-development program for the hydrogen bomb.

815. VON HIPPEL, Frank. "The Myths of Edward Teller."
Bulletin of the Atomic Scientists 39 (March 1983):
6-12.

Systematically destroys Teller's November 1982 Reader's Digest article, "Dangerous Myths about Nuclear Arms," in which Teller pursued his longstanding love affair with the bomb, coupled with assurances (of the sort he has long deployed) that while nuclear war would be unpleasant, it wouldn't be as bad as serious negotiations toward disarmament.

• X •

They Administered the Bomb:
The Atomic Energy Commission

202 • The Atomic Papers

816. ALLARDICE, Corbin and Trapnell, Edward R.   The
      Atomic Energy Commission.   Praeger, 1974.   236 p.

The authors were on the staff of Major General Groves, commander of the Manhattan Project; both went on to employment
with the A. E. C. , and theirs is an uncritical insiders' history
of the agency.

817. FORD, Daniel F.   The Cult of the Atom: The Secret
      Papers of the Atomic Energy Commission.   Simon
      & Schuster, 1982.   273 p.

A readable exposé based on materials Ford obtained through
the Freedom of Information Act showing what he considers
the A. E. C. 's and then the Nuclear Regulatory Commission's
deliberate sidestepping of nuclear safeguard enforcement in
favor of leaving the job to private industry.

818. HEWLETT, Richard G. and Anderson, Oscar E. , Jr.
      The New World, 1939/1946: Volume I: A History
      of the United States Atomic Energy Commission.
      Pennsylvania State University Press, 1962.   766 p.

An official history.   The authors were the first to have access
to a large amount of classified material on the bomb and the
A. E. C.   The most complete account in one place of the
bomb's development, the decision to drop it on Japan, and
the turmoil over post-war atomic control.   A grand total of
9 lines of text are devoted to the immolation of Hiroshima
and Nagasaki.

819. _____ and Duncan, Francis.   Atomic Shield, 1947/
      1952: Volume II: A History of the United States
      Atomic Energy Commission.   Pennsylvania State Uni-
      versity Press, 1969.   718 p.

From the appointment of David Lilienthal and the Oppenheimer
controversy, the Russian bomb in 1949, the contention over
development of the H-bomb, to questions of control and many
other issues; based on A. E. C. and other federal files.   Formidable both in scope and depth, if not often lively.

820. LILIENTHAL, David E.   The Journals of David E.
      Lilienthal.   Harper, 1964.   2v. , 734, 666 p.

See especially volume 2, The Atomic Energy Years, 1945-50.
As the A. E. C. 's first chairman, and as one primarily devoted
to a vision of plenty furnished by nuclear power rather than

to the waste and danger of the developing arms race, Lilienthal's recollections of atomic events and the people associated with them are a vital part of the record.

821. METZGER, H. Peter. The Atomic Establishment. Simon & Schuster, 1973. 274 p.

Attacks the A. E. C. for ineptitude and indifference concerning reactor safety, atomic testing, fallout, waste disposal, and many other areas under its responsibility. Includes close to 600 references which help buttress charges of A. E. C. culpability in ignoring public health.

822. ORLANS, Harold. Contracting for Atoms: A Study of Public Issues Posed by the Atomic Energy Commission's Contracting for Research, Development, and Managerial Services. Brookings Institution, 1967. 242 p.

Based on interviews with A. E. C. officials, contractors, examination of both public and private documents. How contractors were chosen, connections between "big science" and academia, administration of contracts. Includes discussion of nuclear weapons development.

823. SEABORG, Glenn T. Man and Atom: Building a New World through Nuclear Technology. Dutton, 1971. 411 p.

A rationale for the A. E. C.'s pursuit of peaceful uses of nuclear power.

824. STRAUSS, Lewis L. Men and Decisions. Doubleday, 1962. 468 p.

The former A. E. C. chairman relates his life and times, with forays into decisions on the atomic and hydrogen bombs, the Oppenheimer security case, nuclear testing and fallout, and more. See especially the chapter "A Thousand Years of Regret, " on the atomic bombing of Japan "at the end of a war already won. "

825. TEMPLE, David S. Atomic Energy: A Constructive Proposal. Duell, 1955. 165 p.

Argues that the A. E. C. should be under the control of one person subject to influence by the public; objects to the Commission's independence.

● ● ●

"I do not think we shall be any better off because of the bomb.   But the alternatives seem clear.   Only through the monopoly of atomic force by world government can we hope to abolish war. "

--Robert M. Hutchins,
1945.   Item 818, p.   416.

● ● ●

• XI •

They Stole the Bomb (Or Did They?):
The Atomic Spies

826. DE TOLEDANO, Ralph. The Greatest Plot in History:
      How the Reds Stole the A-Bomb. Duell, 1963.
      306 p.

An involved tale of atomic spying, resting on the condescending and provincial notion common in the U.S. that the bomb
was a secret capable of being kept, and that the Russians
simply didn't have the requisite brains to obtain the bomb
without "stealing" it.

827. _____. Spies, Dupes and Diplomats. Duell, 1952.
      244 p.

The right-wing journalist provides an excited, sloppy overview
of Soviet spying; agents and comsymps are everywhere.

828. EVANS, Medford. The Secret War for the A-Bomb.
      Regnery, 1953. 302 p.

Full-fledged McCarthy-era anti-communist indignation over
the various atomic spies, with accusations that those who
favor international control of atomic energy are "fatheads, "
and claims that what the U.S. should do is build more bombs,
right now.

829. HYDE, H. Montgomery. The Atom Bomb Spies. Athe-
      neum, 1980. 339 p.

A work generally superior to others on the subject, partly
because Hyde had access to previously-published materials,
but also because he was able to use formerly-classified FBI,
British, and Canadian documents, along with information from
interviews of government officials. Hyde portrays the atomic
spies not as devils but as human beings with varying motives.
His sympathy for the Rosenbergs is noteworthy, although he
does not acquit them of guilt. Footnoted, with a good selected bibliography.

830. MOOREHEAD, Alan. The Traitors. Harper & Row,
      1963. 236 p.

Though not as foamy as Pilat's The Atom Spies (item 832),
this work, first published in 1952, takes a similarly self-
righteous attitude toward accused atomic spies Allan Nunn
May, Klaus Fuchs, and Bruno Pontecorvo. Based on fewer
than a dozen sources, it barely surpasses the Pilat book in
its effort as journalism, let alone scholarship.

831. NEWMAN, Bernard. Soviet Atomic Spies. Robert
     Hale, 1952. 239 p.

One more Cold War spy book, this one from England, based
on the dubious belief that the Soviet Union may have taken a
decade to develop the bomb without employing its spy forces.
The author concentrates on "the use made of local communists by Russian Intelligence chiefs." Has a scanty bibliography.

832. PILAT, Oliver. The Atom Spies. Putnam's, 1952.
     312 p.

A popular and fist-clenching anti-communist treatment of the
Rosenbergs and others implicated in stealing the "secret" of
fission from the U.S. According to Pilat, one requires a
"strong stomach" to endure personal contact with the Russians.
Such remarks, along with his confident recreation of dialog
among the accused to which he was not privy and his omission of sources leaves this book valuable only as a tool for
prying into the psychology of the era. For that it is very
useful. The reviewer for Saturday Review wrote, "I com-
mend this book to the attention of the junior Senator from
Wisconsin, and his supporters." For those new to the subject, this refers to communist witch-hunter Sen. Joe Mc-
Carthy.

833. RADOSH, Ronald and Milton, Joyce. The Rosenberg
     File: A Search for the Truth. Holt, Rinehart &
     Winston, 1983. 608 p.

Probably the basic book on this famous--and infamous-- atomic spy case. Based on material obtained under the Freedom
of Information Act and on several hundred interviews; the
authors conclude that the Rosenbergs were executed to the
propaganda advantage of both East and West, that Julius was
indeed a Soviet agent, that his wife Ethel was largely rail-
roaded by the FBI in an effort to put pressure on her husband.

834. REUBEN, William. The Atom Spy Hoax. Action
     Books, 1955. 504 p.

An angry attempt to discredit the U.S. campaign against
atomic spies, particularly pursuit of the case against the
Rosenbergs. Illuminates one area of the intense controversy
over the couple.

835. SCHNEIR, Walter and Schneir, Miriam. Invitation to

an Inquest: A New Look at the Rosenberg-Sobell Case. Dell, 1968. 487 p.

The Schneirs maintain that the Rosenbergs were framed. Recently re-issued with additional material. Should be read in conjunction with Radosh's and Milton's The Rosenberg File (item 833).

836. WEXLEY, John. Judgment of Julius and Ethel Rosenberg. Cameron & Kahn, 1955. 672 p.

A long (practically interminable) defense of the Rosenbergs; "Even when one tries valiantly to accept the credibility of the prosecution's case, one is met too often with the implausible." Detailed index. Includes a chronology, 1945-1953, of significant events in or related to the case.

• XII •

They Said We Could Hide from the Bomb:
The Civil Defense Advocates

Oft-Quoted Moscow Joke:
       "What should you do if you hear the air-raid sirens?"
       "What?"
       "Wrap yourself in a sheet and walk slowly toward the nearest grave yard."
       "Why slowly?"
       "So as not to cause a panic."

837. ALBRIGHT, Gifford H., ed. Planning Atomic Shelters: Guidebook for Architects & Engineers. Pennsylvania State University Press, 1961. 196 p.

The product of a research contract between the U.S. Naval Civil Engineering Laboratory and Penn State's Shelter Research and Study Program. Released at the height of our most recent shelter mania.

838. BRELIS, Dean. Run, Dig or Stay? A Search for an Answer to the Fallout Question. Beacon Press, 1962. 196 p.

We might want to remember that the "fallout question," in fact pretty much the whole question of "civil defense," is one open only to Americans of economic means and non-urban situations which would allow the consideration and construction of shelters. Millions of Americans trapped in cities and without financial resources are obviously out of the picture. There is no place to hide on Broadway when you're on welfare. Brelis covers "the great debate" over bomb and fallout shelters of the late 1950s and early '60s, with statements from both shelter proponents and disparagers. He argues that the shelter represents "not a will to live ... anyone going into a shelter must know that whether he comes out or not is a matter of chance--of pure, insecure chance over which he has no control, no aptitude to meet because when those shelter doors close behind him, he is hiding." Brelis has an alternative to holing up (or down), lighting out for the territory, or merely cringing. It consists of keeping the peace. (Clearly a dangerous man.)

839. DENTLER, Robert A. and Cutright, Phillips. Hostage America: Human Aspects of a Nuclear Attack and a Program of Prevention. Beacon Press, 1963. 167 p.

Contends that civil defense is a hopeless charade, recovery from nuclear attack would be at best improbable, at worst impossible; the only sane route is to support nuclear disarmament.

840. FRANK, Pat. How to Survive the H-Bomb and Why. Lippincott, 1962. 160 p.

Frank's novel Alas, Babylon (item 1044) portrayed survival of nuclear war in what is now a fairly unconvincing fashion, and this exercise in how and why achieves no better results-- but is still interesting for its psychological perspectives.

841. FRYKLUND, Richard. 100 Million Lives: Maximum
Survival in a Nuclear War. Macmillan, 1962. 175 p.

Argues that because total war would prove intolerable, the
U. S. and Soviet Union may adopt a "limited" nuclear war
strategy. Written at a popular level, and now badly dated
because of changes (read "massive growth") in nuclear armaments. Useful as a tool for examining the sorts of semi-
optimistic nuclear war thinking delivered to the public in the
early 1960s.

842. GERSTELL, Richard. How to Survive an Atomic
Bomb. Combat Forces Press, 1950. 150 p.

Run-of-the-mill civil defense Pollyanna-izing by a consultant
to the Civil Defense Office of the National Security Resources
Board.

843. GOURE, Leon. Civil Defense in the Soviet Union.
University of California Press, 1962. 207 p.

Goure finds, based on personal visits to Russian cities and
examination of written records, some preoccupation with civil
defense, consisting chiefly of an extension of the WW II-
vintage air attack shelter system--a system largely useless
against nuclear blasts. Also notes indifference and public
pessimism regarding the shelters' efficacy.

844. GRAY, Dwight E. and Martens, John. Radiation
Monitoring in Atomic Defense. Van Nostrand, 1951.
122 p.

For civil defense workers, an early how-to book.

845. KEARNY, Cresson H. Nuclear War Survival Skills.
NWS Research Bureau, 1980. 232 p.

Another in the line of books assuring us that getting H-
bombed isn't as bad as we've been led to believe if we only
remember to take along the shovels and the port-a-johns.
Strictly for survivalists; information on how to build your
basic shelter, how to survive without doctors, etc. Plenty
of illustrations of oddly-happy looking (white) families sitting
in their trenches and so on. Edward Teller informs us in a
cover blurb that this book "takes a long overdue step in edu-
cating the American people. " This from the same man who
reported a successful (i. e., it went off) bomb test at Eniwetok
with the excited, fatherly message, "It's a boy!"

846. KINDALL, Sylvian G. Total Atomic Defense. Richard
      B. Smith, 1952. 224 p.

What we need is "an indestructible capital city" to replace
Washington, D. C., so that, even if the rest of the nation is
reduced to randomly-colliding atoms, those responsible for
the event "will be able to live and work without the constant
fear that any moment they may be blasted into eternity."
Who could want less for them? Cities in general might also
be dispersed on a broader geographic basis, so that "more
bombs" will be required to destroy them. We all have
"more bombs."

847. LEYSON, Burr W. Atomic Energy in War and Peace.
      Dutton, 1951. 217 p.

A former Army pilot with air-raid safety knowledge misses
the point of nuclear destructive capacity when he writes that
three-quarters of atomic casualties could be avoided through
adequate shelters. His emphasis is overwhelmingly on war,
not peace; not bad as a sample of the "you and your family
can survive the bomb" gruel served up to the American public in the 1950s, and again, with variations, in the 1980s.

848. MARTIN, Thomas L. and Latham, Donald C. Strategy
      for Survival. University of Arizona Press, 1963.
      389 p.

A scholarly treatment and championing of systematic construction of community shelters.

849. MAWRENCE, Col. Mel. You Can Survive the Bomb.
      Quadrangle Books, 1961. 194 p.

Well, you see, the destructive effects of nuclear bombs are
highly over-rated. Why, you could practically survive a
direct hit if you just bothered to hide in the cellar for a few
days. With sufficient bombs now in the Soviet arsenal to
deposit one on every U. S. city with a population of 5-10,000
and up, Mawrence's rosy estimation of what it would take to
survive nuclear war seems a little awry, and his assertion
that "for the first time in four generations we face the moral
problems our forefathers faced when they took their families
into the wilderness" is nothing less than fantastic. The em-
bossed cloth cover of this book features a quasi-religious
portrayal of a man, woman, and baby, clearly safe within a
trinity of circles. Truly offensive.

850. SEVERUD, Fred N. and Merrill, Anthony F. The Bomb, Survival and You: Protection for People, Buildings, Equipment. Reinhold, 1954. 264 p.

More typical 1950s "you can live through the bomb" material.

851. TELLER, Edward. The Legacy of Hiroshima. Doubleday, 1962. 325 p.

Teller once again dismisses disarmament, test-bans, and co-existence, and pleads for more bombs, bigger and better bombs, and more shelters. He lacks only pompons in his nuclear cheerleader's role. Generally unnerving, but does feature some grotesque and unintended black humor (writers like Teller and Herman Kahn don't seem capable of saying anything funny intentionally), e. g., although we may be offended, at first, by the sight of fallout-induced mutations, they will ultimately prove beneficial.

852. UNIVERSITY of Michigan. Survey Research Center. Public Thinking about Warfare and Civil Defense. University of Michigan, 1951. 263 p.

Subtitled "A study based upon an intensive interview sample survey of people in eleven major cities, September-October, 1950." Covers public attitudes regarding "general worry," "anticipation of war," "perceptions of what an atomic attack would be like," civil defense attitudes, etc. Interesting not only for what it reveals about the respondents, but for what it shows about the authors, e. g., they identify "prayer" as a "Non-constructive or flight response" in the event one hears that atomic attack is imminent. Given twenty minutes before twenty megatons burst above one's head, one might consider the consolations of prayer rather more constructive than the fruits of any number of other possible actions.

853. WIGNER, Eugene P., ed. Who Speaks for Civil Defense? Scribner's, 1968. 125 p.

Wigner does, for one; to get a concise idea of his point of view, begin with the "Letter to the President" on page 114, a document signed by the editor and numerous other civil defense advocates, including the ubiquitous Herman Kahn and Edward Teller. The letter points to various issues, such as fallout protection and missile defense, that they believe require attention. The statement in the opening of the letter is not without value, questionable or otherwise: "A rational United States Government enhanced our national security by demon-

strating its willingness to risk nuclear war in October, 1962."
That Soviet humiliation in the Missile Crisis led directly to
a severely exacerbated arms race and a consequent diminu-
tion of U.S. security might occur to the reader yielding to
the lure of hindsight. One might also think, moreover, that
a quantity of foresight would not prove completely impossible.

854.   . Survival and the Bomb: Methods of Civil
        Defense. Indiana University Press, 1969. 307 p.

A baker's dozen essays pertinent to the idea that we can hide
away from the bomb and its effects for a few weeks, then
come out later to pick up the pieces, radiant though they may
be.

● Periodical Articles ●

855. "Civil Defense in the Nuclear Age." Society 20
        (Sept. -Oct. 1983): 7-29.

A collection of pro and con civil defense articles. Louis
Rene Beres's is the major piece in opposition, followed by
James L. Holton's "In Defense of Civil Defense."

856. GEIGER, H. Jack. "The Illusion of 'Survival'." Bul-
        letin of the Atomic Scientists 37 (June-July 1981):
        16-20.

Attempts to imagine the consequences of a 20-megaton nuclear
attack on San Francisco. Contends that all means of responding to medical emergency would be destroyed, and that survivors would be left without food, water or drugs.

857. NELSON, Lin. "Offenses of Civil Defense: The Mili-
        tarization of Life and the Exploitation of Women. "
        New Women's Times 8 (Nov. 1982): 1+

Attacks the Crisis Relocation Plan as absurd and unworkable
--it wouldn't work in a surprise attack, attack could come
while evacuees are en route, missiles could easily be re-
targeted on host areas, etc. The Crisis Relocation Plan is
nothing more than "the ultimate drill for death." Argues
that officials will attempt to persuade women to fulfill their
"natural" function by helping prepare the amenities of relocation life.

858. SCHOONMAKER, Mary Ellen. "Helter Shelter." In
        These Times 6 (June 2, 1982): 24+

Describes the general civic abandonment of the fallout shelters constructed in the 1950s and early 1960s, and the Reagan Crisis Relocation Plan now in vogue among the civil defense set. To the author, the C. R. P. "comes down to running rather than hiding. "

859. WILSON, Deb. "After the Blast. " Open Road 14
     (Summer 1982): 12.

An amusing article on a group of Canadian artists who set up a mock civil defense information center in a Vancouver storefront, paraded the sidewalk in radiation suits, and persuaded many that the display was officially sanctioned. The artists wish to link antinuclear protest with environmental, feminist and native issues.

● ● ●

> "Well, I said please--please don't drop--
> Don't drop that A-bomb on me!"
>   --Joe McDonald, "The
>   Bomb Song, " circa 1967.

● ● ●

● XIII ●

The Time We Almost Did It:
The Cuban Missile Crisis

"They're nuts.   One lady's working four shopping carts at once.   Another lady bought twelve packages of detergents. What's she going to do, wash up after the bomb?"

> --A North Hollywood grocer
> on panic buying during the
> Missile Crisis.   Item 864,
> p. 193.

860. ABEL, Elie. The Missiles of October: The Story of the Cuban Missile Crisis, 1962. MacGibbon & Kee, 1966. 204 p.

A day-by-day account of the Crisis, October 14-28. Creditably written, though the lack of footnotes and bibliography pretty much confines it to the popular history genre. Published in the U.S. by Lippincott in 1966 as The Missile Crisis.

861. ALLISON, Graham T. Essence of Decision: Explaining the Cuban Missile Crisis. Little, Brown, 1971. 338 p.

A complicated but valuable investigation of the Crisis which relies on three hypothetical explanatory views, one from the vantage of traditional diplomacy, one from that of organizational behavior theory, the third involving the results of bargaining among governmental officials, each with his own interests and quantity of leverage among the others. Comes down to a picture of the decision-making process as less clear-cut than the one presented in the popular media ("We gave them an ultimatum and they backed down--" or, as the Detroit Free Press so jingoistically put it in mile-high print, "Nik Knuckles Under.") The author speculates on both Soviet and American leadership.

862. CHAYES, Abram. The Cuban Missile Crisis: International Crises and the Role of Law. Oxford University Press, 1974. 157 p.

Chayes was the Legal Adviser with the Department of State during the Crisis; he focuses here on the choice of the naval blockade instead of greater or lesser military tactics, the decision to seek an authorizing resolution from the Organization of American States, and "the manner and method" of the approach to the United Nations.

863. DANIEL, James and Hubbell, John G. Strike in the West: The Complete Story of the Cuban Crisis. Holt, 1963. 180 p.

Contends that the Kennedy administration managed a triumph of foreign policy by persuading the Soviets to withdraw the missile launchers in place on Cuban soil. The authors excoriate Canadian Prime Minister John Diefenbaker for refusing to accept U.S. nuclear weapons, condemning Canada's rejection of these armaments as "woolly thinking."

864. DETZER, David. The Brink: Cuban Missile Crisis, 1962. Crowell, 1979. 299 p.

A very readable account of the crisis, well-researched and at the same time lively. Gives a good sense of popular reaction to the common belief that WW III was coming within the week. Good bibliography.

865. DINERSTEIN, Herbert S. The Making of a Missile Crisis: October, 1962. Johns Hopkins University Press, 1976. 302 p.

Examines the connection between the Crisis and the "Guatemalan Crisis" of 1954, when the Department of State announced that Soviet arms were being shipped to Guatemalan insurgents. A thoughtful discussion of U.S., Soviet, and Latin American perceptions, misperceptions, and resulting actions, particularly vital in light of Central American issues in the 1980s. Dinerstein concludes that, had the ideologically-obsessed Eisenhower administration refrained from its evident assistance in the overthrow of the socialist Guatemalan government, then the Cuban Missile Crisis would not have occurred, and Castro would "have shuttled between Soviet and American cliency as Nasser and Sadat have done."

866. DIVINE, Robert A., ed. The Cuban Missile Crisis. Quadrangle, 1971. 248 p.

Sixteen articles from across the ideological spectrum on various facets of the Crisis. Authors include Stewart Alsop, I. F. Stone, John F. Kennedy and Nikita Khrushchev.

867. KENNEDY, Robert F. Thirteen Days: A Memoir of the Cuban Missile Crisis. Norton, 1969. 224 p.

Kennedy was unable to finish this book, but his presence among the decision makers during the crisis lends it qualities of immediacy and authenticity few other treatments can possess.

868. PACHTER, Henry M. Collision Course: The Cuban Missile Crisis and Coexistence. Praeger, 1963. 261 p.

A readable presentation; includes documentary material on U.S. relations with Cuba and Latin America, some of which seems of less than keen importance to the subject at hand.

• XIV •

The Bomb and the Cross: Christian Perspectives

"What message do we give our children if we avoid taking up
the issue with them? We tell them, I think, that we don't
care very much about human survival, or that the situation
is hopeless, or ... someone else's responsibility, or that the
best way of dealing with a problem is to put it out of your
mind. "

> --Tom Roderick, "Nuclear
> Warfare: What Shall We
> Tell the Kids?" Chris-
> tianity and Crisis, April
> 18, 1983, p. 142.

869. DRESNER, Samuel H. God, Man & Atomic War. Living Books, 1966. 227 p.

Echoes Einstein when he says that "only a change in man himself" can prevent nuclear war. Identifies contemporary cultural problems, from juvenile crime to political cynicism, as rooted in sense of helpless anticipation of extinction. Founded in religious beliefs that the author interprets as requiring individual action toward insuring our survival. "Those who go on living just as they lived before have not grasped the danger. Merely to conceive it intellectually does not mean that it has been absorbed into the reality of one's life."

870. FREUND, Ronald. What One Person Can Do to Help Prevent Nuclear War. Twenty-Third Publications, 1982. 185 p.

The author, a peaceworker for over a decade, opens with an anecdotal account of his "nuclear childhood," surveys the arms race, discusses the deeply-felt fear of nuclear war shared by most of the public, and, relying on case histories, points out how one person can help turn back the threat. Written from a Catholic's point of view, it is entirely appropriate for a non-Catholic reader. Accessible and smoothly composed, especially good for young adults.

871. GOODWIN, Geoffrey L., ed. Ethics and Nuclear Deterrence. St. Martin's, 1982. 199 p.

Essays on deterrence, unilateral disarmament as based in Christian tradition, a call for deep strategic cuts as a "moral imperative," etc.

872. HEYER, Robert, ed. Nuclear Disarmament: Key Statements of Popes, Bishops, Councils and Churches. Paulist Press, 1982. 278 p.

Sixty-seven statements which can be seen leading to the U.S. Catholic bishops' pastoral letter on peace and nuclear arms of May, 1983.

873. HIEBERT, Erwin N. The Impact of Atomic Energy. Faith and Life Press, 1961. 302 p.

Overview of nuclear developments, followed by discussion of attitudes and ideas on disarmament held by governments, scientists, and various religious groups. Lengthy quotations from representatives of the latter.

874. HOLLENBACH, David. Nuclear Ethics: A Christian Moral
Imperative. Paulist Press, 1983. 100 p.

A Catholic professor of moral theology examines historical
and theological aspects of pacifism and "just war" theory,
and discusses policies of nuclear deterrence and warfighting.
Concludes that, although both pacifist and "just war" approaches must be represented within the Church, "no use of nuclear
weapons is justifiable in the circumstances of the present international political and military order."

875. KEYS, Donald, ed. God and the H-Bomb. Bellmea-
dows Press, 1962. 224 p.

Protestant, Catholic, and Jewish theologians inquire into the
morality of the bomb. The general sentiment is toward pacifism.

876. KNOX, Ronald Arbuthnott. God and the Atom. Sheed,
1946. 166 p.

Regrets that the U.S. did not demonstrate the bomb to the
Japanese in a non-lethal fashion. Counsels the maintenance
of hope, or its façade, for a future in spite of the bomb.

877. NATIONAL Conference of Catholic Bishops. The Challenge of Peace: God's Promise and Our Response;
A Pastoral Letter on War and Peace, May 3, 1983.
U.S. Catholic Conference Office of Publishing Services, 1983. 116 p.

The much-debated letter on nuclear weapons and the arms
race; an attempt "to live up to the call of Jesus to be peace-
makers in our own time."

878. O'BRIEN, William V. Nuclear War, Deterrence and
Morality. Newman Press, 1967. 120 p.

No "higher cause" can justify an unlimited nuclear war, says
the author in this statement on both traditional and contemporary Catholic thought. "The Church intends to propose to
our age over and over again, in season and out of season,
the Apostle's message: 'Behold, now is the acceptable time'
for a change of heart, 'behold, now is the day of salvation.' "

879. SMITH, Thomas V. Atomic Power and Moral Faith.
Claremont College, 1946. 56 p.

Two lectures calling for the latter in the face of the former.

880. STEIN, Walter. Nuclear Deterrence and Christian
Conscience. Merlin, 1961. 151 p.

A half-dozen essays addressing issues of defense in relation
to conscience, faith, war, and murder, from a Roman Catholic perspective. "Faith is compelled to take stock of its
own reality, asking itself whether it dares pronounce the
promise that the Gates of Hell shall not prevail, whilst preparing to massacre the innocent in the defence of the things
of God."

• XV •

Children Under the Bomb

881. The Child Study Association of America. Children and
      the Threat of Nuclear War. Duell, 1964. 148 p.

Intended for parents, this is a basic introduction, with articles
on children's perceptions of war, their attitudes toward civil
defense drills; also includes information on fallout hazards,
shelters, etc.

● Periodical Articles ●

882. BECKER, Susan. "Helping Children Think about the
      Unthinkable." Instructor 93 (Sept. 1983): 86-89.

Ideas on teaching children about nuclear issues from those
active in the field. Includes a short resource list for curricu-
lum development.

883. BESTOR, Barbara and Kirsch, Vanessa. "Freezing
      Nukes, Forming Friendships." Sojourner 8 (April
      1983): 4.

Two Cambridge, Mass., high school students discuss their
awakening to nuclear realities--one through a dream of atomic
war, the other through a film on the subject--and the friend-
ship they formed through common interest in antinuclear action. "We do believe that we have a future, but know that
we must take responsibility for assuring it ourselves."

884. CLOSE, David. "Children's View of World Conflict:
      Notes from a Newfoundland Survey." Peace Re-
      search: The Canadian Journal of Peace Studies 15
      (Jan. 1983): 9-14.

Reports on a 1979 survey of children in grades 5, 8, and 11
intended to measure attitudes toward U.S.-Soviet behavior
and war, especially nuclear war. Shows among other findings
a declining readiness to embrace bellicosity over the grade-
span, a steadily-growing awareness of the costs of war, and
a refusal to assign blame for world problems on either nation.

885. CLOUD, Kate. "Will There be a World for Our Chil-
      dren?" Sojourner 8 (March 1983): 15+

A mother's reflections on her own television introduction to the
nuclear threat during the Cuban Missile Crisis, and her young
son's similar initiation during the TMI accident.

886. "Educators and the Nuclear Threat: It's Your Move."
Phi Delta Kappan 64 (April 1983): 527-551.

A good group of articles under the above title, including Terry
Herndon's "A Teacher Speaks of Peace," Stanley M. Elam's
"Educators and the Nuclear Threat," Daniel B. Fleming's
"Nuclear War in High School History Textbooks," and others.

887. FRYMILLER, Kathleen M. "Energy Education: Responding to the Nuclear Power Controversy." Young
Children 37 (May 1982): 3-11.

The response is based on the assumption that nuclear power
and nuclear weapons are both menaces. Suggestions for cur-
riculum activities concerning renewable energy sources, pollution, conservation; brief bibliography citing, among other
material, some studies linking radiation to health defects in
children.

888. MAYRAND, Theresa. "The Nuclear Dilemma: Where
Can We Go for Help?" The Science Teacher 50
(April 1983): 27-31.

Summarizes the urgency of the nuclear arms situation, suggests ways to work nuclear war into class discussion, provides an annotated list of organizations and resources dedicated
to halting the arms race and preventing war.

889. MOLANDER, Roger and Woodward, E. "How to Teach
Nuclear War to High School Students." Educational
Leadership 40 (May 1983): 44-48.

Molander, Executive Director of Ground Zero, and Woodward,
the organization's Director of Public Affairs, contend that examining "how a nuclear war might start and how one might be
prevented" is the best way for teachers to present the subject
to their students. They offer a half-dozen brief scenarios
for nuclear war, and discuss ways to keep the scenarios from
coming true.

890. SCHIRMER, Peggy. "Helping Children Deal with the
Nuclear Threat." Interracial Books for Children
Bulletin 13 (Nos. 6/7, 1982): 4+

A discussion intended chiefly for teachers with suggestions for
integrating nuclear war issues into the classroom--for, as
Schirmer points out, even very young children "are aware of
the nuclear arms race" through television and other means.

891. SCHWEBEL, Milton. "Effects of the Nuclear War
Threat on Children and Teenagers: Implications for
Professionals." American Journal of Orthopsy-
chiatry 52 (Oct. 1982): 608-618.

Shows that children are widely aware of the nuclear war
threat, which the author believes helps lead to anxiety and
various socio-psychological problems. Includes a plan for
helping the young deal with the threat in a constructive manner.

892. "Social Responsibility." Physics Education 18 (May
1983).

This British journal contains several articles under the above feature dealing with the implications for physics teachers' commitment to peace education. See especially the essay by Sakae
Shimizu (emeritus professor of physics, Kyoto University) on his
exploratory trip to Hiroshima shortly after the bombing.

893. WIGUTOFF, Sharon and Herscovici, Sergiu. "Militarism
in Textbooks: An Analysis." Interracial Books for
Children Bulletin 13 (Nos. 6-7, 1982): 15-17.

How public school textbooks present militarism, regarding
both nuclear and conventional war.

894. WINTER, Metta L. "Taming the Technological Beast:
The Debate on Nuclear Education." School Library
Journal 30 (Sept. 1983): 36-40.

Disputes various superficially comforting assumptions, including
the one holding children immune to distress over new technologies,
especially nuclear; emphasis on the need for responsible education rather than traditional avoidance of the issues.

● ● ●

Now you've thrown the worst fear that can ever be
hurled,
Fear to bring children into the world;
For threatenin' my babies, unborn and unnamed--
You ain't worth the blood that runs through your
veins.

--Bob Dylan, "Masters of
War," Columbia Records,
1963

● ● ●

• XVI •

Three Mile Island:
Political, Health, and Economic Fallout

895. CANTELON, Philip L. and Williams, Robert C. Crisis
Contained: The Department of Energy at Three Mile
Island. Southern Illinois University Press, 1982.
213 p.

The authors describe the TMI accident, which they call a
"minor loss-of-coolant accident that caused them [the public]
less radiation than their dentist and was less likely to kill
them than their automobile" as of greatest consequence because of the inept way public agencies fed the public jargon-
laden and contradictory explanations of what was going on,
thus contributing to a distrust of technocratic officialdom and
of technology itself. The authors praise the work of D.O.E.
in its reaction to the accident as "the most effective response"
to the situation. The reader might want to keep in mind that
the authors prepared this book under contract to the Department of Energy.

896. DEL TREDICI, Robert. The People of Three Mile
Island: Interviews and Photos. Sierra Club, 1980.
127 p.

Nearly forty interviews with a variety of people concerned
with the TMI accident. A mixture of informed opinion, hear-
say, denial, and fear runs through the interviews; a good look
at the psychological impact of a nuclear accident.

897. FORD, Daniel F. Three Mile Island: Thirty Minutes
to Meltdown. Penguin Books, 1982. 271 p.

A detailed account of the breakdown, focusing on what happened, how, and why. The author is a former executive
director of the Union of Concerned Scientists.

898. GRAY, Mike and Rosen, Ira. The Warning: Accident
at Three Mile Island. Norton, 1982. 287 p.

Gray wrote the script for the film "The China Syndrome";
Rosen is a producer for "60 Minutes." Their book provides
lively coverage of the TMI accident, though its thriller-like
approach limits its utility as a source for serious inquiry.

899. KEISLING, Bill. Three Mile Island: Turning Point.
Veritas Books, 1980. 184 p.

A journalistic account of the accident, couched in an antinuclear point of view.

900. LEPPZER, Robert. Voices from Three Mile Island:
    The People Speak Out. Crossing Press, 1980.
    86 p.

A staunchly antinuclear book compiled from taped interviews
with TMI-area residents.

901. MARTIN, Daniel. Three Mile Island. Random House,
    1980. 246 p.

A non-polemical but not uncritical investigation of the reasons
for the TMI accident; includes discussion of public attitudes
toward nuclear power and safety. Martin was a member of
the Public Information Task Force of the President's Commission on the Accident at Three Mile Island. "A Final look at
the performance of government during the accident at Three
Mile Island shows the same fear of honesty--if honesty car-
ries any sign of weakness with it--that had been characteristic of Met Ed in the accident's first two days."

902. MOSS, Thomas H. and Sills, David L., eds. The
    Three Mile Island Nuclear Accident: Lessons &
    Implications. New York Academy of Sciences,
    1981. 343 p.

The result of a conference on TMI held in 1980, sponsored
by the Academy. Approximately eighty contributors provide
essays on a large number of TMI-related issues, grouped
into broad categories of "Background," "Public Information
and Communication," "Societal Reaction," "Major Lessons and
Issues." One of the best books on the accident for breadth
and detail. Frequent bibliographies, but no index.

903. The President's Commission on the Accident at Three
    Mile Island. Report: The Need for Change: The
    Legacy of TMI. U.S. Government Printing Office,
    1979. 201 p.

An overview of the accident, including causes, handling of the
emergency, public and worker health and safety, the public's
right to information, roles of the utility and the Nuclear Regulatory Commission. "Extremely critical" of the N.R.C. (com-
pare with the glowing account of the N.R.C. at TMI by Cantelon and Williams, item 895) finding "a serious lack of communication among the commissioners, those who were attempting to make the decisions about the accident in Bethesda, the
field offices, and those actually on site." Includes numerous
recommendations aimed at insuring that such an accident would
not be repeated.

904.   SILLS, David L., et al., eds.   Accident at Three
       Mile Island: The Human Dimensions.   Westview
       Press, 1982.   258 p.

Revised papers written at the request of the President's Commission on the Accident at TMI.   Covers public perceptions
of nuclear energy, local responses to nuclear plants, interaction of social and technical systems, implications for public
policy.   Based on the idea that the accident was "as much a
social-systems failure as it was an engineering failure."

905.   STEPHENS, Mark.   Three Mile Island.   Random House,
       1981.   245 p.

The author was a public information specialist on the President's Commission.   This is his account of what happened
and why.   His rancor is directed chiefly at administrators
and politicians who, he believes, put financial profit and the
lure of power ahead of consideration for the public good.

●   Periodical Articles   ●

906.   BAUM, Andrew, et al.   "Emotional, Behavioral, and
       Physiological Effects of Chronic Stress at Three
       Mile Island."   Journal of Consulting and Clinical
       Psychology 51 (Aug. 1983):   565-572.

Based on a study of TMI residents compared with those in
vicinities of a coal-fired power plant and a problem-free
nuclear plant, researchers found TMI residents, a year after
the accident, exhibiting more measurable symptoms of stress.

907.   DAVIDSON, Laura M., et al.   "Stress and Control-
       Related Problems at Three Mile Island."   Journal
       of Applied Social Psychology 12 (Sept.-Oct. 1982):
       349-359.

A study involving interviews with and tests on a group of
TMI residents and another group nearly 100 miles away from
any nuclear plant shows that the TMI group experienced a
higher degree of stress and greater loss of control at certain
tasks.

908.   "Financing for TMI Cleanup Finally Falling into
       Place."   Nuclear Industry: The Monthly Magazine
       of the Atomic Industrial Forum 30 (April 1983):
       18-20.

It will cost over $1 billion to clean up the radioactive mess at TMI Unit 2. The responsible utility, General Public Utilities Corporation, had only $300 million to contribute. This article outlines the sources for the remaining funds, including electric utility contributions, the states of Pennsylvania and New Jersey (i.e., the taxpayers of those states), higher charges to regional utility customers, and the federal government (i.e., U.S. taxpayers.) Does this explain that tee-shirt slogan, "We All Live at Three Mile Island?" At any rate, Nuclear Industry seems delighted that the taxes are all falling into place through the TMI siphon.

909. GOLDHABER, Marilyn K., et al. "Spontaneous Abortions after the Three Mile Island Nuclear Accident: A Life Table Analysis." American Journal of Public Health 73 (July 1983): 752-759.

A study based on information regarding pregnant women within five miles of TMI during the months following the accident showed no unusual departure from the norm for spontaneous abortions.

910. MANNING, D. Thompson. "Post-TMI Perceived Risk from Nuclear Power in Three Communities." Nuclear Safety 23 (July-Aug. 1982): 379-384.

Reports and discusses an attitude poll following the accident; findings were that those who did not live near a nuclear plant were almost as distressed over nuclear power as TMI residents, but those who lived in the vicinity of a trouble-free nuclear plant expressed the least distress.

911. NELKIN, Dorothy. "Some Social and Political Dimensions of Nuclear Power: Examples from Three Mile Island." American Political Science Review 75 (March 1981): 132-142.

Uses the TMI accident as a basis for discussing the necessity of understanding technology as a social concept. Focuses on reactions and roles of the nuclear industry, public officials, the regulatory system, the courts, the media, and the scientific community.

912. STILLMAN, Peter G. "Three Mile Island: A Case of Disinformation." Democracy: A Journal of Political Renewal and Radical Change 2 (Fall 1982): 66-78.

Criticizes information exchange among parties responsible for safe operation and response to emergencies at TMI, including the NRC, Metropolitan Edison, and Babcock & Wilcox. "Having misunderstood the system's potential accidents when they designed and regulated it, the experts then misunderstood the course of the accident itself." Skeptical of NRC's ability to adequately prepare for emergencies.

913. WINFIELD-LAIRD, Idee, et al. "Changes in Uranium Plant Community Leaders' Attitudes Toward Nuclear Power: Before and After TMI." Energy 7 (No. 5, 1982): 449-455.

This study of community leaders (in both public and private sectors) in nuclear-plant host communities shows that, in spite of the TMI accident, their attitudes remained receptive toward nuclear power, and held the presence of local plants a positive good.

• XVII •

An Atomic Miscellany

Ooops: "Contrary to the public's perception, the risk of
nuclear war by accident is minute and negligible, provided
that strategic stability is assured.   The focus on the risk of
nuclear war by accident may misrepresent the problem and
misdirect attention from more serious and crucial risks con-
stituting a far greater danger."

--Frei and Catrina, Item
926, p. 165.

914. ADAMS, Benson D. Ballistic Missile Defense. American Elsevier, 1971. 274 p.

A politically oriented examination of U.S. efforts toward an ABM system. Should be useful to anyone researching the issue. Many authorities (Adams is not one of them) believe that any ABM system within the scope of present technology would constitute a hoax, an illusion of defense which could not work.

915. AMERICAN Psychiatric Association. Psychosocial Aspects of Nuclear Development. APA, 1982. 96 p.

A collection of papers from an APA Task Force; covers sociopsychological aspects of the arms race, emotional responses to nuclear issues, Soviet-American relations, nuclear weapons and secrecy, psychological effects of the TMI accident and its media treatment, the effects of nuclear developments on children and adolescents, and a review of the international literature on psychosocial aspects of nuclear power.

916. ARKIN, William M. Research Guide to Current Military and Strategic Affairs. Institute for Policy Studies, 1981. 232 p.

Arkin is Director of the Arms Race and Nuclear Weapons Research Project of the Institute for Policy Studies. In the process of citing and discussing over 1,000 U.S. and foreign government documents, hundreds of periodicals, Congressional hearings, and other sources of military information, he provides countless worthwhile leads to researchers at almost any level. Includes attention to nuclear issues.

917. BARNABY, Charles F. and Boserup, A., eds. Implications of Anti-Ballistic Missile Systems. Humanities Press, 1969. 246 p.

Composed chiefly of papers presented at a Pugwash symposium on the ABM. Barnaby prefaces the papers with chapters on the development and characteristics of ABM systems, and on pro and con arguments regarding them. Individual papers include those on ABM systems and the arms race, effects of ABM on disarmament, strategic balance, "limited" nuclear war, etc.

918. BERES, Louis Rene. Terrorism and Global Security: The Nuclear Threat. Westview Press, 1979. 161 p.

How contemporary terrorists could develop a nuclear threat; how to counter the possibilities.

919. BICKEL, Lennard. The Deadly Element: The Story of Uranium. Stein & Day, 1979. 312 p.

A readable history of uranium from 1780 Berlin to the present. Includes a list of over 70 important scientists concerned with uranium (biographical sketches for each), a short bibliography and index.

920. CHAYES, Abram and Weisner, Jerome B., eds. ABM: An Evaluation of the Decision to Deploy an Anti-Ballistic Missile System. Harper & Row, 1969. 282 p.

The U.S. system was not deployed; the only such system now in place is a primitive one around Moscow. Here scientists, academicians and statesmen ponder the questions turning around the proposed Safeguard anti-missile system. Generally opposed to the system.

921. COCHRAN, Bert. The War System. Macmillan, 1965. 274 p.

The main theme: the partial absorption of various facets of the culture, e.g., the educational system, by the military, thus hindering the work of disarmament.

922. COCKBURN, Andrew. The Threat: Inside the Soviet Military Machine. Random House, 1983. 338 p.

Cockburn relies on interviews with Soviet émigrés, samizdat documents and U.S. intelligence sources to debunk the myth of the Soviet military as flawlessly organized and surpassingly powerful. Contends that the Soviet nuclear forces are no more capable of "winning" a nuclear war than those of the U.S. "Only by understanding the true motivations and actions of the military bureaucrats," he writes, "both in the East and at home, can we hope to frustrate them, and thus avoid a dénouement more terrible and final than 1914." Cockburn has written on defense for many publications.

923. DAVIS, Elmer H. Two Minutes till Midnight. Bobbs, 1955. 207 p.

Argues that nuclear war is at hand. His gloom stems from Russian perfection of the hydrogen bomb in 1954. Good in-

sights on the complex of fears, hopes, and Cold War attitudes
roiling the mind of one intelligent citizen, though his intelligence does not keep him from saying things like "The next
war ... would not destroy civilization unless we lost it."

924. DeVOLPI, Alexander, et al. Born Secret: The H-
     Bomb, the Progressive Case and National Security.
     Pergamon Press, 1981. 305 p.

The authors were all consultants for the defense in the U.S.
government's 1979 case against the Progressive, through which
it sought to prevent publication of Howard Morland's how-to
article on the H-bomb worked out from various unclassified
sources. Discusses the background of the case regarding
nuclear secrecy and the public's right to know, covers legal
arguments and connections with the proliferation problem.
Morland wrote the article to bring to public attention the
issues of secrecy surrounding the nuclear establishment. The
title alludes to the "born secret" interpretation of the Atomic
Energy Act, under which a researcher may combine information from unclassified sources in a way that produces a "legi-
timately" classifiable concept. The authors are critical of
the Act and its application. An appendix offers Morland's
original article, which finally appeared in the November,
1979 Progressive. A thorough examination of a case with
significant national security and First-Amendment implications. [See also item 947.]

925. FREEMAN, Leslie J. Nuclear Witnesses: Insiders
     Speak Out. Norton, 1981. 330 p.

Transcribed interviews with 16 people involved in the nuclear
business. Talks with engineers, physicists, the widows of
uranium miners, and others. Preceded by a chronology of
nuclear events, 1895-present.

926. FREI, Daniel and Catrina, Christian. Risks of Unin-
     tentional Nuclear War. Rowman & Allanheld, 1983.
     255 p.

A study carried out under the auspices of the United Nations
Institute for Disarmament Research. Treats not accidental
war, "but rather nuclear war based on false assumptions,
i.e. on misjudgment or miscalculation by the persons legiti-
mately authorized to decide on the use of nuclear weapons."
Discusses strategic policies such as "launch on warning"
which could set off a nuclear war; the arms race and strategic
stability, the failure of deterrence, nuclear accidents and

proliferation as they all contribute to the risks of unintentional war. Each main issue receives concise summarization. Excellent bibliography.

927. GOFMAN, John W. Radiation & Human Health. Sierra Club, 1981. 908 p.

Gofman has a long chain of establishment achievements (Professor Emeritus of Medical Physics at the University of California, co-discoverer of uranium-233, Manhattan Project veteran, founder of the Lawrence Livermore Laboratory's Biomedical Research Division) which lend credibility to his case against official estimates of a tolerable exposure level to radiation. Pro-nuclear advocates find his arguments infuriating, and it's easy to see why. This is probably the most comprehensive examination between two covers of the effects of low-level radiation. Gofman has sought to coordinate data from "every valid existing study" in the process of arguing that estimates of a "safe" level of exposure have been set too low. He does not deal with the effects of massive radiation doses resulting from nuclear weapons blasts or from nuclear plant disasters, but dwells at length on the health hazards associated with low-level exposure. Long bibliography and index.

928. GOULDING, Phil G. Confirm or Deny: Informing the People on National Security. Harper & Row, 1970. 369 p.

The author was Assistant Secretary of Defense for Public Affairs under Robert McNamara. This is his insider's view of what the press and public are told--or not told--about Department of Defense functions. Includes chapters on the ABM system and on the B-52 crash and scattering of hydrogen bombs around Palomares, Spain in 1966.

929. HIGHAM, Robin, ed. A Guide to the Sources of United States Military History. Archon Books, 1975. 559 p.

Outstanding access source to books, journal articles, and U.S. documents on all phases of U.S. military history, includes a large section on "The Department of Defense, 1945-1973" and a shorter (ca. 250 items) but interesting chapter on "Science and Technology in the 20th Century," among other useful features. Bibliographies are preceded by bibliographical essays.

930. _____ and Mrozek, Donald J., eds. A Guide to the
    Sources of United States Military History: Supple-
    ment I. Archon Books, 1981. 300 p.

Updates information in the main edition noted above, and includes new material on nuclear war and arms control.

931. HOOK, Sidney. Fail-Safe Fallacy. Stein & Day, 1963.
    32 p.

Cold warrior Hook lambastes Burdick's Fail-Safe (item 1023)
as full of technical ineptitude, defeatist, and an encouragement to the Russians.

● ● ●

"Peace is our profession."
                        --Motto, U.S. Strategic Air
                        Command

● ● ●

932. HUBLER, Richard G. SAC: The Strategic Air Com-
    mand. Duell, 1958. 280 p.

A popular history of SAC, then a dozen years old.

933. KINTNER, William R., ed. Safeguard: Why the ABM
    Makes Sense. Hawthorn, 1969. 413 p.

Praise for the Nixon-proposed anti-missile system from the
editor, Secretary of Defense Melvin Laird, Senators Henry
Jackson and Howard Baker, academic strategist Albert Wohlstetter, and others.

934. KNORR, Klaus. On the Uses of Military Power in the
    Nuclear Age. Princeton University Press, 1966.
    185 p.

On the obsolescence of war and the need for world community,
considering the threat of nuclear destruction.

935. KOLODZIEJ, Edward A. Uncommon Defense and
    Congress, 1945-1963. Ohio State University Press,
    1966. 630 p.

Congressional influence on military policy and weapons systems; describes Congressional participation in shaping defense

policy and analyzes Congressional decisions "as they have been recorded in its review and passage of the annual appropriations bills for the defense establishment." Includes passages on nuclear weapons, the one-time U.S. atomic monopoly, nuclear war, and strategic policy.

936. LANG, Daniel. The Man in the Thick Lead Suit. Oxford University Press, 1954. 207 p.

Articles which originally appeared in The New Yorker on topics ranging from flying saucers to civil defense. Lang interviews uranium miners and nuclear physicists, with a diverse bunch in between. Human interest is paramount.

937. LARUS, Joel. Nuclear Weapon Safety and the Common Defense. Ohio State University Press, 1967. 171 p.

An examination of the nuclear powers' ability to handle accidents involving nuclear weapons which endanger life and property. The conclusions are comforting to a point, owing to the considerable safeguards against accidental detonation built into nuclear warheads. Larus anticipates problems as older nuclear powers relax their vigilance over weapons-handling and as new nuclear powers engage in carelessness through haste or financial constraints.

938. LEFEVER, Ernest W. and Hunt, E. Stephen, eds. The Apocalyptic Premise: Nuclear Arms Debated. Ethics and Public Policy Center, 1982. 417 p.

Thirty-one essays "by statesmen, scholars, religious leaders, and journalists" on arms control, the peace movement, the churches and nuclear arms, and official views. Any anthology able to contain the opinions of radical lefty Sidney Lens and the right-wing fulminating of Reader's Digest writer John Barron has something going for it. Opinions from all over the ideological spectrum here, and though some are dubiously included (e.g., Barron's preposterous Digest piece in which he accuses anti-nuclear advocates of being Kremlin dupes), most of the others are chosen with some care.

939. LEWIS, Flora. One of Our H-Bombs is Missing. McGraw, 1967. 270 p.

More than one, in fact. An account of the aftermath of the 1966 mid-air explosion over Palomares, Spain, which destroyed a B-52, a tanker plane--and dropped four H-bombs, three near the town, one out at sea. A journalistic look at the recovery operation, local reaction, and implications of the accident.

940. LIDDELL HART, B. H. Why Don't We Learn From History? Hawthorn, 1971. 95 p.

First published in 1944, this short work by the prolific war historian makes the familiar charge that technological advances have outstripped the capacity of morality to accommodate them short of suicide. A provocative book for one weighing arguments on the nuclear question; see especially the final part, "War and Peace," where Hart pithily analyzes, among other topics, the desire for power, the shortsightedness of expediency, the importance of keeping promises, and "the germs of war."

● ● ●

"In general, then, those who survived ... were the people who ignored their friends crying out in extremis ... selfish, self-centered, guided by instinct and not civilization ... and we know it, we who have survived."
--T. Nagai, Nagasaki survivor, Item 505, p. 46.

● ● ●

941. LILIENTHAL, David E. Change, Hope, and the Bomb. Princeton University Press, 1963. 168 p.

"I offer one man's faith that a world of change is a world of hope." Lilienthal argues against disarmament negotiations; the way to peace lies "in other areas." A conservative, anticommunist book.

942. LIPSCHUTZ, Ronnie D. Radioactive Waste: Politics, Technology and Risk. Ballinger, 1980. 247 p.

This report from the Union of Concerned Scientists discusses radiation hazards and present efforts to manage hot waste. Advises that the job be taken away from the Department of Energy and turned over to a new, independent agency, thus eliminating "formidable obstacles to finding and developing a safe, sound solution to the radioactive waste problem."

943. LOEB, Paul. Nuclear Culture: Living and Working in the World's Largest Atomic Complex. Coward, McCann & Geoghegan, 1982. 255 p.

On life at Washington State's Hanford Nuclear Reservation, half the size of Rhode Island and the employer of 13, 000 atomic workers, where a nearby highschool football team call themselves "The Bombers" and wear helmets adorned with mushroom clouds. Loeb interviews many of the people in the three cities providing the Hanford labor force. The citizens of Richland, Kennewick, and Pasco discuss their ideas, perceptions, and field their rationalizations about their work in one of the nation's major nuclear weapons facilities. In an anecdotal style.

944. McPHEE, John. The Curve of Binding Energy. Farrar, Straus, 1974. 231 p.

Biographical attention to nuclear physicist Theodore B. Taylor allows McPhee to dwell on the likelihood of nuclear terrorism.

945. MEDVEDEV, Zhores A. Nuclear Disaster in the Urals. Norton, 1979. 214 p.

Soviet dissident scientist Medvedev discusses a late 1950s nuclear waste dump explosion in the southern Urals which he contends killed hundreds of people and contaminated more than 1, 000 square kilometers. Information on the catastrophe has long been repressed by both Soviet and Western officials. A number of CIA documents on the explosion are reproduced here courtesy of the Freedom of Information Act.

946. MERTON, Thomas. Original Child Bomb: Points for Meditation to be Scratched on the Walls of a Cave. New Directions, 1963. 20 p.

A poem by the pacifist Trappist monk on the Hiroshima bombing. Conveys a driving anger in a restrained text which makes considerable effective use of unusually significant points in the first bomb's history. "Original Child" was the name given the bomb by the Japanese, for they "recognized that it was the first of its kind."

947. MORLAND, Howard. The Secret That Exploded. Random House, 1981. 288 p.

Free-lance journalist Morland poked through available unclassified information and taught himself how to build an H-bomb. He wrote up the investigation for The Progressive, hoping to bring the whole issue of nuclear establishment secrecy to public attention. The government made Morland's work a cause célèbre by attempting to censor the issue with his article in it. This is the author's story of the case; see also item 924.

948. MOSS, Norman. The Politics of Uranium. Universe Books, 1982. 239 p.

A well-researched study of uranium from 1945 on; covers political, military, and economic issues. Argues that the peaceful uses of uranium cannot be separated from the weapons proliferation problem.

949. MURRAY, Raymond L. Understanding Radioactive Waste. Battelle Press, 1982. 117 p.

An adequate introduction to the subject, though the author, who served on the Manhattan Project, is clearly pro-nuclear in spite of his claim to an "unbiased" presentation. Includes a short appendix annotating sources.

● ● ●

"I'd drop a low-yield atomic bomb on Chinese supply lines in North Vietnam. "
> --Barry Goldwater in News-
> week, May 20, 1963.

● ● ●

950. MYERS, Edward. The Chosen Few: Surviving the Nuclear Holocaust. South Bend, 1982. 177 p.

A journalistic treatment of the "survivalists, " the people who believe that the best way to deal with the threat of nuclear war is not to keep the war from happening, but to prepare to live through its inevitable occurrence. Includes bibliography.

951. NELKIN, Dorothy. The University and Military Research: Moral Politics at MIT. Cornell University Press, 1972. 195 p.

Another examination of the extent to which scientists and technologists are responsible for the applications of their work. Catalyst for the book is the Massachusetts Institute of Technology's 1970 divestment of its Instrumentation Laboratory, then receiving close to $60 million annually from the Department of Defense and NASA. The Laboratory designed inertial guidance systems for ballistic missiles. Of particular interest given current competition among universities for pieces of the defense budget.

952. NIEBURG, Harold L. Nuclear Secrecy and Foreign Policy. Public Affairs Press, 1964. 255 p.

Criticizes our obsession with nuclear secrecy as a hindrance to U.S. options in response to Soviet moves, and an impediment to effective management of conventional weapons. For very different perspectives on this secrecy, see items 924, 947.

953. PECK, Merton J. and Scherer, Frederic M. The Weapons Acquisition Process: An Economic Analysis. Graduate School of Business, Harvard University, 1962. 736 p.

Includes coverage of many nuclear weapons systems--bombers, missiles, etc. The questions dealt with here are not of the "Should we build them?" sort as much as of the "How can we build them well?" variety.

954. POWERS, Thomas. Thinking About the Next War. Knopf, 1982. 153 p.

A superb collection of 19 essays published in Commonweal, 1976-1982, on multiple aspects of the nuclear specter. Informative, thought-provoking, and moving; e.g., in "What to Tell the Kids," in which Powers broods on how to tell his three children about nuclear war. One of the first books on the subject that any concerned citizen should read.

955. PRINGLE, Peter and Spigelman, James. The Nuclear Barons. Holt, Rinehart & Winston, 1981. 578 p.

A popular history of nuclear power, weaponry, and strategy; concentrates on personalities and politics rather than technology.

956. RYAN, William L. and Summerlin, Sam. The China Cloud: America's Tragic Blunder and China's Rise to Nuclear Power. Little, Brown, 1968. 309 p.

An illuminating account of one backlash effect of the Cold War; the book relates the manner in which close to a hundred Chinese aerodynamicists, physicists, and other scientists were driven from the U.S. during the 1940s and 1950s--back to China, where they helped develop that nation's nuclear weapons status long before it would have been otherwise obtainable. According to the authors, almost half of China's most eminent scientists received their training at such institutions as M. I. T., Harvard, Michigan, and Yale. Includes a good bibliography on China's drive to the nuclear kingdom, and an appendix giving a breakdown of U. S. universities where specific Chinese scientists studied.

957. SANDERS, Ralph. Project Plowshare: The Development of the Peaceful Use of Nuclear Weapons. Public Affairs Press, 1962. 206 p.

Documents the atomic pipedream that civilized nuclear blasts were to have a promising future.

958. SKOLNIKOFF, Eugene B. Science, Technology, and American Foreign Policy. MIT Press, 1967. 330 p.

Among other issues concerning the author is the need for international cooperation in the control of nuclear power, and his anger at U. S. nuclear testing. An interesting if not specifically nuclear feature is his discussion of the several opportunities the U. S. missed in the late 1950s and early 1960s to take advantage of Soviet proposals for joint study and exploration of space. What political advantages might have accrued, one wonders, had the two nations cooperated in putting men on the moon?

959. SLUSSER, Robert M. The Berlin Crisis of 1961: Soviet-American Relations and the Struggle for Power in the Kremlin, June-November 1961. Johns Hopkins University Press, 1973. 510 p.

The second Berlin Crisis featured a number of public pronouncements on what nuclear matters might ensue, including Marshal Malinovsky's threat to Great Britain and West Germany regarding the ease with which they could be obliterated by "really very few multimegaton nuclear bombs" which would "kill you instantly in your lairs!" The first major crisis of East and West presided over by their ability to demolish one another pretty thoroughly in rather brief time. The subject index permits ready access to nuclear topics.

960. STEINBERG, Gerald M. Satellite Reconnaissance: The Role of Informal Bargaining. Praeger, 1983. 201 p.

Reviews the international acceptance of reconnaissance satel-
lites; concludes that formal arms negotiations have little
chance of success, but that, given the success of informal
negotiations over satellite reconnaissance, similar beneficial
results may be obtained through informal negotiations in strategic areas.

961. STEINBERG, Rafael. Postscript from Hiroshima.
Random House, 1966. 119 p.

How the city rebuilt itself from the wreckage of the bomb;
based in large part on interviews with survivors.

962. STERNGLASS, Ernest. Secret Fallout: Low-Level
Radiation from Hiroshima to Three Mile Island.
McGraw-Hill, 1981. 306 p.

The author, a professor of radiation physics, concludes that
low-level radiation, beginning with that from nuclear bomb
tests, has led to genetic defects, greater infant mortality,
mental retardation and other ailments.

963. U.S. Department of Defense. Soviet Military Power.
U.S. Government Printing Office, 1981. 99 p.

The standard U.S. propaganda tool portraying the U.S.S.R.
as the major global military threat. [See also item 964.]

964. U.S.S.R. Ministry of Defense. Whence the Threat to
Peace? Imported Publications, 1981. 78 p.

The standard Soviet propaganda tool portraying the U.S. as
the major global military threat. [See also item 963.]

965. WALKER, Charles A., et al., eds. Too Hot to
Handle? Social and Policy Issues in the Management of Radioactive Wastes. Yale University Press,
1983. 209 p.

Intended to provide a basis for understanding the history of
radioactive waste management in the U.S., the nation's nuclear power prospects, the technological aspects of waste production and control, biological effects of radiation, public
perceptions of the situation, and institutional control of waste
management. The many references, most to recent work,
will encourage further research.

966. WILLRICH, Mason and Lester, Richard K. Radioactive

Waste Management and Regulation.   Free Press,
1977.   138 p.

An accessible discussion of the problem; includes coverage of
the inter-relationship between military and civilian nuclear
waste.

967.   WOITO, Robert.   To End War: A New Approach to
         International Conflict.   Pilgrim, 1982.   6th edition.
         755 p.

A handbook for those who seriously reflect on the issues of
war and peace and wish to work in behalf of the latter.   In
three major sections, "Ideas," "Contexts," and "Action," the
author discusses--among other topics--the nature of the war
institution, arms control and disarmament, roles of the U.S.
and the U.S.S.R., peace research, personal options for the
concerned citizen, and much more.   Each section includes
substantial support for further inquiry in the form of annotated
bibliographies.   The "Action" section also includes a long,
annotated list of peace organizations.   A basic tool for anyone
who believes that "security" based on nuclear deterrence is
probably not the best that we can do, and perhaps a tool sufficient to undermine the assumption that deterrence is the best
we can do.

968.   YANARELLA, Ernest J.   The Missile Defense Contro-
         versy: Strategy, Technology and Politics, 1955-1972.
         University Press of Kentucky, 1977.   236 p.

An historical treatment hinging on the idea that technological
advances stimulate the arms race as much or more than political considerations.

● Periodical Articles ●

969.   BATES, Al.   "The Dubious Legacy of Oak Ridge."
         Critical Mass: Public Citizen's Energy Journal 8
         (Aug. 1983): 8+

A report on high levels of radioactive contamination in the
ecosystems surrounding the Oak Ridge, Tennessee Laboratory, the world's biggest nuclear weapons factory.   Among
the material fouling lake and river water in the area--to
levels several thousand times greater than normal background:
plutonium, americium, strontium, cesium, and cobalt.   State
and federal authorities are taking belated action on the problem, which has been developing for four decades.

970. COCKBURN, Andrew. "Graphic Evidence ... of Nuclear Confusion." Columbia Journalism Review 22
(May-June 1983): 38-41.

Critical analysis of charts published in The New York Times,
Scientific American and other sources purporting to illustrate
Soviet-U.S. nuclear strength and vulnerability.

971. "Co-Existence or No Existence." Labor Today 20
(Oct. 1981): 6-7.

A spread in this Chicago-based labor paper on the dubious
eventuality of a Russian first-strike, the economic burdens of
the arms race on union members, and the overall ghastliness
of nuclear weapons' effects.

972. "Conflict Resolution & Peacemaking." National Forum
63 (Fall 1983).

A thematic issue with close to twenty short articles related to
contemporary international conflict. Includes Coretta Scott
King's plea for a National Peace Academy, Noam Chomsky on
the disarmament debate, Edward Teller begging for more
nukes (in the form of both power and bombs), and other pieces
from various viewpoints.

973. COX, David. "The Cruise Testing Argument." International Perspectives: The Canadian Journal on
World Affairs (July-August 1983): 3-5.

Presents the U.S.-Canadian agreement for flight-testing of the
Cruise over Canadian territory as a potential back door for
other U.S. military testing in Canada sans public debate.
Politely requests that the Canadian government make these
moves more open to public inquiry and influence.

974. GORDON, Gail M. and Levinson, Steven C. "Uranium
Mining in Northwest New Jersey." Journal of Public Health Policy 4 (March 1983): 56-63.

On the citizens movement which led to New Jersey's 1981 law
providing for a 7-year ban on uranium mining in the state.
The movement was provoked by intentions of multinational oil
companies to explore for uranium in northwest N.J. Gives
some background on hazardous wastes associated with uranium
mining.

975. HALLE, Louis J. "A Hopeful Future for Mankind."
Foreign Affairs 58 (Summer 1980): 1129-1136.

Because there is a good chance that we shall all blow ourselves up, or pollute ourselves into oblivion, Halle says that
we should colonize outer space to insure humanity's survival
in the event that blow or pollute we do.   Believes that a global effort to colonize space would ease international tensions.
It probably would, but pursued with the understanding that the
purpose was to get some of us out into the void before laying
waste to the planet, those tensions would most likely leap
up.

976.   HOLLENBACH, David.   "Nuclear Weapons Policy and
        Christian Conscience."   New Catholic World 226
        (Jan. -Feb. 1983):   17-20.

Discusses Christian bases for both pacifist and just-war positions; believes "that these criteria compel just war thinkers
to conclude that the military and political realities of the
nuclear age make all use of nuclear weapons incompatible with
Christian conscience."   Ponders the difficult obligation of
Catholics to pursue both peace and justice in a nuclear world.

977.   KAPLAN, David E.   "When Incidents are Accidents:
        The Silent Saga of the Nuclear Navy."   Oceans 16
        (July-Aug. 1983):   26-33.

An exposé of a generally-overlooked nuclear hazard: reactor
accidents on atomic submarines.   The author describes numerous accidents involving radiation release and other problems with both U.S. and Soviet subs, cites U.S. official reference to "catastrophic" reactor accidents aboard the latter.
In the secrecy pervading military operations (the U.S. Navy
has no "accidents"; it has "incidents") the clearest information about the U.S. fleet can often be obtained from Soviet
sources, and vice-versa.   Also discusses naval ocean dumping
of radioactive waste.

978.   KAPLAN, Fred.   "Going Native without a Field Map:
        The Press Plunges into Limited Nuclear War."
        Columbia Journalism Review 19 (Jan-Feb. 1981):
        23-29.

On the press's confused and misleading coverage of the "limited" nuclear war, a concept brought to boil by President Carter's Presidential Directive 59 in July, 1980, which, though a
refinement of strategy developed under Robert McNamara, encourages "the delusion ... that we can fight, rationally control, and win a nuclear war."   A good look at the media's

adherence to the official Washington line of the moment, however deluded it may be.

979.   KIRSHIN, I. I.   "Prevention of World Nuclear War: The
        Global Problem of Our Time." Soviet Studies in
        Philosophy No. 3 (Winter 1979-1980):   83-99.

The straight Moscow line on the socialist "struggle for peace, "
the desirability of disarmament vs. the need to remain armed
against the capitalist threat, etc.   With very minor rewriting
and the substitution of the terms "democratic" for "socialist"
and "U.S." for "Soviet, " this piece would easily pass as a
current statement of U.S. policy.   The enemy lives in the
mirror.

980.   LAMARSH, John R.   "China's Nuclear Program." Bul-
        letin of the Atomic Scientists 36 (May 1980):   28-31.

Describes the program; states that China should abandon atmospheric testing of nuclear weapons and adhere to the Non-
Proliferation Treaty as qualifications for receiving U.S. assistance with reactor development.

981.   LEE, Kai N.   "A Federalist Strategy for Nuclear Waste
        Management." Science 208 (May 16, 1980):   679-
        684.

On federal plans to rely on "consultation and concurrence"
with state governments to set up nuclear waste repositories;
argues for a "siting jury" combining high-level technical skills
with sensitivity to state and local interests to take the responsibility for such facilities.

982.   LOVELL, John P.   "The Idiom of National Security. "
        Journal of Political & Military Sociology 11 (Spring
        1983):   35-51.

Describes the way in which all groups interested in strategic
affairs, regardless of the programs they support, tend to
move toward syntactic modes of considerable abstraction and
simplification when defending their positions.   Identifies several categories of "National Security Subcultures, " ranging
from the super-hardline "Technocrats" to the "Consciousness
III Disarmers. "

983.   McCLORY, Robert.   "Church Groups Preach Peace. "
        In These Times 6 (June 2-15, 1982):   3.

On the religious roots of the current peace movement, especially among mainstream groups--Catholics, Baptists,
evangelists--not previously noted for antinuclear commitment.
Includes attention to backlash from conservative clergy and
from Moral Majority champions of nuclear triumph.

984. MANOFF, Robert K. "Covering the Bomb: The Nu-
      clear Story and the News." Working Papers Maga-
      zine 10 (May-June 1983): 18-27.

A good essay on media coverage of nuclear weapons, from
Hiroshima to the Freeze and the Catholic bishops' pastoral
letter on the bomb. Argues that the press has been largely
a servant of state assumptions and preferences in its nuclear
reporting.

985. NAIDU, M. V. "Economics Behind Cruise Missile
      Testing in Canada." Peace Research: The Cana-
      dian Journal of Peace Studies 15 (Sept. 1983): 2-20.

Detailed economic analysis leads to the conclusion that "the
force behind the permission for the testing of the American
cruise missile in Canada is the militarization of the Canadian industry and the Americanization of the Canadian economy."

986. NEFF, Thomas L. and Jacoby, Henry D. "World
      Uranium: Softening Markets and Rising Security."
      Technology Review 83 (Jan. 1981): 18-30.

A "soft" buyer's market for uranium will probably prevail
over the next two decades. With growing supplies, nonproliferation will become more difficult.

987. NEWCOMBE, Hanna. "Approaches to a Nuclear-Free
      Future." Peace Research Reviews 9 Nos. 2 and 3,
      (May 1982).

Two issues of the Dundas, Ontario Peace Research Institute's
journal; opens with a review of literature on the Non-Proliferation Treaty, nuclear-free and demilitarized zones and no-
first-use agreements; works through disarmament inspection
schemes and proposals for new kinds of disarmament organization. Extensive references to published material; would be
helpful for a thorough investigation of covered topics.

988. "Nuclear Arms Education." Physics Today. 36
      (March 1983): 23-59.

A special section; Herbert York writes on arms control, Leo Sartorion on the effects of the bomb, Barbara Levi on U.S. and Soviet nuclear arsenals, etc.

989.   O'BRIEN, William V.   "The Peace Debate and American Catholics."   The Washington Quarterly (Spring 1982): 219-222.

Brief exegesis of Catholic teaching on nuclear deterrence and on efforts of American Catholic bishops to grapple with the nuclear issue.   Criticizes Church policy as "incomplete" and its effects "uncertain."   Finds nuclear deterrence a morally defensible policy.

990.   OGLESBY, Carl.   "Life at the End of the Road."   New Age 9 (Sept. 1983):   42+

Reports on a June, 1983 conference in Rhode Island, "Facing Apocalypse," attended by 125 people--most disciples of Jungian psychology--dedicated to the question of what is the best way to face the bomb.   Some called for fatalism, some for ac- tion--and some for recognition that the bomb is not the prob- lem: the problem is the world political orientation which makes its use conceivable.

991.   PETERS, 1st Lt. Ralph H.   "Forward Defense: Time to Break the Concrete?"   Army 33 (March 1983): 30-36.

Lieutenant Peters contends that "chronic underestimates of NATO's battlefield capabilities" are a consequence of the al- liance's traditional "forward defense," a commitment to holding advancing opponents along a line close to the border, specifically, that of West Germany.   Believes that a defense oriented deeper within the country and free of a linear view would be more effective and also reduce the risk of nuclear confrontation.

992.   PILARSKI, Jan.   "The Next Battleground: Waste Trans- port Mobilizes Citizen Activists."   Critical Mass: Public Citizen's Energy Journal 8 (Feb. 1983): 9+

Discusses present methods of shipping radioactive waste; questions the NRC's safety standards on such shipment.   The Nuclear Waste Policy Act of 1982, though opposed by many environmentalists, does allow local legal challenges to waste shipments through populated areas.

993. POSEN, Barry R. "Inadvertent Nuclear War? Escalation and NATO's Northern Flank." International Security 7 (Fall 1982): 28-54.

Calls American notions about avoidance of nuclear escalation in a European war "dangerous and unwarranted." Poses the northern flank of NATO, where Soviet submarine forces are susceptible to conventional NATO assault, as a catalyst for unintended nuclear war. Because the U.S. does not share the Soviet Union's geographical defense problems, U.S. planners find it hard to appreciate the threat to Soviet strategic forces that Soviets see NATO's conventional forces embodying. Calls rethinking of conventional war assumptions "essential," and suggests ways to lessen danger of inadvertent nuclear war.

994. ROGERS, Carl R. "A Psychologist Looks at Nuclear War: Its Threat, Its Possible Prevention." Journal of Humanistic Psychology 22 (Fall 1982): 9-20.

The noted psychologist dwells briefly on what he regards as the terrible hopelessness the threat of nuclear war has inflicted on our youth, and then calls for massive public pressure against the government's drift toward that war through carelessness and trivialization of its consequences. Believes that improved international communication is possible--citing the Camp David meeting of Carter, Begin, and Sadat as a good example.

995. SABIN, Philip A. G. " 'World War Three': A Historical Mirage?" Futures: The Journal of Forecasting and Planning 4 (Aug. 1983): 272-280.

Sabin argues that contemporary military and political thinking is over-influenced by historical experience of "total war," leading to a common vision of WW III as an utterly absurd suicidal spasm. Says that neither conventional nor nuclear conflict between the superpowers is a rational military option; "the whole notion of a potential Third World War is of dubious value" for strategic purposes.

996. SCHAEFER, Virginia. "The Pentagon's Computer Game." Science for the People 13 (Nov. 1981): 25-30.

Explication of LOW (Launch on Warning) ICBM strategy, a computer-controlled system designed to insure that missiles could be launched before destruction by opposing missiles

already on their way. Though not now in effect (as far as
we know) LOW remains an option. On the dangers of sur-
rendering the decision-making process to machines. Includes
notes on past military computer errors and references to
other material.

997. "Should Physicians Prepare for War?" Hastings
     Center Report 12 (April 1982): 15-21.

Four articles in reaction to two connected events: the Defense Department's efforts to line up 50,000 U.S. hospital
beds for overseas war casualties, and the refusal of San
Francisco's Contra Costa Hospital to cooperate, on the grounds
that this plan "would offer tacit approval for the planning of
a nuclear war." The authors examine the issue of physicians'
responsibility and reach different conclusions.

998. SINGLAUB, Major General John K. "Liberation: An
     Alternative to Nuclear War." Asian Outlook 18
     (July 1983): 5-7.

The retired Major-General is under the impression that internal dissent, properly encouraged by the West, could bring
down communist governments without resort to the bomb.
Calls for stronger CIA and for retargeting nuclear missiles
now aimed at targets in Eastern Europe onto Soviet territory
(apparently does not put complete faith in political persuasion),
and for no restraint on aid to anti-communist governments.

999. "The Struggle for Global Security." Graduate Woman
     76 (May-June 1982).

A single-topic issue of this journal from the American Association of University Women dealing with the search for peace
in the nuclear woods. Rear Admiral Gene R. LaRacque,
U.S.N. (Ret.) writes of the growing antinuclear awareness;
Nancy Ramsey of the Women's International League for Peace
and Freedom poses eleven questions for the citizen concerned
about nuclear war; etc.

1000. "Symposium on Nuclear Waste Management." Natural
      Resources Journal 21 (Oct. 1981): 302 p.

Essays on high-level radioactive waste, policy issues, emergency preparedness, effects on property values, non-proliferation aspects and more.

1001. TOBIAS, Sheilah, et al. "Dilemmas of Modern

Weaponry." Humanities in Society 5 (Winter-Spring 1982): 67-82.

On the interrelations of technology, political decision making and defense. Discusses various sticking points of strategic warfare, e.g., would a U.S. President really retaliate for a first strike killing 20 million, knowing that such retaliation would result in far greater death? Welcomes J. Schell's Fate of the Earth (item 542) as a tool which has helped pry the issue of weapons and their effects out of the hands of "experts" and set it on the public table for close scrutiny.

1002.   TYSOE, Maryon.   "The Psychology of Nuclear Accidents."   New Society 63 (Mar. 31, 1983):   505-507.

Discusses the difficulty in accurate psychological perceptions of risk involving nuclear weapons, e.g., in their vulnerability to terrorist action.   Cites various blunders concerning nuclear weapons management; points out that as time of decision-making shrinks (a serious Cruise missile factor), the hazard of accidental missile launch expands.

1003.   WASILEWSKI, Valeria.   "Medical Planning for Nuclear War."   Monthly Review 33 (Jan. 1982): 19-26.

The author, a physician, attacks the U.S. "Civil Military Contingency Hospital System," designed to provide beds in the U.S. for what is apparently--though not identified as such by official sources--a "limited" nuclear war abroad.   Analyzes Department of Defense wishful thinking and obfuscation of the issue.   [See also item 997.]

1004.   WASSERMAN, Harvey.   "Ode to an Unsung Hero: Dr. Ernest Sternglass."   New Age 7 (April 1982):   42-43.

A profile of one of the first authorities to raise the alarm over the harmful effects of low-level radiation.   [See also item 962.]

1005.   "What We Can Do."   Bulletin of the Atomic Scientists 37 (June-July 1981):   20-21.

Measures physicians can take, including informing the public about the likely consequences of nuclear war, to keep such war from happening.

1006. "Women for Peace and Disarmament." Socialist International Women Bulletin No. 2 (1982): 32 p.

Includes articles on European nuclear-free zones, the economics of the arms race, benefits of disarmament in the Third World, historical look at popular peace movements, etc.

1007. ZAGANO, Phyllis, ed. "The Nuclear Arms Debate." Book Forum 6 (No. 3, 1983): 284-384.

An entire issue devoted to the title topic, with essays grouped in four categories: "Historical and International Considerations"; "Political, Sociological and Economic Views"; "Morality and Nuclear Arms"; and "Propaganda Pro and Con." Various perspectives represented, from pacifism to rationalization of nuclear weapons by an Air Force General. Includes a long, unannotated bibliography of books on nuclear weapons and disarmament published 1980-1982.

● XVIII ●

The Art of Fission:
Novels and Stories with Nuclear Themes

1008. ADLER, Warren. The Trans-Siberian Express. Putnam's, 1977. 310 p.

A cast of thriller-generic characters accompany an American
doctor by rail across Siberia after he has administered to an
ailing Soviet head of state. Aside from diversion furnished
by trainboard relationships, we wonder whether the Soviet
Union and China will come to nuclear blows.

1009. ALDISS, Brian W. Greybeard. Harcourt, Brace,
1964. 245 p.

By the second decade of the 21st century, a nuclear disaster
involving "space bombs" has left humanity sterile; apparently
no children, save a few hopeless freaks and monsters, have
been born since 1981. The population grows steadily older,
and the end of the race looks near. Hope surfaces for a
future in a new breed of feral youth, however. A good job
by Aldiss, both in his evocation of Nature's reclamation of
the sparsely populated earth and of the fears and frustrations
endured by the ageing survivors of the "Big Accident." Set
primarily along the Thames.

1010. AMRINE, Michael. Secret. Houghton, 1950. 311 p.

A behind-the-scenes atomic travelog and argument for international control of atomic energy. Follows Benjamin Franklin
Halverson, called from peaceful to martial research, from
Oak Ridge to Hiroshima and Washington, D.C. Heavier on
ideas than on character; one of the main themes is that of
the scientist's responsibility as a citizen of the world rather
than of a particular nation.

1011. ASIMOV, Isaac. "Breeds There a Man ...?" In his
Nightfall and Other Stories, p. 94-128. Doubleday,
1969.

An atomic scientist whose services are required to design an
anti-Bomb force field believes that humans are the bacteria-
like experimental creatures of a superior order. Part of this
story's interest now lies in the sense of imminent nuclear attack it encourages, a sense common in 1950s atomic fiction.
(First appeared in the June, 1951 Astounding Science Fiction.)

1012. _____. "Paté de Foie Gras." In his Where Do
We Go from Here, p. 323-346. Doubleday, 1971.

A lightweight novelty tale. A goose, mutated through irradia-

tion from bomb test fallout, lays golden eggs--and is immune
to gamma rays. (First published in Astounding Science Fiction in 1956.)

1013. BLISH, James. The Day after Judgment. Doubleday,
1971. 166 p.

In a world pulverized by hydrogen bombs, where survivors
outside of the Strategic Air Command post far below Denver
are few, the Infernal City of Dis raises its head in Death
Valley. This has not been WW III, but Armageddon, and Sa-
tan has apparently won.

1014. BONE, J. F. "Triggerman." In Prologue to Analog,
p. 206-218. Edited by John W. Campbell. Doubleday, 1962.

The "triggerman," a military official responsible for firing
U.S. ICBMs, disobeys orders to fire after a missile wipes
out Washington, D.C. The "missile" proves to have been a
meteor. Portrayal of the officer's dilemma, and his imagining that of his Soviet counterpart, is well handled.

1015. BRACKETT, Leigh. The Long Tomorrow. Doubleday,
1955. 222 p.

Sixty years after "the Destruction," the technophobic Men-
nonites have gained control of the government of what was the
United States. Young Len Colter, possessed by curiosity
about the pre-Destruction world, discovers a small community
harboring a nuclear research center dedicated to making atomic reactions, and nuclear war, impossible. Written from the
point of view that once knowledge is attained, it cannot be
forgotten--only contended with.

1016. BRADBURY, Ray. "The Garbage Collector." In his
Twice Twenty-Two, p. 180-185. Doubleday, 1966.

A highly effective relation of a garbage worker's atomic epi-
phany in 1951, provoked by his city's plan to use garbage
trucks to haul away the dead after a nuclear attack. "Oh
Christ," he says, "it just doesn't seem right a man, a human
being, should ever let himself get used to any idea like that."

1017. _____. "The Highway." In his The Illustrated
Man, p. 58-62. Doubleday, 1951.

A Mexican peasant, Hernando, pauses from his job in the field

to watch a stream of automobiles racing north, back to the
U.S. Hernando learns from some young people, also on the
way back, that atomic war has broken out in the North. It
is "the end of the world." When they leave, Hernando re-
turns to his plow, the wind blowing the scent of the jungle to
him. "What do they mean, 'the world'?" he says.

1018. _____. The Martian Chronicles. Doubleday, 1951.
          222 p.

In this generally despairing classic of science fiction and
fantasy, colonists from Earth establish a budding civilization
on Mars. The stories in the collection focus on the characters' inability and refusal to transcend the moral limitations that plague humankind on Earth, and which lead to that
planet's nuclear extinction. Bradbury holds out some small
hope at the end in a little family's realization that they are
no longer of Earth, but are the real Martians.

1019. BRINTON, Henry. Purple-6. Walker & Company,
          1963. 207 p.

An ICBM is on the way to England, and is due shortly. Shall
we set off the last war in response? A fairly routine atomic
thriller.

1020. BRYANT, Edward. "Jody After the War." In Orbit
          10, p. 80-87. Edited by Damon Knight. Putnam's,
          1972.

The fear here is one running through so many post-holocaust
stories: that of producing genetically unsound children. Jody
is a young woman who survived the nuclear incineration of
Pittsburgh in a Sino-American war; now, in spite of her love
for the story's narrator, she feels compelled to shun a sexual
relation.

1021. BUCHARD, Robert. Thirty Seconds Over New York.
          Morrow, 1970. 218 p.

A nuclear thriller of the terrorist persuasion. The Chinese
communists plant an atomic bomb aboard a Boeing airliner
headed for New York City. They intend to raze the greatest
symbol of the capitalist system, in conjunction with the contemporary extravagancies of the Cultural Revolution. The
technique of the attack is more credible than its motivation.
Translated from the French.

1022. BUCK, Pearl S. Command the Morning. Day, 1959.
317 p.

Novelistic treatment of the development of the bomb, especially as it involves the moral problems of the scientists responsible for it. The Accident, by Dexter Masters (item 1078)
provides better coverage of similar ground.

1023. BURDICK, Eugene and Wheeler, Harvey. Fail-Safe.
McGraw, 1963. 286 p.

Accidental war looms as American bombers mistakenly head
for Moscow to lay their atomic eggs. Caused a certain sen-
sation as one of the first books to point out in popular terms
(the thriller) that we might blow ourselves up without intending
to. The chief villain here, aside from human foolishness,
is the computerized defense system, acting almost independently. The tradeoff solution devised to avoid general war
after Moscow's vaporization entails the deposition of four
twenty-megaton bombs over New York City--by the U.S. Air
Force itself. This scenario may be no more bizarre than
some others inherent in nuclear arms. (The basis for an
excellent film in 1964.)

1024. CAIDIN, Martin. Almost Midnight. Bantam, 1974.
218 p.

Nuclear blackmail is the subject here, not of the political
variety but of the financial kind. Unless the U.S. pays a
hundred million dollar ransom demand, five U.S. cities will
be demolished by bombs stolen from the U.S. strategic arsenal. Caidin's 1950-1954 stint as an analyst of the effects of
nuclear bombs for the State of New York helps lend credibility
to the tale.

1025. _____. Long Night. Dodd, 1956. 242 p.

Comparable to Philip Wylie's civil defense lectures (items
1128-30), Long Night focuses on the fictional town of Harring-
ton, victim with many others of a Soviet nuclear blitz. Fire-
storms rage, heroism and cowardice are manifest--and the
message is that through clear-headed resolution, a city can be
salvaged by its residents after nuclear bombing. Incredibly
ignores the effects of radiation poisoning on both land and
people, and assumes that nuclear war would be like conventional war, only rather worse and much quicker. One can
only wonder what effect such a book would have had on a
naïve reader in the mid-1950s.

1026. CALLISON, Brian. An Act of War. Dutton, 1977.
      206 p.

Run-of-the-mill nuclear nonsense: the Russian Navy impounds
a British ship at a Baltic port, unaware that within her lies
a very live and eager hydrogen bomb. Our hero's job: keep
it from going off.

1027. CAMPBELL, John W., Jr. [Don A. Stuart]. "Atomic
      Power." In The Best of Science Fiction, p. 140-
      151. Edited by Groff Conklin. Crown, 1946.

A reasonably berserk story based on the notion that the Earth
is but an atomic particle in some universe beyond our grasp.
This arrangement leads to an interaction between universes
which breaks down the gravitational system of our own. The
destruction of all that we know can be reversed only by the
suitable application of--atomic power! Doesn't make a lot of
sense, but it's amusing. Published originally in 1934 in
Astounding Science Fiction.

1028. CARD, Orson Scott. "Deep Breathing Exercises."
      In his Unaccompanied Sonata and Other Stories, p.
      72-81. Dial Press, 1981.

A man finds that he can foresee the deaths of others by close
attention to their breathing. He proceeds to realize that the
city of Denver is to be immolated by a nuclear burst. A
frightening story imbued with ironic fatalism.

1029. CARTER, Mary Arkley. Minutes of the Night. Little,
      1965. 304 p.

An "old line" communist revolution in China threatens international holocaust, and the residents of California (and else-
where, no doubt) become crazed with fear. Minutes is far
more about fear than it is about the bomb; fear, panic, the
breakdown of civilized routine under the threat of imminent
death. Contains several good passages, including a striking
confrontation in a doorway between a grinning fool-for-Christ
and a man who wants to ask some simple, rational questions
--but ends up threatening the cant-prattling missionary with a
firearm. A serious novel several cuts above the atomic
average.

1030. CARTMILL, Cleve. "Deadline." In The Best of
      Science Fiction, p. 67-88. Edited by Groff Conklin.
      Crown, 1946.

"Deadline" was first published in the March, 1944 issue of Astounding Science Fiction, and caused a minor stir foreshadowing the brouhaha over Howard Morland's H-bomb article, finally published in the November, 1979 issue of The Progressive. (See Morland's The Secret That Exploded, item 947, for his account of the latter affair.) A few days after Cartmill's story came out, military intelligence officials approached both the author and the magazine's editorial office, convinced that someone connected with the Manhattan Project had been releasing classified information. How else could Cartmill's bomb story have been so accurate?

The story, concerning an atomic bomb which might have been used to terminate a war on some distant planet, was peculiarly on the mark in most of its technical details involving construction and detonation of the bomb. Also of note here is the fear that detonating the bomb would cause a chain reaction that would destroy the entire planet. Some of the atomic scientists who built the actual bomb considered this a distant but real possibility--that the first "successful" atomic test might indeed fry the whole earth. Aside from its technical considerations, "Deadline" isn't much as fiction, but in this instance it hardly matters.

1031. CHEVALIER, Haakon. The Man Who Would Play God. Putnam's, 1959. 449 p.

A fictional portrayal of J. Robert Oppenheimer by one of his acquaintances. Sebastian Bloch is a communist-sympathizing physicist who plays a prominent part in developing the atomic bomb (referred to here, for no especially good reason, as "the Bolt"). Traces Bloch's genuine admiration for communist ideals, and his eventual disillusionment, with passages devoted to atomic spying and scientists' anguish over the bomb's use. Chevalier was implicated by Oppenheimer as having sought atomic data to pass on to the Soviet Union. A roman-à-clef whose rationale is a little hard to understand.

1032. CLARK, Ronald W. Queen Victoria's Bomb: The Disclosures of Professor Franklin Huxtable. Morrow, 1968. 234 p.

Clark plays with history to illustrate current nuclear dilemmas. After inventing the bomb, Huxtable has growing doubts that it will indeed halt war forever. A fantasy peopled by various historic characters, from Gladstone to Florence Nightingale.

1033. COLLINS, Larry and Lapierre, Dominique. The Fifth Horseman. Simon & Schuster, 1980. 478 p.

Libyan terrorists plant a nuclear bomb in a barrel in a New York City warehouse, and the race to prevent its detonation is on. Entertaining, credible, somewhat overlong. Reasonably effective use of real-life characters.

1034. COPPEL, Alfred. The Dragon. Harcourt, Brace, Jovanovich, 1977. 438 p.

The Chinese devise an antimissile laser; the Soviets hope to knock it out of service. Adequate thriller of the hard-line school.

1035. _____. The Hastings Conspiracy. Holt, Rinehart & Winston, 1980. 346 p.

The importance of England as a staging-base for U.S. support of NATO operations is the crux of the plot; for the researcher investigating the current political and military situation, the popular right-of-center (well right-of-center) perceptions of Soviet military ambitions and nuclear intentions, this novel should be useful.

1036. CORY, Desmond. Sunburst. Walker & Company, 1971. 253 p.

Set in Spain, involves nuclear blackmail by its military, with the threat directed at Europe. A blend of conventional spy thriller and serious fiction.

1037. CROSBY, John. Dear Judgment. Stein & Day, 1978. 244 p.

Mafia capo di tutti capi Cosimo Belardi steals two advanced U.S. fighters equipped with nuclear weapons. He plans to auction them to the highest bidder: the Air Force, a billionaire recluse, or a foreign power interested in improving its military stature. Not as silly as it sounds.

1038. DAWKINS, Cecil. "The Buffalo Farm." In her The Quiet Enemy, p. 30-55. Atheneum, 1963.

A small crowd gathers at a last-chance gas station and half-baked zoo in Nevada, where the proprietor sells sunglasses at inflated prices--to protect the eyes of the gathering from the light of a forthcoming A-bomb test. "Big Blast," says the sign. "See it here." A very effective story which might have been better without the lunatic Christ figure brought in at the end.

1039. DEL REY, Lester. Nerves. Ballantine, 1956. 153 p.

Reactor meltdown follows from a foolhardy isotope experiment at the "National Atomics" plant in Missouri, and a runaway reaction threatens mass annihilation. Scientists must figure out how to stop it "before it's too late." Not the ammo-against-nukes that it might sound like; more a triumph-of-the-scientist tale. (First published as a short story in Astounding Science Fiction, September, 1942.)

1040. DICK, Philip K. Dr. Bloodmoney, or, How We Got Along after the Bomb. Ace, 1965. 222 p.

Nuclear was has reduced the society of the 1980s to little more than a primitive clutching for the essentials of survival. A believable and well-wrought novel, for the most part, with some memorable scenes, including a space traveller marooned in perpetual earth orbit broadcasting inspirational selections of music and literature to the survivors below.

1041. DISCH, Thomas M. "Casablanca." In his Fun with Your New Head, p. 184-207. Doubleday, 1971.

Mr. and Mrs. Richmond, on vacation in Casablanca, find their American funds in light demand after the U.S. has been destroyed by nuclear war. An ironic, if not nasty, depiction of aggressive provincialism.

1042. DRURY, Allen. The Hill of Summer: A Novel of the Soviet Conquest. Doubleday, 1981. 484 p.

A bloated, boring and unreadable soapbox from which Drury shrills his warnings about perceived Soviet ambition and alleged U.S. military flaccidity, useful only as one more fictional manifestation of the renewed Cold War mentality which gripped the U.S. on Reagan's accession to the presidency.

1043. ELLIOTT, George P. David Knudsen. Random House, 1962. 339 p.

Professional photographer Knudsen is irradiated during a Pacific bomb test. His physicist father happens to also be one of the "fathers" of the atomic bomb. The central issue of this novel of self-examination is Knudsen's quite rational fear of having children; his fear leads him to persuade his pregnant wife to obtain an abortion. Through the father-son and wife-husband relations, Elliot explores the meanings of life in a nuclear world.

1044. FRANK, Pat. Alas, Babylon. Lippincott, 1959.
253 p.

A very readable account of nuclear war's aftermath, with
most of the action taking place in a rural Florida community.
If such a war as a "limited" nuclear war were actually fought,
the effects on the survivors, and their responses, would probably resemble many of those here. It takes a few weeks for
the new reality to set in, but when it does, with lawlessness,
vigilantism, and shortages of goods, it settles down hard.

1045. _____. Forbidden Area. Lippincott, 1956.
221 p.

Who can resist a Cold War bomb novel whose jacket calls it
"guaranteed to split the most obdurate atom of reader restraint and cause a nationwide fallout of enthusiasm?" Was
someone in the Lippincott marketing department suffering a
case of terminal black humor? As for the story, Russia
attempts a blitz of the U.S. before American ICBMs can be
perfected, a perfection Frank evidently thought would make
war impossible because of guaranteed retaliation against any
aggressor. Frank is more literate than most who write in
the peace-through-armaments-to-the-eyeballs mode, and Forbidden Area is an interesting look at mid-1950s bomb-thought
and popular perception of the Soviet Union.

1046. _____. Mr. Adam. Lippincott, 1946. 252 p.

That's "Adam," not "atom." A humorous satire based on the
sudden sterility of the world's males owing to the explosion
of nuclear plants at "Bohrville," Mississippi. Time has removed this book from the category of the amusing, but it is
still useful for a glimpse into immediate postwar ideas and
attitudes on the nuclear issue.

1047. GEORGE, Peter. Commander-1. Delacorte Press,
1965. 254 p.

Following the annihilation of the U.S., the Soviet Union and
the People's Republic of China in nuclear war initiated by the
latter, an American submarine commander with ambitions to
become "World Leader" sets up with his crew a fascist regime
on a remote island. Told partly in diary form through ex-
tracts from Commander Geraghty's journal, partly in flash-
back to explain the Chinese plan, partly in conventional narrative. By the co-author of the film "Dr. Strangelove." [See
also next entry.]

1048. _____ . Two Hours to Doom. Boardman, 1958.
192 p.

Published as Red Alert by Ace paperbacks in 1959, this
serious treatment of George's longstanding concern over unintentional nuclear war features an Air Force general who,
in his misplaced faith in preventive war, starts WW III. The
tale mutated into one of the blackest of the film comedies of
the 1960s, "Dr. Strangelove, or, How I Learned to Stop
Worrying and Love the Bomb." Following George's introduction to director Stanley Kubrick, the two combined with Terry
Southern to rewrite the novel for the screen. The book's
unusual history continued when George wrote a novelization
of the film, giving it the Dr. Strangelove title (published by
Bantam in 1964).

Peter George committed suicide in 1966, according to some
reports while working on yet another novel of nuclear war.
George's other work may pass from memory, but his part
in creating "Dr. Strangelove," one of the great classics of
cinematic satire, assures him some attention, at least until
his vision proves accurate in the final detail.

1049. Goldston, Robert. The Shore Dimly Seen. Random
House, 1963. 241 p.

The few passengers and crew aboard a yacht in the Atlantic
have reason to believe that nuclear war has broken out,
leaving much of the world in ruins. The big question:
should they maintain course for the U.S. and take their
chances with what might be left, or head for South America?

1050. GORDON, Donald. Flight of the Bat. Morrow, 1964.
222 p.

Russia announces its military superiority through simultaneous
deposit in major Western capitals of unarmed rockets. The
Allies must demonstrate equality, surrender, or start nuclear war. A technological thriller and propaganda brief for
maintaining manned bombers; turns on the successful penetra-
tion of Russian defenses by "the Bat," an experimental low-
level Royal Air Force bomber.

1051. GRAVES, Robert. "Christmas Truce." In his Col-
lected Short Stories, p. 100-118. Doubleday, 1964.

Through an anecdote of trench warfare, a World War I veteran
assures a young bomb protestor that "Only fear can keep the

peace.... [T]hank your lucky stars that the Russians have H-bombs and that the Yanks have H-bombs, stacks of 'em...." This sentiment is not, however, the final one of the tale.

1052. GRAY, Anthony. The Penetrators. Putnam's, 1965. 314 p.

A tract-as-novel urging that the U.S. upgrade its strategic bomber fleet with faster, more sophisticated craft rather than relying exclusively on ICBMs as a deterrent force. Gray's rationale includes the then-dubious accuracy of ballistic missiles, the impossibility of recalling them once launched, and the alternative for conventional bombing afforded by manned craft.

1053. GRIFFITH, Maxwell. Gadget Maker. Lippincott, 1955. 438 p.

Traces the career of an M.I.T. graduate who proceeds from work on civilian aircraft before WW II to an important role in postwar ballistic missile development. Concludes with a successful missile test referred to as "a beautiful shoot." Although not directly concerned with nuclear weapons, the novel offers glimpses into the state of mind which embraces and encourages advances in military technology, one of the driving wheels of the arms race. The author makes a few negative remarks about militarism, but his basic appeal is to the technological romance of R & D, and an effective military free of inter-service rivalry.

1054. HACKETT, John. The Third World War: August, 1985. Macmillian, 1979. 368 p.

A widely-influential and engrossing novel designed to solicit sympathy for a militarily stronger NATO, and especially a stronger Great Britain. WW III goes off following Soviet invasion of Yugoslavia, provocations in the Persian Gulf and South Africa, and assault on Western Europe. The bloody business ends with the nuclear trade-off of an exterminated Birmingham, England for an incinerated Minsk. The destruction of Minsk, together with Soviet setbacks in conventional war, leads to the dissolution of the U.S.S.R. A fascinating example of wishful thinking raised to dangerous and self-deluding heights.

1055. _____. The Third World War: The Untold Story. Macmillan, 1982. 372 p.

A sequel to Hackett's earlier book, based on the same san-
guine anticipations, the same reverence for military preparedness, and the same contempt for seekers of peace and
disarmament. Isn't the invocation of Lenin's famous dismissal of the latter groups as "useful fools" wearing a little thin
in the hands of Western military fans? One doesn't note much
credence placed by most of the West in Lenin's other animad-
versions, so what is the peculiar attractiveness of his dictum
in this area to authorities like Hackett? Is it merely that
Lenin and Western warhawks think alike in several respects,
i. e. , wrong?

1056. HALDEMAN, Joe. "To Howard Hughes: A Modest
Proposal. " In his Infinite Dreams, p. 47-67.
St. Martin's Press, 1978.

One of the very few funny bomb stories; a recluse billionaire
plants 29 Hiroshima-size bombs in chief cities around the
world, and threatens to set them off unless all nations surrender their nuclear weapons within three days--which they
do, and peace breaks out. Not at all believable after it's
over, but fun while it lasts.

1057. HARDY, Ronald. The Face of Jalanth. Putnam's,
1973. 253 p.

A small international force trained by the Indian military
plants hydrogen bombs on Mt. Jalanth, overlooking China's
major nuclear missile installation. The plan is to simulate
a natural disaster which will destroy the site and set China's
nuclear program back several years. The site is destroyed,
and authorities take the event as a natural disaster, but ironic
consequences follow. A competent thriller, and another possible face of nuclear terrorism.

1058. HARRIS, John Beynon [John Wyndham]. The Chrysalids.
In The John Wyndham Omnibus, p. 385-532. Simon
& Schuster, 1964.

Combines a variation on the revival of civilization after nuclear war with conflict between cultures at different technological levels and some dubious business about telepathy. The
rationalization of the holocaust as just punishment by God and
the society's subsequent rigid fundamentalism, with dire sanc-
tions visited upon even inadvertent transgressors, are the
book's most interesting features. Includes the post-atomic
definition of man: "And any creature that shall seem to be
human, but is not formed thus is not human.... It is a

blasphemy against the true Image of God, and hateful in the sight of God." A difficult precept for radiation mutants to accommodate. First published in the U.S. in 1955 as Re-Birth.

1059. HARRIS, Leonard. The Masada Plan. Crown, 1976.
        314 p.

A standard mainstream political thriller. Arab nations attack an isolated Israel, which may trigger nuclear war in an effort to preserve itself. The possibility of hidden nuclear bombs going off in various world capitals contributes to the entertainment.

• • •

A Child's Letter to Reagan: "I think that nuclear bombs are very very very bad.... if you keep makeing them you will want to try them out. So why don't you stop makeing them?"
                              --Mary Brinkmeyen, age 6
                              Southern Exposure, July-
                              Aug. 1983, p. 51.

• • •

1060. HEINLEIN, Robert [Anson MacDonald]. "Blowups Happen." In The Best of Science Fiction, p. 103-139. Edited by Groff Conklin. Crown, 1946.

First published in Astounding Science Fiction in 1940, set sometime in the unspecified future after a period referred to as the "Crazy Years." A huge atomic power plant located in the Arizona desert provides energy for most of the nation's enterprises, but the heart of the plant is a nuclear "bomb" requiring constant surveillance lest it embark on a runaway chain reaction and destroy a large portion of the planet. The title alludes not only to the potential of such plants to cause unscheduled excitement, but to the emotional breakdowns frequently suffered by the personnel assigned to monitor the "bomb." Technically far from accurate, but not at all far from depicting the psychological pressures accompanying the real bomb which burst five years after this story's publication.

1061. _____. Farnham's Freehold. Putnam's, 1964.
        315 p.

The first sixty pages feature an excellent depiction of how a

family might endure a nuclear attack deep within a well-built
and well-provisioned shelter. What follows is pure fantasy,
with speculation on parallel worlds once the Farnhams are
transported (apparently) to a lush, unpopulated earth, followed
by an interlude with French-speaking blacks and generally
incredible goings-on. Reads as though Heinlein didn't know
what to do after blowing up the world.

1062. _____. "Solution Unsatisfactory." In The Best
of Science Fiction, p. 3-35. Edited by Groff Conklin. Crown, 1946.

Published in 1941, this is another remarkable tale of prescience regarding the threat of nuclear weapons. The weapon
in this case is a radioactive dust capable of destroying all
life in large areas; the U.S. uses it to halt a European war,
then to impose global peace--temporarily interrupted by a
four-day "dust war" with Russia. The story ends with the
world at uncomfortable peace under the military dictatorship
of a U.S. strongman. Among other points of interest is the
imposition of the Pax Americana, a situation envisioned by
many who advocated "preventive" war against Russia during
the U.S.'s brief atomic monopoly.

1063. HOBAN, Russell. Riddley Walker. Summit Books,
1981. 220 p.

Acclaimed widely for its linguistic brilliance--Hoban has in-
vented a new English more fully-realized than that Anthony
Burgess employed in A Clockwork Orange--Riddley Walker's
title character lives in a distant future perplexed and obsessed
with the power that drove their mysterious ancestors, who
destroyed their civilization with what was clearly nuclear war.
This little book, with its gifted creation of a primitive future
society and its concern with human values--what represents
real power?--is one of the outstanding works of atomic fiction.

1064. IBUSE, Masuji. Black Rain. Kodansha, 1970.
300 p.

Although in the form of a novel, Black Rain is closely based
on the actual experiences of a group of people victimized or
affected by the Hiroshima bomb. Relies on the war-time
journal of one Shigematsu Shizuma. Related with characteristic Japanese emotional restraint, effectively translated by John
Bester. Similar in some respects to Edita Morris's Flowers
of Hiroshima and Seeds of Hiroshima, but the author's back-

ground and use of sources gives Black Rain undeniable authority and accuracy of tone. (The title refers to the black rain which fell on Hiroshima following the bombing.)

1065. JONES, Dennis. Rubicon One. Beaufort Books, 1983.
      309 p.

A better-than-average nuclear thriller, but with its genuine admonitory attitude toward the bomb more than a thriller as well. Israel's enemies, abetted by the Kremlin, are armed with nuclear weapons; an aggressive KGB controls the Soviet government. The U.S.'s scenario-setting computer advises initiation of "Rubicon One," a plan for destabilizing the Soviet leadership in the hope of averting widespread war. As the crisis concludes, an accidentally-triggered nuclear bomb destroys much of Damascus, an event which comes close to starting the global war the U.S. hoped to avoid.

1066. JONES, Dennis F. Colossus. Putnam's, 1967.
      256 p.

Human subservience to technology reaches an acme when two supercomputers, the U.S.'s "Colossus" and the Soviets' "Guardian"--both designed to provide complete military security--spurn their national allegiances and force their operators to allow their minds to merge. Nuclear blackmail, with ICBMs bursting in both nations, forms the machinery's chief tactic for obtaining its ends. (Filmed as "The Forbin Project.")

1067. KING, Harold. Four Days. Bobbs-Merrill, 1976.
      352 p.

Stalin's death provokes threatening global military events, including full-scale SAC drills at President Eisenhower's order. Historical fiction with imaginary accounts of actual people.

1068. KING, Stephen. The Dead Zone. Viking, 1979.
      426 p.

The reluctant hero, Johnny Smith, develops a discomforting ability to see flashes of the future; he must choose whether to use his power to help unmask a psychopathic politician whose election as President would bring a nuclear war. Probably this prolific and generally under-rated author's best novel, with good characterization, focus on plot, and attention to private needs and desires versus public responsibilities.

1069. KIRST, Hans H. The Seventh Day. Doubleday,
1959. 424 p.

Nuclear war precipitated by rebellion in the German Democratic Republic, for which the U.S.S.R. blames West Germany, destroys civilization within a week. The ironic analogy
to Genesis is not unintended. Believable, unsettling, and
relatively hopeless. First published in Germany in 1957.

1070. KORNBLUTH, Cyril M. Not This August. Doubleday, 1955. 190 p.

An economically-written and quite gripping story of an Ameri-
can rebellion against Soviet occupation tropps in the mid-1960s.
Kornbluth's post-conquest U.S. --"The People's Democratic
Republic of North America"--is far better conceived than attempts in a similar vein, such as in Douglas Terman's Free
Flight (item 1119), because Kornbluth is a far better writer.
The rebellion depends for its success on the launching of a
nuclear-armed satellite able to destroy the largest Soviet and
Chinese cities; plutonium for the bombs comes from a supply
spirited away by physicists in the U.S.'s final hour. Two
weaknesses: the conquest is no longer strategically convincing,
and the hero's renunciation of violence at the end is too summary to be credible. Otherwise a good portrait of insurrec-
tionary determination, and a good look at mid-1950's U.S.
perceptions of the Soviet threat.

1071. KUTTNER, Henry. Mutant. Gnome, 1953. 210 p.

One effect of "the Blowup," the last nuclear war, has been a
mutation involving telepathic ability. The abnormally-gifted
"Baldies" find it difficult to associate with normal human
beings. The Baldies, in fact, regard the latter as sub-
normal. Although the author goes to some lengths to lay out
a society as it might exist after nuclear war--cities, for
example, are no longer permitted, for they might prove politically adventurous; instead, little towns each specializing
in one form of art or industry are all that remains of urbani-
ty--the chief concern here is mutation and telepathy.

1072. LANGLEY, Robert. The War of the Running Fox.
Scribner, 1979. 183 p.

Uninspired business concerning an attempt by white Rhodesian
commandos to steal British plutonium, with nuclear blackmail
in behalf of Rhodesia their intent.

1073. LANHAM, Edwin. The Clock at 8:16: A Novel about
Hiroshima 25 Years Later. Doubleday, 1970.
357 p.

A love affair between an American soldier serving in Vietnam
and a survivor of the Hiroshima bomb. The title-time refers
to the moment of the blast. "Only my eyes saw that day,"
says the young woman, "and they made photos and put them
away in small envelope in my head where later my thinking
took them out one by one to be seen again on dark nights
when I wake up and scream for my mother."

1074. LEIBER, Fritz. "A Bad Day for Sales." In Men and
Machines: Ten Stories of Science Fiction, p. 31-
39. Edited by Robert Silverberg. Meredith Press,
1968.

In the not-too-distant future, a robot vending machine continues to work his pitch to an urban crowd which has been
largely incinerated by an ICBM. Robot and missile combine
to illuminate two aspects of our technological hubris and
absurdity. First appeared in 1953 in Galaxy Science Fiction,
has lost none of its punch.

1075. McMAHON, Thomas. Principles of American Nuclear
Chemistry: A Novel. Little, 1970. 246 p.

Timmy McLaurin, son of one of the first bomb's makers, reflects on his youth among the atomic scientists at Los Alamos,
1943-45, and on the spent possibilities of a world at peace.
An unusual, original, and low-keyed novel.

1076. MARTINO, Joseph. "Pushbutton War." In Prologue
to Analog, p. 259-281. Edited by John W. Campbell. Doubleday, 1962.

Somewhere in the Arctic, U.S. pilots fly ICBM-interceptors.
The story focuses on one pilot's decision-making difficulties
as he destroys an incoming warhead. Another reminder that
no matter what the computers say, human history lies at the
mercy of human hands.

1077. MASON, Colin. Hostage. Walker, 1973. 221 p.

Israeli terrorists blow up Cairo with pilfered U.S. nuclear
bombs, the Soviet Union seizes Egypt and holds Sydney,
Australia as a nuclear hostage to force the U.S. to abandon
Israel.

1078. MASTERS, Dexter. The Accident. Knopf, 1955. 406 p.

Based on an actual, lethal radiation accident involving several atomic scientists at Los Alamos in 1946. Although the narrative is strongest when concentrating on the dying Louis Saxl (the Canadian Louis Slotin in real life), the questions raised throughout the book on the moral issues of the bomb's development and use, the roles of scientists as military adjuncts, and the overall history of the bomb remain as vital as ever.

1079. MEADOWS, Patrick. "Countercommandment." In Analog 5, p. 153-168. Edited by John W. Campbell. Doubleday, 1967.

Centralized computers have taken over the ICBM launch functions in both East and West--but their ability to "think" upon the texts of their makers' religious and philosophical documents renders launch impossible. A typical piece of science fiction "if only it were so" work.

1080. MERLE, Robert. Malevil. Simon & Schuster, 1973. 575 p.

Easter, 1977: most of the civilized world blows itself up, leaving but scattered survivors, including a group of friends in the remote French chateau, "Malevil," who escape the bomb because of their fortuitous presence in the cellar. The bulk of this very bulky but enjoyable book concerns the rebuilding of society, with previous centuries' cultural evolution compressed into a few years. Evolution appears stuck in a groove, however, for when we leave our friends, they are busy planning how to improve their armaments. Translated from the French.

1081. MERRIL, Judith. Shadow on the Hearth. Doubleday, 1950. 277 p.

The author, best known as an editor of science fiction anthologies, provides in her first novel a description of a woman's efforts to protect her family after an atomic attack on New York City. Given the power of today's thermonuclear versus the mere atomic bombs of the early 1950s, the scenario of the attack is no longer likely, unless carried out by a terrorist group. The portrayal of people under stress is carried off well, though, and Merril's exposition of then-current ideas about the bomb is valuable.

1082. _____ . "That Only a Mother." In Science Fiction Hall of Fame, p. 279-287. Edited by Robert
Silverberg. Doubleday, 1970.

First published in 1948, this is a well-written story about a
young, pregnant woman whose husband was exposed to radiation. It is also one of the most--perhaps the most--shocking
treatments of genetic mutation in the entire canon of atomic
fiction, its effect achieved by Merril's restraint and by her
skillful evocation of sympathy for the new mother. No parent
of young children could forget this story, or wonder at the
wisdom of reading it, so wrenching is its conclusion.

1083. MILLER, Walter M. Canticle for Leibowitz. Lippincott, 1960. 320 p.

Another of the handful of atomic fiction keystones (assuming
that more than one keystone is a possibility; it is, if we
imagine such stones supporting a bridge of many arches from
an era of war to one of peace.) Nuclear war has nearly
wiped out humanity; Isaac Leibowitz founds a monastery in
what was the U.S. Southwest in an attempt to retain knowledge
against a widespread anti-intellectual movement. Many centuries later, history has repeated itself, and the atom has
again been put to use against the earth. A spacecraft bearing
the knowledge protected by the monastery, along with a small
group of passengers, departs for the stars.

On its face grim and depressing, Canticle's depth of concern,
consideration of ideas of state, morality, knowledge and reli-
giosity, along with the author's stylistic skill, have made it
one of the science fiction genre's most durable works.

1084. MOORE, Ward. "Lot's Daughter." In A Decade of
Fantasy and Science Fiction, p. 292-324. Edited
by Robert P. Mills. Doubleday, 1960.

A northern California survivor of atomic war meditates on
the exigencies of post-holocaust existence. Thoughtful handling
of both major issues (How does one try to rebuild civilization?) and minor (What does one do with an infected tooth
in a world without dentists?) Compresses many ideas into a
short space.

1085. MORRIS, Edita. Flowers of Hiroshima. Viking, 1960.
187 p.

A tale of bomb survivors. Effectively raises one's awareness

regarding the hideousness of the bomb and of war in general.
As in Seeds of Hiroshima, Morris affects a style which has
vague "Oriental" attributes. Flowers also turns its attention
to the genetic consequences of exposure to radiation, and the
fear of giving birth to deformed children.

1086. _____. The Seeds of Hiroshima. George Braziller,
          1965. 118 p.

"The seeds of Hiroshima are tainted and they will blow about
the world for centuries to come," reflects one of Morris's
characters upon the birth of a deformed infant. The baby's
gestation serves as the dramatic focus. Morris's presentation of the first-person narrative through a Japanese woman
is a questionable choice, but once taken is well executed.
The "monster's" mother commits suicide in behalf of freedom
from fear of the bomb. A useful compendium of insights into
the minds of atomic survivors.

1087. MURPHY, Robert. "Fallout Island." In The Post
          Reader of Fantasy and Science Fiction, p. 17-28.
          Edited by the Saturday Evening Post. Doubleday,
          1964.

An implicitly admonitory, if not particularly well-written,
story of bizarre mutation reversing the flow of evolution on
a remote island soaked by radiation from bomb testing.

1088. NORTON, Andre. Star Man's Son, 2250 A.D.. Har-
          court, Brace, 1952. 248 p.

Another study in post-atomic holocaust primitivism and heroism. Young Fors and his telepathic cat pursue fearful ad-
ventures in the badlands of mid-America, radioactive since
the "Great Blow-up" two centuries earlier. "We who were
meant to roam the stars go now on foot on a ravaged earth."
Norton is best known for her fantasy, the Witchworld saga,
but this early work is readable and not without moments
arousing the imagination, e.g., Fors's discovery of colored
pencils in an old shop in an abandoned city. "He sharpened
two with his hunting knife and made glorious red and green
lines on the dusty floor." As in so many other fictions
growing from bomb-consciousness, this one also makes the
issue of mutation a central topic.

1089. PANGBORN, Edgar. Davy. Garland Pub. Co., 1975.
          266 p.

This is a reprint of the Ballantine edition of 1964. Set three centuries after nuclear war, what is left of the U.S. is a medieval society, with walled cities, slavery, and execution-by-fire for anyone who tries to retrieve the scientific knowl-edge of the "Old Time." An engagingly-conceived picture of future culture in what used to be upstate New York, centering on 14-year old Davy's coming of age. Once again, one of the lingering problems is the "evil that Old Time set adrift, that came down through the generations," the threat of muta-tion. Here the mutants are known as "mues."

1090. PETESCH, Natalie L. M. "How I Saved Mickey from the Bomb." In her After the First Death There is No Other, p. 136-154. University of Iowa Press, 1974.

An excellent and uneasy fantasy; Gabriel de Miabeau, a highly-articulate French poodle, recounts a meeting concerned with neighborhood civil defense against the bomb. Gabriel was not impressed with the proceedings.

1091. POHL, Frederik. "Three Portraits and a Prayer." In The Best of Frederik Pohl, p. 40-52. Edited by Lester Del Rey. Doubleday, 1975.

A utilities baron who covets political power sets up two-dozen fusion power plants as nuclear bombs for blackmail purposes. First published in the August, 1962 Galaxy Magazine.

1092. PORTER, Joe Ashby. "Nadine, The Supermarket, The Story Ends." In his Kentucky Stories, p. 69-88. Johns Hopkins University Press, 1983.

A perplexing but effective combination of three different but subtly-related stories told from a woman's point of view. "Nadine" rises from humble beginnings to the Presidency; the narrator makes a trip through the supermarket, where she finds lipsticked obscenities in peculiar places (and in a color no longer quite fashionable); to top it off, civilization-demolish-ing war of the nuclear variety spreads with strange delibera-tion across the world. The narrator and her kin are left to view the ruins on television. (An impossibility, but it doesn't matter.) A strong, complicated story that invites re-reading.

1093. PRIEST, Christopher. Darkening Island. Harper & Row, 1972. 147 p.

In this often violent, cold-voiced first-person narrative, a young English college lecturer relates a disjointed impression of Great Britain torn by civil war, a war prompted by the arrival of two million refugees from Africa. With nuclear weapons evidently supplied by the major powers, the African nations have annihilated themselves and made the continent uninhabitable; starving refugees flee to any available country. The sense of chaos, lack of reliable information for either characters or reader, and sundering of personal relations here is strongly reminiscent of Shame, Ingmar Bergman's almost unbearably depressing 1968 film, which also dealt with civil war. Priest's is a completely believable version of future possibilities given nuclear proliferation.

1094.   PROCHNAU, William.   Trinity's Child.   Putnam's,
        1983.   400 p.

An intense and nerve-wracking novel predicated on a BOOB (Bolt Out of the Blue) Soviet nuclear attack on the U.S. The attack is intended as a preventive measure to relieve the Soviet Union of the economic burden of matching the U.S. arms buildup, though it initially embraces only SAC bases, some missile silos and a few other token targets, but it gets out of hand fairly rapidly. Before the shooting stops (leaving 40,000 unused nuclear weapons still at the ready), 100 million Americans and Russians are dead. Action is about evenly divided between the U.S. government's flailing around trying to maintain control, and the interrelations among crew members on a B-52 headed for Russia.

The ring of verisimilitude is clear and strong. Prochnau has written prize-winning articles on nuclear war for the Seattle Post-Intelligencer and the Washington Post. His accounts of nuclear war operational procedures and crucial sites, such as the Omaha command center, are based on first-hand observation. Prochnau regards nuclear war as "inevitable." His novel is very good; it is also very close to hopeless.

1095.   RASCOVICH, Mark.   The Bedford Incident.   Atheneum,
        1963.   337 p.

The Bedford, an American destroyer, accidentally torpedoes a Russian submarine during a protracted bit of Cold-War maneuvering. The progress toward the accident shows with considerable persuasiveness the mental tensions inherent in "peacetime" military exercises, and the innocuous means (in this case a misunderstood order) through which an "accidental" nuclear war might be set off.

1096. ROSE, Mark. "We Would See a Sign." In Spectrum
III, p. 161-166. Edited by Kingsley Amis and
Robert Conquest. Harcourt, Brace & World, 1964.

An effective portrait of the man responsible for destroying
"all Asia" through nuclear attack. He now lives in the post-
holocaust ruins of Bayonne, New Jersey, where the pathetic,
mutant survivors regard him with religious awe. An interesting investigation of personal guilt and public reaction.

1097. ROSHWALD, Mordecai. Level Seven. McGraw, 1960.
186 p.

Dedication "To Dwight and Nikita"; the novel's title refers to
an ICBM command center nearly a mile below ground oc-
cupied by 500 men and women who are never permitted access to the surface. The nationality of the center is unspecified, but Level Seven possesses a twin in an enemy
nation. The holocaust starts by accident, most of humanity
is abruptly obliterated, and the rest--including those in Level
Seven--die slowly and gruesomely. Narrated in the form of
a diary kept by a Level Seven functionary. A sincere and
serious work whose lack of artistry does not much get in the
way.

1098. SCHOONOVER, Lawrence. Central Passage. Sloane,
1962. 246 p.

A religious-political fanatic starts "The Twenty Minute War" with
nuclear sabotage in the Panama Canal. Resulting global climatic
changes through diversion of ocean currents cause "The Big Ice."
War and weather are of more interest than the remaining focus on
superintelligent but doomed children.

1099. SCORTIA, Thomas N. Earthwreck! Fawcett, 1974.
224 p.

A straight SF premise: American and Russian astronauts
watch from their respective space stations as the Earth below
destroys itself in a nuclear war. The choice they face is
death or cooperation, to be fulfilled with colonization of Mars.

1100. _____ and Robinson, Frank M. The Prometheus
Crisis. Doubleday, 1975. 321 p.

A readable thriller based on a reactor explosion at a huge
new northern California nuclear plant, the world's largest.
Intended as a didactic novel, this is the sort of work that

makes pro-nuclear authorities (or opinion leaders) grind their teeth over alleged scientific inaccuracies.

1101. SETLOWE, Rick. The Brink. Arthur Field, 1976. 244 p.

On the actions and fears of U.S. Navy fighter pilots during the Quemoy-Matsu Crisis in the Straits of Taiwan in 1960, when the possibility of nuclear attack on the Chinese mainland was close at hand. The author was an officer on the U.S.S. Midway during its involvement in the crisis; his narrative thus possesses considerable credibility, and is well told.

1102. SHIRAS, Wilmar H. Children of the Atom. Gnome, 1953. 216 p.

Through the effects of radiation poisoning, a group of children has mutated into superior intelligences who can only feel comfortable when in the company of their mutated peers. Following discovery of the condition by a psychiatrist, the book follows the gathering of the children and their preparation for a life of extraordinary achievement. Unusual in that most atomic fictions portray mutations as either debilitating, regarded by society as signs of inferiority, or both.

1103. SHUTE, Nevil. On the Beach. Morrow, 1957. 320 p.

In spite of mixed reviews, one of the seminal works of bomb-consciousness. Civilization is extinguished through nuclear war, with Australians the last to go. Serialized in comic-strip form in many newspapers, convinced a number of ten-year olds (including this bibliography's compiler) that they would not see their 14th birthdays.

1104. SIMAK, Clifford D. "Lobby." In The Best of Science Fiction, p. 89-102. Edited by Groff Conklin. Crown, 1946.

In a story which more-or-less anticipates a reverse image of the historical record, Simak posits the conventional power utilities' readiness to do anything, including murder, to protect their interests against the development of nuclear power, envisioned by Simak as a building block of both prosperity and world government. First published in 1944.

1105. SIMPSON, George E. and Burger, Neal R. Fair Warning. Dell, 1981. 528 p.

An "alternate history"--or nearly so--regarding an effort by
American nuclear scientists to warn Japan about the bomb in
hopes of eliciting Japan's surrender rather than the "rain of
ruin" Truman promised after Hiroshima. Alternate histories
are for a certain taste which finds speculation on what might
have been as compelling as on what might still be; Fair
Warning, with its large cast of characters taken from real
life and its fictional depiction of actual historical events, is
above average in the genre. (The love-interest passages
simply get in the way, however, and should have been left
out.)

1106. SINCLAIR, Andrew. The Project. Simon & Schuster,
       1960. 186 p.

A strange book in which some renegade scientists fire a
nuclear missile from the Australian Outback at Russia, hoping
to precipitate WW III. There is some symbolic connection
here between unhealthy sex and the urge to kill, a connection one cannot help making when contemplating those sleekly
erect ICBMs poised in their tubes. Too much affected dialog,
not entertaining as a thriller (nor meant to be), and unsuc-
cessful as satire.

1107. SNOW, C. P. Corridors of Power. Scribner's, 1964.
       403 p.

Conservative Minister Roger Quaife's campaign to relieve
Britain of its place in the nuclear arms race leads to his
fall from power and the failure of his nuclear aims.

1108. _____. The New Men. Scribner's, 1955. 311 p.

A British companion to Dexter Masters's The Accident (item
1078). On the relations of English scientists and government
officials working on development of the first atomic bomb.
The bomb's use on Japan is the catalyst for a heightened
scrutiny of the work's moral nature. More polished than
The Accident, but less compelling. "You can't expect decency from any collection of people with power in their hands,
but surely you can expect a modicum of sense.... They
can't drop the bomb."

1109. SOTRELL, Robert. Social Firebreak: World War III,
       June 12, 1986. Select Publications, 1982. 260 p.

A radical's answer to John Hackett (items 1054-55). Treats
a potentially provocative theme: the advent of widespread

revolution spurred by tactical nuclear war in Europe. Although it remains of interest because of its ideas, Sotrell's story fails to engage the reader on an artistic level. It focuses on the common soldier's experience, so might have exploited considerable sympathy, but is not competently written.

1110. SOUTHWELL, Samuel B. If All the Rebels Die. Doubleday, 1966. 400 p.

Russia has attacked the U.S. with nuclear weapons and forced its surrender. Russian forces occupy the country. The stout citizens of one small town continue to resist. Similar in some respects to Kornbluth's Not This August, (item 1070), but the latter is more interesting.

1111. SPINRAD, Norman. "The Big Flash." In Orbit 5, p. 199-222. Edited by Damon Knight. Putnam's, 1969.

A punk rock apotheosis and the triumph of the death wish. The "Four Horsemen," a rock band with a stage show religiously devoted to the bomb, soon have the public going about wearing buttons with the command "Do it!" superimposed over a mushroom cloud. A story of mass psychological yearning and manipulation that is both believable and frightening.

1112. _____. "The Equalizer." In 100 Years of Science Fiction, p. 269-277. Edited by Damon Knight. Victor Gollancz, 1970.

An Israeli scientist and a military officer argue about whether the former's discovery of a new superbomb represents Israel's salvation, or the planet's doom. "One thing we can be sure of," said one, "whatever we decide will be wrong."

1113. STANTON, Paul. Village of Stars. Mill, 1961. 241 p.

A British jet bomber, carrying a nuclear bomb capable of devastating 40,000 square miles, is patrolling above the Black Sea. Ordered to arm the bomb during an international crisis, the crew cannot disarm it when the crisis abates. The bomb will detonate at an altitude of 5,500 feet. Predictable difficulties ensue. The author is an experienced military pilot.

1114. STAPP, Robert. A More Perfect Union. Harper's Magazine Press, 1970. 375 p.

A U.N. -engineered treaty provides for substantial and general
nuclear disarmament by 1981. An era of peace seems at
hand, except, perhaps, for the threat posed the U.S. by the
Confederate States of America. The fascist Confederacy,
allowed to stand firm in its secession by Lincoln to avoid
the Civil War, wants access to the Pacific, and possesses a
nuclear stockpile of over 3,000 warheads. Even with the
new treaty imposition of a 1,000 mile limit on delivery
vehicles, the Confederacy can easily destroy the U.S. A
better than usual alternate history.

1115. STOCKTON, Frank R. The Great War Syndicate.
        Literature House, 1970. 191 p.

This novel, first published in 1889, presages a great deal.
A group of American scientists, the "Syndicate," take control of U.S. fortunes in a brief war with Great Britain. It
is brief, for these scientists have developed a weapon known
as the "Instantaneous Motor Bomb" whose effects strongly
resemble those of small atomic bombs. Great Britain,
recognizing that an altogether new sort of war has been in-
augurated by this bomb, capitulates following a demonstration
shot on an isolated fort. An Anglo-American bomb monopoly
is born.

1116. SWANWICK, Michael. "Mummer Kiss." In Universe
        II, p. 159-192. Edited by Terry Carr. Doubleday,
        1981.

A moody portrayal of the breakdown and reorganization of
society following a nuclear plant reactor meltdown. Set many
years after the disaster, the story details credible social and
political developments in the northeastern U.S. radioactive
"Drift" zone. Well written, provocative and ominous. A
woman reporter plays a major part in the action.

1117. SZILARD, Leo. "The Voice of the Dolphins." In
        his The Voice of the Dolphins and Other Stories,
        p. 19-71. Simon & Schuster, 1961.

A tour-de-force of socio-political fiction in the guise of a
historical account of successful world disarmament in the late
1980s. The author, one of the pioneering atomic scientists
who campaigned against the nuclear arms race, foresees the
post-1965 nuclear stalemate between the U.S. and the Soviet
Union, describes what has become the common doubt about
the credibility of U.S. nuclear "deterrence" in conflicts which
do not threaten the existence of the U.S. as a nation; his

ideas of "limited atomic war," mobile missiles, the perceived need for augmented conventional forces in a nuclear
world are similarly eye-opening in light of the story's date
of publication. Impressive as is his gift for looking ahead
into the nuclear future is his grasp of the psychological rami-
fications of disarmament. That he saw the world movement
in favor of disarmament reaching an apex in the mid-1980s
is almost eerily on the nose.

1118. TERMAN, Douglas C. First Strike. Scribner's,
        1979. 368 p.

A New Cold War thriller and admonition. The Russians en-
list an ambitious, soft-headed American politician in a scheme
to render the U.S. weak through disarmament. The author's
background as a launch crew commander for Atlas ICBMs
provides some technical credibility, but his politics are black
& white, his characterizations the same, and his grasp of
strategic issues is strangely limp.

1119. _____. Free Flight. Pocket Books, 1981. 346 p.

Terman dishes up another helping of melodramatic, macho
Cold War hash; this time the U.S. has indeed succumbed to
a Soviet first-strike; the Spirit of America lives on in the
character of one "Mallen," who likes to say tough stuff like
"Let the bastards come and get me." Terman has nothing
special to say, but his books do permit a glimpse of a 1980s
parallel to the hysterical Cold War novels of a generation
earlier, and for that reason cannot be dismissed.

1120. TREW, Anthony. Ultimatum. St. Martin's, 1976.
        223 p.

Another nuclear blackmail thriller. Palestinian terrorists
secrete a bomb somewhere in London, and promise to set it
off unless the U.S. and the U.K. accept an independent Pale-
stine on presently-Israeli territory.

1121. TUCKER, Wilson. The Long Loud Silence. Rinehart
        & Co., 1952. 217 p.

Atomic and bacteriological warfare has laid ruin to the eastern
half of the U.S. The depiction of ordinary people reduced to
a scavenging, near-savage struggle for mere survival in a
post-war wasteland is convincing enough. Comparable in some
respects--though far bleaker than--George Stewart's late-'40s
plague novel, Earth Abides.

1122. _____. Time Bomb. Rinehart & Co., 1955.
184 p.

A weird amalgam of political assassination, the ascent of
American fascism (the Sons of America being the chief vehi-
cle), telepathy, the gutting of the federal budget programs
for social services in favor of a military buildup, all culminating in the destruction of the Soviet Union by surprise nuclear attack--and a ruling that communists in the U.S. be
shot on sight. One might wish to make certain connections
between some of these points and contemporary developments.

1123. VONNEGUT, Kurt, Jr. Cat's Cradle. Holt, Rinehart
& Winston, 1963. 231 p.

Vonnegut's funniest novel. The narrator, John (or Jonah),
while writing a book called The Day the World Ended on the
Hiroshima bombing, stumbles onto the secret of "Ice Nine,"
a catalyst for the instantaneous freezing of all the planet's
water--in short, apocalypse through ice rather than fire.
Ice Nine's inventor also happens to be one of the "fathers"
of the atomic bomb.

1124. WAGER, Walter H. Viper Three. Macmillan, 1971.
257 p.

Five escaped killers commandeer an ICBM station in Montana
and threaten to launch if they don't get what they want: ransom, and the President as hostage.

1125. WELLS, H. G. The World Set Free. Scribners,
1926. 250 p.

This is volume 21 of the Atlantic Edition of Wells's works.
Written in 1913 and published before the outbreak of WW I, it
is an astonishing novel. After opening with a brief survey of
humanity's involvement with various kinds of energy, Wells
has his fictional scientist, Holsten, achieve a successful
"atomic disintegration" in 1933. Holsten recognizes some of
the potential of the event, but has "a vague idea" that it
might be wise to keep his findings securely under his hat.

In spite of Holsten's misgivings, the world by the 1950s runs
primarily on atomic energy. Nation states persist, and terrible war breaks out, a war characterized by the indiscriminate
use of "atomic bombs," as Wells names them. He refers to
what came to be known as "chain reaction" as "continuing explosive." Wells understandably underestimates the bomb's

power, but "these atomic bombs which science burst upon
the world" are powerful enough: when a bombardier looked
down at the results of a blast, "it was like looking down upon
the crater of a small volcano. " The tremendous damage inflicted by the atomic bombs encourages national leaders to
dissolve national autonomy, and peace reigns.

"For long decades, " writes Wells, "the combative side in
human affairs had been monstrously exaggerated by the accidents of political separation. . . . An enormous proportion of
the force that sustained armaments had been nothing more
aggressive than the fear of war and warlike neighbors. "

Wells was far from optimistic, yet he believed that human
reason stood a chance of overcoming the fruits of human rage.
He lived long enough to learn of the non-fictional atomic bomb's
desolation of the Japanese cities, and in the last months of
his life planned a film on the threat of nuclear war. The
World Set Free sounded the warning scarcely a dozen years
after the turn of the last century; it has since been sounded
in greater detail, owing to further information on the effects
of nuclear weapons, but it has never been sounded with greater conviction or foresight. One could do far worse than to
begin a study of the bomb and its implications by reading this
novel.

1126. WHITE, E. B. "The Morning of the Day They Did
       It. " In A Treasury of Great Science Fiction, v. 2,
       p. 322-333. Edited by Anthony Boucher. Double-
       day, 1959.

A television employee since fled to another planet recounts
the destruction of the Earth by the personnel aboard a U.S.
space station equipped with a "liberal supply" of bombs more
powerful than the hydrogen bomb. They "do it" out of sheer
boredom and lack of emotional connection with the planet,
spread out below them like a vast target. Among White's
ideas is the distancing of everyone from reality: all dote
upon television, trusting more in the image of the things than
in things themselves. The detachment of the space station
occupants is no more than the culmination of earthly alienation. First published in The New Yorker in 1950.

1127. WILLIAMS, Tennessee. "The Knightly Quest. " In
       his The Knightly Quest and Other Stories, p. 1-104.
       New Directions, 1966.

A frequently very funny novella portraying the residents of a

small southern town going about their oblivious business as
a secrecy-wrapped government "Project" "engaged all day and
all night in some marvelous mystery weapon of annihilation"
adds layers of fascist overcoating to the town milieu.   Funny
and deadly perceptive.   Williams's satire fillets the ominous
absurdity of nuclear weapons manufacture, but even more so
the happy idiocy of those who allow it to persist in their own
backyards.

1128.   WYLIE, Philip.   "The Answer."   In The Post Reader
        of Fantasy and Science Fiction, p. 275-311.   Edited
        by The Saturday Evening Post.   Doubleday, 1964.

First published in 1955, this work is chiefly of value as an
illustration of Cold War high anxiety.   The conceit is ludi-
crous: atomic tests by the U.S. and the Soviet Union lead
to surprising casualties--fallen angels.   The sort with wings.
Don't miss Wylie's Soviet Premier, in the throes of perfect
atheism, giving the boot (literally) to a dead angel.   Silly,
but Wylie's clear fear of imminent attack by the Russians
illuminates the psychology of the early 1950s.

1129.   _____ .   Tomorrow!   Rinehart & Co., 1954.
        372 p.

A politically naïve and strategically ignorant apologia--exhor-
tation, in fact--for the U.S. pursuing every available avenue
toward nuclear supremacy and effective civil defense.   The
climax is a nuclear blitz of the U.S., and the softheads who
thought they could buy peace without bombs and shelters meet
their just fate.   Peace comes to hand, at last, through the
utter extermination of the Soviet Union, and, with that, "the
last great obstacle to freedom had been removed from the
human path."   The entire book equals the vicious simple-
mindedness of this conception.   Considering Wylie's status
as a best-selling author, no study of Cold War nuclear psychology would be complete without reference to Tomorrow!

1130.   _____ .   Triumph.   Doubleday, 1963.   277 p.

More nuclear-alarmist potboiling from Wylie, though he
sounds more worried here than in his dismal Tomorrow!
Here fourteen Americans hole up underground for a couple of
years, pending rescue by Australians after Russia incinerates
the U.S.   The publisher tells us that Wylie's "statement of
Communist reasoning behind Russia's instigation of mass destruction will inspire nodding assent--and fear--in each reader."
The Russians, we learn, are willing to see their homeland

destroyed and irradiated, all of Europe wasted, because they have cleverly secreted a few thousand of their most select citizens--who will joyously rule over the ashes--in safe shelters in the Ural mountains and below the sea. Horrendous from any point of view, but, again, an important tool for understanding why we now have 30,000 nuclear warheads at our disposal.

● ● ●

Behold, I send you forth as sheep in the midst of wolves: be ye therefore wise as serpents, and harmless as doves.
--Matthew 10:16

● ● ●

SUBJECT INDEX

This index is of the "quick and dirty" variety, and is meant only to supplement access afforded by the bibliography's main subject divisions. (The "Miscellany" chapter should be fairly well covered here, however.) Items noted in the index may not necessarily be the only ones to deal with the subjects they appear under; almost any book on strategic policy, e.g., will discuss U.S.-Soviet relations and nuclear deterrence; almost any book on nuclear power will discuss radiation. Indexed items represent the compiler's completely subjective opinion of what the reader may be looking for--and want in a hurry--or what may be buried in the mass of material.

References are to item numbers. The last chapter, "The Art of Fission," is not covered by the subject index.

Academics for Nuclear Disarmament (Group) 597
Acheson, Dean 93
Amarillo, Texas 593, 610
American Association of University Women 999
Anders, Gunther 22
Anderson, John 577
Andropov, Yuri 288, 489
Antiballistic Missile Systems 914, 917, 920, 928, 933, 968
Antinuclear Weapons Movement [See also related entries under "Nuclear War" and "Nuclear Weapons"]: analysis 288, 569, 600; and Middle East 605; and theater 602; Canada 523, 561, 597, 601; criticism of 555, 575, 581, 605; demonstrations, media coverage 595; gay and lesbian role 564, 595; Great Britain 536, 547, 548; literature review 987; origins 536, 559, 983; poetry 518, 615; religious roots 983; U.S. social context 571, 579; West Germany 592, 598, 606-608, 613; Western Europe 272, 535, 548, 549, 574, 588, 620; Western Europe, media coverage 609
Arms Control [See also "Disarmament"]: and Congress 452; bibliography 414; history 406, 409, 424, 426, 435, 442, 453, 466; legal aspects 411, 432, 476; "linkage" 486; mathematical models 454; psychological aspects 494, 501; SALT [Strategic Arms Limitation Talks] 279, 436-438, 447, 459, 473; SALT, Soviet views 135, 451; SALT II 146, 450, 485, 488; START [Strategic Arms Reduction Talks] 493, 495; verification 444, 496
Arms Race: economic aspects 335; history 300, 304, 323, 329; psychological aspects 341; public attitudes 187; secrecy 321; Soviet Union 318, 342; technological aspects 301, 312, 319
"Assault Breaker" weapon system 336
Atomic Energy Act, 1946 66, 89
Atomic Energy Commission, criticism of 51, 54 [see also Chapter X]
Atomic Scientists [see also Chapter IX]: antiwar movement 3, 533, 802, 804, 805; FBI involvement 814; Great Britain 812
Atomic veterans 73, 75, 84

Ballistic missiles see "Missiles, nuclear"
Barnard, Chester 88
Baruch, Bernard 442
Belisle, Mavis 611
Berlin Crisis, 1961 959
Bethe, Hans 781
Bohr, Niels 796

Caldicott, Helen 577
California, 1982 Freeze referendum 576

Campaign for Nuclear Disarmament 536, 578
Cayuga Lake 757
Christian Democrats [W. Germany] 598
Civil defense 16, 50, [see also Chapter XII]
Civil Military Contingency Hospital System 1003
Cohen-Joppa, Jack and Felice 571
Committee for Nuclear Free Europe 607
Committee of Atom Bomb Survivors in the U.S.A. 96
Cruise missile see "Missiles, nuclear"

Deterrence, conventional--preferable to nuclear 199, 202, 224, 247, 264, 273, 430
Deterrence, nuclear [See also many items in Chapter II]: historical risk of war 291; paradox of 274; psychological aspects 152; utilitarian ethics 268, 270
Detroit, nuclear attack on 87
Direct Action (Group) 523, 561, 596
Disarmament [See also "Arms Control"]: bibliographies 414, 967, 1007; Japanese views 490; legal aspects 411, 444, 476; mathematical models 454; Soviet views 412, 439, 440, 475; unilateral 487, 491, 530, 563; yearbooks 462, 464, 467

ELF communications system 566
Eatherly, Claude 22, 42
Einstein, Albert 785
Electronic warfare 277 [see also "Nuclear War" and "Nuclear Weapons," subheading "Command and control systems"]
"Enola Gay" 22, 42, 60, 81
European Nuclear Disarmament 548, 573, 620

Fail Safe (criticism of the novel) 931
Falklands Crisis 399
Fallout, radioactive 26, 27, 54, 69,

86, 233, 510, 511, 539
Fate of the Earth, criticism of 422, 619, 1001
Fermi, Enrico 789, 793
Fermi nuclear plant 741
"Finletter Report" 237
Fires, from nuclear war 100
Forsberg, Randall 521
"Forward Defense" [W. Germany] 991
"Franck Report" 791

Gay-Lesbian Action for Disarmament (Group) 601
The "Golden Rule" (boat) 508, 539
Green Party [W. Germany] 592, 598, 606, 608
Groton, CT 604
Guided missiles see "Missiles, nuclear"

Hahn, Otto 43
Hanford Nuclear Reservation 943
Harvest of Justice 618
Hiatt, Dr. Howard H. 569
Hiroshima 1, 17, 39, 58, 59, 81, 946, 961; survivors 44, 58, 59, 68, 82, 94; U.S. victims 96
Hydrogen bomb 23, 56, 78, 93, 322, 509, 809, 923, 924

ICBMs see "Missiles, nuclear"
Intelligence, U.S.--and Soviet intentions 137, 214
International Atomic Energy Agency 376
International Nuclear Fuel Cycle Evaluation 404
Interventionism and nuclear war 583

"Jonah House" (Group) 604
Jungian psychology and nuclear war 990
"Just War" 234

Kennan, George F., criticism of 497
Kennewick, WA 943

Keyes, Ken 582
Khrushchev, Nikita 456
King, Coretta Scott 972

"Launch on Warning" 996
Lawrence, Ernest O. 787
Leningrad, nuclear attack on 87
Lifton, Robert J. 602
Lilienthal, David 88
"Lilienthal Report" 88
"Limited" nuclear war 120, 165,
  176, 177, 179, 201, 220, 221;
  criticism of 205, 262, 263,
  276, 286, 557, 558; media
  coverage 978
Litton Systems 561, 596, 601
London, nuclear attack on 32
Los Alamos, N. M. 5, 48
The "Lucky Dragon" (boat) 54

McGill Study Group for Peace &
  Disarmament 92
McMahon-Douglas Bill 66
McNamara, Robert S. 168
Massachusetts Institute of Tech-
  nology 951
"Massive Retaliation" 208, 232
Matthiesen, Leroy 593, 610
Mayer, Norman 560
"Missile Gap" 112, 300
Missiles, nuclear: accuracy 275,
  267; "bias" factor 267; Cruise
  missile 153, 278, 292, 298--
  Canadian flight testing: 973,
  985--in Italy: 617--protest:
  538, 601, 617--sabotage: 561,
  596; ICBM Development 297,
  313; "Launch on Warning" 996;
  MIRV 316; in Montana 572;
  MX 238, 287, 311, 315, 328, 343;
  Pershing II 278, 292, 500; SS-20
  258
Morland, Howard 924
Montana, ICBM protests 572

NUTS [Nuclear Utilization Target
  Selection] 266, 269
Nagai, Takashi 76
Nagasaki 14, 17, 62, 63, 76; sur-
  vivors 63, 82, 94, 97; U.S. vic-
  tims 96
National security, and educational in-
  stitutions 192

NATO [see also many of the books
  noted in Chapter II] 247, 249,
  250, 257, 258, 261, 272, 277,
  284, 292, 607
Neutron bomb 306, 307, 337
New Jersey, uranium mining 974
New York City, nuclear attack on 20
Nonproliferation see "Nuclear
  Weapons--Proliferation"
Nuclear Energy Women (Group) 728
Nuclear Free Zones 273, 418, 478,
  479
Nuclear Non-Proliferation Treaty,
  history 379
Nuclear Power: accidents 652, 661,
  690, 715, 722, 741, 945; advocacy
  polemics 623, 663, 683; antinuclear movement--history 739,
  764--origins 633, 753, 769--
  Western Europe 757; California
  729; Canada 632, 634, 701; cancer
  mortality 706; capitalism 776;
  China (People's Republic) 666,
  980; civil liberties 750; Congress
  622, 688, 777; cost-benefit analysis 711; Cuba 721; directory of
  groups 667; Eastern Europe 666;
  economics 681, 752, 771; environmental aspects 641, 677, 679,
  729, 758; ethics 682; France 632,
  719, 720; fuel cycle 645, 693,
  767; fusion power 646; future of
  684, 687, 692; Great Britain 621,
  628, 632; human factors engineering 702, 703; India 727; Japan
  723; labor/antinuclear coalition
  751; Latin America 717; legal
  aspects 720, 731, 733; lightwater
  reactors 625; media coverage
  621, 700; moratoria 672, 695;
  Nigeria 712; plants--decommission-
  ing 651, 674--decontamination
  674--licensing process 686,
  710, 725--offshore 694--securi-
  ty 627--siting 653, 657, 737--
  vulnerability to acts of war
  676, 754; public opinion 707;
  public relations 728, 772, 773;
  reactor proposals 708; regulation
  673, 678, 726; safety study 689,
  778; South Korea 775; Soviet Union
  632, 659, 666, 705, 714, 718,
  730; Sweden 655, 696; technology
  transfer 669; television ads 772;
  Third World 724; "turnkey" system 698; waste disposal see
  "Radioactive Waste" below. West
  Germany 632, 720; Western
  Europe 671; Workers 716, 770,

925, 936, 943
Nuclear Resister 571, 618
Nuclear Test Ban see "Test Ban"
Nuclear theft 366, 385
Nuclear War: accidental 393; Canada 92; children 68, 341, 954 [see also Chapter XV]; command & control systems 113, 285, 290; "decapitation" 285, 290; effects see "Nuclear Weapons--Effects"; escalation of 114, 164, 166; interventionism 583; limited see " 'Limited' Nuclear War" above; Middle East 248, 281, 340; Philippines 95; physicians' movement 502, 505, 513, 569, 584, 589, 997, 1003, 1005; plans for 119, 252, 253, 283, 1003; psychological aspects 334, 591, 994; public opinion 296, 423, 587, 852; Rapid Deployment Force 344; scenarios 106, 118, 164, 166, 511; Soviet Marxism 230; Soviet views 265, 289, 526, 979; strategists of 147, 167, 188, 218, 225; "survivalists" 950; theater (the stage) 602; unintentional 926, 993, 1002;
Nuclear Weapons: accidents 928, 937, 939, 945, 1002; acquisitions, history 953; Berlin Crisis, 1961 959; bibliographies 204, 916, 929, 930, 1007; broadening functions (beyond deterrence) 280, 282; Canada 30, 523, 973, 985; Catholic Church 989 [see also Chapter XIV]; children 68 [see also Chapter XV]; China (People's Republic) 190, 209, 216, 305, 418, 431, 956; command & control systems 277; directories 41, 70; education 988 [see also Chapter XV]; effects 14, 17, 20, 29, 32, 37, 45, 58, 59, 64, 65, 80, 85, 87, 90, 100, 502, 505, 513, 542; electronic warfare 277; foreign policy 9, 10, 38; France 180; Free Zones see "Nuclear Free Zones" above; Freeze Movement 288, 515, 521, 522, 552-554, 565, 576, 577, 580, 590, 616--criticism of 570, 594; general war, end of 138, 154, 186, 445, 934, 995; Germany 170; Great Britain 8, 15, 30, 31, 255,

259; Japan, decision to bomb 1, 2, 6, 7, 24, 25, 28, 36, 47, 77, 786, 818, 824; labor unions 562, 612; legal aspects 256, 924; media coverage 924, 947, 970; Nazi Germany 43; Pacific Ocean 99, 566, 567; philosophical view 528; protest against [see also "Antinuclear Weapons Movement"] 508, 510; psychological aspects 61, 62, 251; public attitudes & opinion 18, 53, 284; Reagan administration 116, 122, 132, 223, 238, 265, 275, 288, 338, 339, 345, 399, 401, 422, 489, 492, 493, 498, 499, 515, 519, 521, 527, 554, 556, 569, 590, 857, 858; religious perspectives [see also Chapter XIV] 551, 976; satire 527, 531; secrecy 51, 53, 54, 924, 947, 952; Soviet Union, history 19, 98; speeches, 1945 4; "tactical" 159, 231, 239, 284; terrorism 918, 944; testing 8, 27, 49, 54, 55, 73, 233--victims of 54, 73, 75, 84, 91, 99; U.S., history 3, 5, 7, 9, 11, 819, 955 (among many others)
Nuclear Weapons Proliferation [see also Chapter IV]: Argentina 356, 364, 401; Australia 365, 370; bibliography 357; Black Africa 399; Brazil 364, 401; Canada 356; Chile 401; fuel leasing 389; India 363, 365, 370, 378, 382; Indonesia 370; Iraq 382; Iran 370; Israel 356, 365, 382; Italy 356; Japan 356, 360, 364, 365, 370; Middle East 371; Pakistan 370, 382; Philippines 370; South Africa 351, 356, 364, 365; South Asia 364; South Korea 370; Soviet Policy 396; Taiwan 356, 370; West Germany 356; war, possibility of 359; white collar crime 355; "Nuclearism" 157, 532, 915

Oak Ridge, Tenn., Laboratory 969
Oppenheimer, J. Robert 88, 779, 782, 787, 795, 803, 806, 809
Osaka Association of A-Bomb Victims 94

Palomares, Spain 928, 939

Pantex Plant 593, 610
Pasco, WA 943
Peace movement [see also "Anti-
nuclear Weapons Movement"]:
Directory 504; Bibliography 967
Peace Museum, Chicago 568
Physicians for Social Responsibility
584
Presidential Directive 59, 283,
286
Progressive magazine 924, 947
Project Plowshare 957
Project Sherwood 624
Propaganda, Soviet, and U.S.
military 964
Propaganda, U.S., and Soviet
military 963
"Psychic numbing" 585
"Purex" reprocessing system 403

Radford, Arthur 208
Radiation effects [see also "Nu-
clear Weapons--Effects"]: 74,
91, 744, 927, 962
Radioactive waste 631, 655, 942,
945, 949, 965, 966, 981, 992,
1000
Rapid Deployment Force 344
"Rasmussen Report" 689, 715, 778
Reader's Digest 815
Richland, WA 943
Richmond, VA 579
"Ripley's Believe It or Not" parody
599
Rosenberg, Julius and Ethel 829,
833 and others in Chapter XI

SALT see "Arms Control"
San Francisco, nuclear attack on
856
San Onofre nuclear plant 706
Satellite reconnaissance 477, 960
Schell, Jonathan 422, 619
Schlafly, Phyllis 577
Scientists, ethical responsibility
[see also Chapter IX] 811
"Scowcroft Commission Report"
238, 287
Seabrook nuclear plant 686
Silkwood, Karen 685, 742, 765
Sino-Soviet Relations 305
The "Smyth Report" 79
"Soviet Threat" 345, 607, 922
Soviet Union, military, U.S. percep-
tions 142

Space colonization 975
Space, military uses 293, 314, 326,
327, 333, 338, 339
Space, Soviet proposals for U.S. -
Soviet cooperation 958
Sternglass, Ernest 1004
Strategic Air Command 213, 932
Strategic Arms Limitation Talks
see "Arms Control"
Strategic Arms Reduction Talks see
"Arms Control"
Strategic issues, bibliography 916
Strategic Policy: attitudes toward
156, 982; Australia 260; France
200; Great Britain 210, 226;
Japan 128, 490; NATO see
"NATO" above; Soviet 108, 125,
126, 139, 140, 145, 160, 175,
229
Strategists see "Nuclear War--
Strategists of"
Submarines, nuclear--accidents 977
Szilard, Leo 805, 813

Taylor, Theodore B. 944
Technology, as cause of war 940
Teller, Edward 782, 809, 815
Test Ban: comprehensive 481, 557;
criticism 468; history 420; Treaty
of 1963 209, 419, 426, 443, 445,
456
Third World and militarization 332
Thomas, Charles 88
Tibbets, Paul 42
Townes Committee 275
"Trident Nein" (Group) 604
Truman, Harry 1, 36, 77, 93 (and
many others in Chapter I)

Unilateral disarmament see "Dis-
armament"
Union of Concerned Scientists 522
U.S. Arms Control and Disarmament
Agency 416
U.S. -China relations 150, 190
U.S. Committee for Energy Aware-
ness 728, 772
U.S. military, bibliographies 916,
929, 930
U.S. -Soviet relations 130, 132, 171,
173, 207, 324
U.S. -Soviet relations, psychological
aspects 274, 480, 501, 532, 979
Universities and military research
951

Ural mountains, nuclear accident
  in 945
Uranium 919, 948, 974

Weinberger, Caspar, criticism
  of 422

Winne, Harry 88
Women: and civil defense 857; and
  nuclear power 728, 773, 774;
  and the peace movement 1006
Woodson, Helen 618
World government 514, 516, 546

• AUTHOR INDEX •

This index also includes the names of many writers whose work appears in anthologies noted in the bibliography. References are to item number.

Abbotts, John 756
Abel, Elie 860
Abshire, David M. 101
Adams, Benson D. 914
Adams, Ruth 502
Addinall, Eric 621
Adler, Alice 552, 553
Adler, Carl G. 769
Adler, Warren 1008
Agnelli, Giovanni 246
Agnew, Harold M. 389
Agrawal, Mahendra 482
Albert, Michael 503
Albright, Gifford H. 837
Aldiss, Brian W. 1009
Aliano, Richard A. 102
Allardice, Corbin 816
Allen, Richard V. 101
Allison, Graham T. 861
Alperovitz, Gar 1
Alsop, Joseph 779
Alsop, Stewart 779, 866
Althoff, Philip 366
American Library Assoc., Social
  Responsibilities Rountable 504
American Psychiatric Association
  915
Amrine, Michael 2, 1010
Anderson, Oscar E., Jr. 818
Arkin, William M. 916
Aron, Raymond 103
Aronow, Sault 505
Asimov, Isaac 1011, 1012
Athanasiou, Tom 555
Atomic Scientists of Chicago 3
Ausubel, Nathan 4
Aviel, S. David 622

Badash, Laurence 5
Bagne, Paul 770
Bailey, Charles W. 47
Baker, David 293
Baker, Earl J. 694

Baker, Howard 933
Baker, John C. 108
Baker, Paul R. 6
Baldwin, Hanson W. 23, 104, 294
Barash, David P. 506
Barkenbus, J.N. 404
Barker, Robert B. 481
Barnaby, Charles F. 295, 296, 346,
  917
Barnet, Richard J. 406
Barron, John 938
Barton, John H. 407, 408
Batchelder, Robert C. 7
Bates, Al 969
Bates, Don G. 92
Baum, Andrew 906
Baxter, James Phinney 3d 780
Beard, Edmund 297
Beaton, Leonard 347
Bechhoefer, Bernhard G. 409
Becker, Susan 882
Beckmann, Petr 623
Beilenson, Laurence W. 105
Benedict, Robert 695
Bennett, Bruce 298
Bennett, John C. 507
Benoit, Emile 410
Beres, Louis R. 106, 107, 556-558, 918
Berg, Per 478
Berger, John 732
Bergman, Lars 696
Berman, Harold J. 411
Berman, Robert P. 108
Bernstein, Barton J. 93
Bernstein, Jeremy 781
Bertin, Leonard 8
Bestor, Barbara 883
Bethe, Hans 810
Betts, Richard K. 298
Bickel, Lennard 919
Bickerstaff, Julia 697
Bigelow, Albert 508
Bishop, Amasa S. 624
Blackett, Patrick M.S. 109-111
Blair, Clay, Jr. 78

Blechman, Barry M.   216, 479
Blish, James   1013
Bloomfield, Lincoln P.   412
Blumberg, Stanley A.   782
Boardman, Robert   348
Bobrow, Davis B.   299
Bodansky, David   680
Bone, J. F.   1014
Boserup, A.   917
Bottome, Edgar M.   112, 300
Boulding, Kenneth E.   410, 439
Boulton, David   509
Boyte, Harry C.   559
Bracken, Paul   113
Brackett, Leigh   1015
Bradbury, Ray   1016-1018
Bradford, George   560
Bradley, David J.   510
Brelis, Dean   838
Brenner, Michael J.   349
Briggs, Raymond   511
Brinton, Henry   1019
Brito, Dagobert L.   393
Brodie, Bernard   9, 114, 115, 301
Brodie, Fawn   301
Brown, Harold   116
Brown, Harrison S.   783
Brown, Neville   117
Brubaker, Bob   561
Bruin, Janet   94
Bryant, Edward   1020
Buchan, Alistair   350
Buchard, Robert   1021
Buck, Pearl S.   1022
Bulletin of the Atomic Scientists   784
Bundy, McGeorge   247
Bupp, Irvin C.   402, 625
Burdick, Eugene   1023
Burger, Neal R.   1105
Burn, Duncan L.   626
Burness, H. S.   698
Burns, E. L. M.   413
Burns, Richard D.   414
Burt, Richard A.   415
Bush, Vannevar   10, 11

Cadwell, Jerry J.   627
Caidin, Martin   1024, 1025
Calder, Nigel   118
Caldicott, Helen   512
Callison, Brian   1026
Campbell, John W., Jr.   1027
Cantelon, Philip L.   895
Cantor, Ileen   333
Card, Orson Scott   1028

Carlton, David   302
Carter, Mary Arkley   1029
Cartmill, Cleve   1030
Catrina, Christian   926
Cave-Brown, Anthony   12, 119
Cervenka, Zdenek   351
Chalfont, Alun   563
Challener, Richard D.   235
Chant, Christopher   41
Chapman, Duane   771
Chapman, John L.   303
Chase, Stuart   13
Chayes, Abram   862, 920
Chevalier, Haakon   1031
Chicken, John C.   628
Child Study Association of America   881
Chinnock, Frank W.   14
Chivian, Eric   513
Chomsky, Noam   248
Clark, Grenville   514
Clark, Ian C.   120
Clark, Jil   564
Clark, Ronald W.   15, 304, 785, 1032
Clarke, Duncan L.   416
Clemens, Walter C.   305, 417
Close, David   884
Cloud, Kate   885
Clough, Ralph N.   418
Coale, Ansley J.   16
Cochran, Bert   921
Cochran, Thomas B.   699
Cockburn, Andrew   922, 970
Coffey, Joseph I.   121
Cohen, Bernard L.   629, 700
Cohen, S. T.   239, 306, 307
Cohen, Sam   249
Cole, Paul M.   515
Collins, John M.   308
Collins, Larry   1033
Comfort, Alex   509
Committee for the Compilation of Materials on Damage Caused by Atomic Bombs   17
Compton, Arthur Holly   786
Conetta, Carl   565
Congressional Quarterly, Inc.   122
Cook, Constance E.   733
Cook, Earl   701
Coppel, Alfred   1034, 1035
Cordes, Colleen   480, 702, 703
Cory, Desmond   1036
Cottrell, Alan   630
Cottrell, Leonard S.   18
Cousins, Norman   516, 517
Cox, Arthur M.   309, 310
Cox, David   973
Croall, Stephen   734
Crosby, John   1037

Cullen, Susan 502
Cunningham, Ann Marie 569
Curtis, Richard 735, 736
Cutright, Phillips 839

Dando, Malcolm R. 123
Daniel, James 863
Darnovsky, Marcy 570
Davidson, Laura M. 907
Davis, Barbara N. 518
Davis, Elmer H. 923
Davis, Nuel P. 787
Davis, W. Kenneth 704
Dawkins, Cecil 1038
Day, Samuel H. 571, 572
de Mesquita, Bruce B. 390
De Toledano, Ralph 826, 827
Dean, Arthur H. 419
Dean, Gordon E. 19
Dean, Roy 250
Deese, David A. 631
Deitchman, Seymour J. 124
Del Rey, Lester 1039
Del Sesto, Steven L. 633
DeLeon, Peter 632
Dellinger, David 503
DelTredici, Robert 896
Deluca, Donald R. 284
Dentler, Robert A. 839
Derian, Jean-Claude 625
Detzer, David 864
Deutsch, Morton 251
DeVolpi, Alexander 352, 924
Devove, Robert 20
DeWitt, Hugh E. 481
Dick, Philip K. 1040
Dietz, David 21, 788
Dinerstein, Herbert S. 125, 865
Disch, Thomas M. 1041
Divine, Robert A. 420, 866
Diwakar, R. R. 482
Doern, G. Bruce 634
Dougherty, James E. 421
Douglass, Joseph 126
Downing, Roger H. 709
Draper, Theodore 422
Drell, Sidney D. 423, 483
Dresner, Samuel H. 869
Drinan, Robert F. 519
Drummond, Hugh 811
Drury, Allen 1042
Duderstadt, James 635
Duncan, Francis 819
Dunn, Keith A. 254
Dunn, Lewis A. 353, 402
Dupuy, Trevor N. 424
Durie, Sheila 354
Dyson, Freeman xiii

Eatherly, Claude 22
Ebbin, Steven 737
Eberhart, Sylvia 18
Edelhertz, Herbert 355
Edwards, David V. 425
Edwards, John 311
Edwards, Rob 354, 812
Einstein, Albert 23, 784
Eliot, George F. 23, 127
Ellington, Henry 621
Elliott, George P. 1043
Emmanuel, Jorge 95
Endicott, John E. 128
Ensign, Tod 84
Enstrom, James E. 706
Enthoven, Alain C. 129
Environmental Action Foundation 738
Epstein, William 356, 426, 520
Etzioni, Amitai 130, 427
Evans, Medford 828
Evers, Ridgely C. 357

Fairchild, Johnson E. 636
Falk, Jim 739
Falk, Richard 532
Fallows, James 131
Faulkner, Peter T. 740
Federation of American Scientists 521
Feis, Herbert 24, 25
Feld, Bernard T. 312
Fermi, Laura 637, 789
Ferrara, Grace M. 638
Ferry, W. H. 573
Firebaugh, M. W. 707
Finletter, Thomas K. 133
Firestone, Bernard J. 132
Flickinger, Richard 574
Foote, Frederick C. 575
Forbes, Henry W. 428
Ford, Daniel F. 522, 817, 897
Ford, Harold P. 134
Foreman, Harry 639
Foster, James 298
Fowler, Eric B. 26
Fowler, John M. 27
Francia, Luis H. 96
Frank, Jerome D. 334
Frank, Lewis A. 135
Frank, Pat 840, 1044-1046
Freed, Fred 28
Freedman, Lawrence 136, 137, 255, 484
Freeman, Leslie J. 925
Freeman, S. David 708
Frei, Daniel 926
Freund, Ronald 870
Fried, John H. E. 256

Fryklund, Richard 841
Frymiller, Kathleen M. 887
Fuller, John G. 741

Galbraith, John K. 335
Gallois, Pierre 138
Galtung, John 658
Gamble, Hays B. 709
Gantz, Lieut. Col. Kenneth F.
  313
Garrison, Jim 742
Garthoff, Raymond L. 139, 140,
  257, 258
Garvey, Gerald 640
Geiger, H. Jack 856
Gelb, Norman 259
Gelber, H. G. 260
George, Alexander L. 141
George, Peter 1047, 1048
Georgetown University Center for
  Strategic Studies 142
Gerstell, Richard 842
Geyer, Alan F. 429
Giangrande, Carole 523
Gilpin, Robert G. 790
Giovannitti, Len 28
Glasstone, Samuel 29, 641, 642
Gliksman, Alex 261
Gofman, John W. 743, 744, 927
Goheen, Robert F. 391
Goldhaber, Marilyn K. 909
Goldschmidt, Bertrand 643
Goldston, Robert 1049
Gollancz, Victor 524
Gompert, David C. 143
Goodwin, Geoffrey L. 144
Gordon, Donald 1050
Gordon, Gail M. 974
Gordon, Michael R. 336, 485
Gordon, Suzanne 576
Goulding, Phil G. 928
Goure, Leon 145, 843
Gowing, Margaret 30, 31
Graham, Daniel O. 146, 314
Graham, Thomas W. 357
Graves, Robert 1051
Gray, Anthony 1052
Gray, Colin S. 215, 262, 315
Gray, Dwight E. 844
Gray, Mike 898
Green, Harold P. 710
Green, Philip 147
Greene, Owen 32
Greenhalgh, Geoffrey 644
Greenwood, Ted 316
Grenon, Michel 645
Griffith, Maxwell 1053

Griffiths, Franklyn 317
Grossman, Karl 745
Groueff, Stephane 33
Ground Zero 525, 526
Groves, Leslie R. 34
Gruber, Carol S. 813
Gsponer, Andre 337
Guertner, Gary 263
Guhin, Michael A. 358
Gyorgy, Anna 746

Hackett, John 1054, 1055
Hadley, Arthur T. 430
Hagen, Lawrence S. 148
Hahn, R. W. 711
Haldeman, Joe 1056
Halle, Louis J. 149, 975
Hallinan, Conn 338
Halperin, Morton H. 150, 151, 431
Hamilton, John A. 486
Hammerman, Gay M. 424
Hardin, Russell 487
Hardy, Ronald 1057
Harkabi, Yehoshafat 152
Harkavy, Robert E. 153, 402
Harris, John Beynon 1058
Harris, Leonard 1059
Harris, Martyn 578
Harvard Nuclear Study Group 154
Hawkins, David 35
Hayes, Dennis 747
Haynes, Richard F. 36
Heer, David M. 37
Heffernan, Patrick 359
Heilbrunn, Otto 155
Heinlein, Robert 314, 1060-1062
Heller, Steven 527
Henderson, Robert D'A 712
Henkin, Louis 432, 433
Heppenheimer, T. A. 646
Herken, Gregg 38
Herscovici, Sergiu 893
Hersey, John R. 39
Hertsgaard, Mark 748
Herzog, Arthur 156
Hewlett, Richard G. 818, 819
Heyer, Robert 872
Hiebert, Erwin N. 873
Higham, Robin 929, 930
Hilgartner, Stephen 157
Hitch, Charles J. 158
Hoban, Russell 1063
Hodgson, P. E. 713
Hoffman, M. David 40
Hoffman, Stanley 154, 350
Hogan, Elizabeth 735, 736
Hogg, Ian 41

Holdren, John P. 392
Hollenbach, David 874, 976
Holloway, David 318
Holst, Johan J. 159
Holsworth, Robert D. 579
Hook, Sidney 931
Horelick, Arnold L. 160
Howard, Michael E. 264
Hoyle, Fred 647, 648
Hoyle, Geoffrey 648
Hubbell, John G. 863
Hubler, Richard G. 932
Hughes, Donald J. 649
Huie, William Bradford 42
Hulett, L.S. 488
Hunt, E. Stephen 938
Hunt, Stanley E. 650
Huntington, Samuel P. 154, 161
Hyde, Montgomery H. 829

Ibuse, Masuji 1064
Imai, Ryukichi 360, 408
Independent Commission on Disarmament and Security Issues 434
Inglis, David R. 749
International Atomic Energy Agency 435, 651-654
Intriligator, Michael D. 393
Irving, David 43

Jackson, Henry 933
Jacobsen, Carl G. 162, 489
Jacoby, Henry D. 986
Japan Broadcasting Corporation 44
Jasani, Bhupendra 361
Jaspers, Karl 528
Jensen, Lloyd 362
Johansson, Thomas B. 655
Jones, David R. 265
Jones, Dennis 1065
Jones, Dennis F. 1066
Jordan, Walter H. 641
Joseph, Paul 266
Judis, John B. 580
Jungk, Robert 750, 791

Kahan, Jerome H. 163
Kahn, Herman 164-166, 212
Kaku, Michio 339, 656
Kamata, Sadao 97
Kaplan, David E. 977
Kaplan, Fred 167, 267, 978

Kaplan, Morton A. 436
Kapur, Ashok 363, 364
Kasper, Raphael 737
Katsumi, Takeoka 490
Katz, Arthur M. 45
Kaufmann, William W. 168, 169
Kavka, Gregory S. 268, 491
Kearny, Cresson H. 845
Keeley, James 348, 581
Keeny, Spurgeon M., Jr. 269
Keisling, Bill 899
Kelleher, Catherine M. 170
Kelly, Orville E. 75
Kelly, William J. 714
Kennan, George F. 171-173, 247
Kennedy, John F. 441, 866
Kennedy, Robert F. 867
Keyes, Ken 529, 582
Keys, Donald 875
Khrushchev, Nikita 441, 866
Kikuchi, Chihiro 635
Kindall, Sylvian G. 846
King, Harold 1067
King, Stephen 1068
King-Hall, Sir Stephen 530
Kintner, William R. 174, 175, 220, 437, 933
Kirchwey, Freda 46
Kirsch, Vanessa 883
Kirshin, I.I. 979
Kirst, Hans H. 1069
Kissinger, Henry A. 176-178, 212
Klare, Michael T. 340, 583
Klema, Ernest D. 657
Klineberg, Otto 658
Klochko, Mikhail 98
Knebel, Fletcher 47
Knorr, Klaus 179, 934
Knox, Ronald A. 876
Kohl, Wilfrid L. 180
Kolodziej, Edward A. 153, 935
Kornbluth, Cyril M. 1070
Kramish, Arnold 659, 660
Krepon, Michael 492
Krosney, Herbert 382
Kunetka, James W. 48
Kuttner, Henry 1071

Labrie, Roger P. 215, 438, 485
Lackey, Douglas P. 270
Laird, Melvin R. 181, 215, 933
Lamarsh, John R. 980
Lamont, Lansing 49
Landman, David 636
Lang, Daniel 50, 182, 792, 936
Langley, Robert 1072

304 • Author Index

Langor, Victor 531
Lanham, Edwin 1073
Lanoue, Ron 752
Lapierre, Dominique 1033
Lapp, Ralph E. 51-54, 183, 319
Larson, Arthur 439
Larson, Thomas B. 440
Larus, Joel 365, 937
Latham, Donald C. 848
Lathrop, J.W. 661
Latil, Pierre de 793
Latler, Albert 233
Laurence, William L. 55-57
Lawrence, Robert M. 365
Leachman, Robert B. 366
Lee, Kai N. 981
Lefever, Ernest W. 441, 938
Legault, Albert 184
Lehman, J.F. 421
Leiber, Fritz 1074
LeMay, Curtis 185
Lens, Sidney 320
Leonard, Jonathan A. 584
Leppzer, Robert 900
Lester, Richard K. 966
Levi, Isaac 715
Levi, Warner 186
Levine, Robert A. 187
Levinson, Steven C. 974
Lewis, Flora 939
Lewis, Richard S. 753
Leyson, Burr W. 847
Libby, Leona M. 794
Licklider, Roy E. 188
Liddell Hart, B.H. 189, 940
Lieberman, Joseph I. 442
Liebow, Averill A. 58
Lifton, Robert J. 59, 532, 585, 586
Lihach, Nadine 716
Lilienthal, David E. 662, 820, 941
Lindsey, George 184
Linebaugh, David 493
Lipman, Harvey 772
Lipschutz, Ronnie D. 942
Lipsey, David 587
Lipton, Judith E. 506
Liu, Leo Yueh-yun 190
Livingston, Robert G. 588
Lodgaard, Sverre 478
Loeb, Paul 943
Lonnroth, Mans 381
Lovell, John P. 982
Lovins, Amory B. 367, 394, 395, 754
Lovins, L. Hunter 367, 754
Lowe, George E. 191

Lown, Bernard 589
Luddemann, Margarete K. 717
Lyons, Gene M. 192

McBride, James H. 443
McClelland, Charles A. 193
McClory, Robert 983
McCracken, Samuel 663
McCullough, Campbell R. 664
MacDonald, Anson 1062
MacDonald, Charles B. 12
McFadden, Dave 590
McGeehan, Robert 271, 272
McGuire, Martin C. 321
Mack, John E. 341
McKean, Roland N. 158
McMahon, Thomas 1075
McNamara, Robert S. 194, 247, 273
McPhee, John 944
Maggs, Peter B. 411
Malcolmson, Robert W. 274
Mallan, Lloyd 195
Mandelbaum, Michael 61, 196, 197
Mann, Martin 665
Mann, Paul S. 275
Manning, D. Thompson 910
Manoff, Robert K. 984
Markey, Edward J. 368
Marschak, Jakob 681
Martens, John 844
Martin, Brian 591
Martin, Daniel 901
Martin, Laurence W. 198
Martin, Thomas L. 848
Martino, Joseph 1076
Marx, Joseph L. 60
Mason, Colin 1077
Masters, Dexter 533, 1078
Mather, Celia 99
Mathieson, R.S. 718
Mattes, Kitty Campbell 534
Mawrence, Col. Mel 849
Mayrand, Theresa 888
Meadows, Patrick 1079
Medaris, John B. 199
Medvedev, Roy 342
Medvedev, Zhores 342, 945
Meller, Eberhard 369
Melman, Seymour 444
Mendl, Wolf 200
Merle, Robert 1080
Merril, Judith 1081, 1082
Merrill, Anthony F. 850
Merton, Thomas 946
Metzger, H. Peter 821
Mewes, Horst 592

Author Index ● 305

Michelmore, Peter 795
Miksche, Ferdinand O. 201, 202
Miller, Byron S. 66
Miller, Merle 62
Miller, Steven E. 343
Miller, Walter M. 1083
Millett, Stephen M. 494
Millis, Walter 439, 445
Mills, C. Wright 203
Mills, Mark P. 719
Milton, Joyce 833
Modelski, George A. 666
Mojtabai, A. G. 593
Molander, Roger 889
Moore, Mark R. 479
Moore, Ruth 796
Moore, Ward 1084
Moorehead, Alan 830
Morland, Howard 947
Morris, Edita 1085, 1086
Morris, Robert 446
Morton, Louis 192
Moss, Norman 322, 948
Moss, Thomas H. 902
Moulton, Harland B. 323
Mountbatten, Louis 276
Mrozek, Donald J. 930
Mueller, Kimberly J. 667
Mullenbach, Philip 668
Muntzing, L. Manning 669
Muravchik, Joshua 594
Murphy, Dervla 755
Murphy, Robert 1087
Murray, Raymond L. 949
Myers, Desaix 670
Myers, Edward 950
Myrdal, Alva 324, 535

Nader, Ralph 756
Nagai, Takashi 63
Naidu, M. V. 985
Nakazawa, Keiji 64
National Conference of Catholic
Bishops 877
National Research Council,
National Academy of Sciences
64
Nau, Henry R. 671
Neff, Thomas L. 986
Nelkin, Dorothy 720, 757, 758,
911, 951
Nelson, Bob 595
Nelson, Lin 773, 857
Nerlich, Uwe 159
Newcombe, Hanna 987

Newhouse, John 447
Newman, Barrie R. 123
Newman, Bernard 831
Newman, James R. 66
Nieburg, Harold L. 952
Nixon, Richard 215
Noel-Baker, Philip 448
Nogee, Joseph L. 396, 460
Norton, Andre 1088
Norton, Deborah 774
Novick, Sheldon 759, 760
Nutting, Anthony 449
Nye, Joseph S., Jr. 154, 399

Oak Ridge Associated Universities,
Institute for Energy Analysis 672
O'Brien, William V. 878, 989
Oglesby, Carl 990
O'Keefe, Bernard J. 205
Okrent, David 673
Olson, McKinley C. 761
O'Neill, John J. 67
Oppenheimer, J. Robert 784, 797
Orlans, Harold 822
Osada, Arata 68
Osborn, Robert 545
Osborne, John 509
Osterhout, Marilyn M. 674
Otis, Todd H. 762
Overholt, William H. 370
Owens, Gwen 782

Pachter, Henry M. 868
Paine, Christopher 344
Pajak, Roger F. 371
Palmer, Bryan 597
Pangborn, Edgar 1089
Panofsky, Wolfgang K. H. 269, 450
Parkin, Frank 536
Parson, Nels A. 206
Patterson, Walter C. 763
Pauling, Linus C. 537
Payne, Keith B. 207, 262
Payne, Samuel B., Jr. 451
Pearce, David 697
Peck, Merton J. 953
Peeters, Paul 208
Pentreath, R. J. 675
Perez-Lopez, Jorge F. 721
Perkins, Dwight H. 431
Perry, Ronald W. 722
Peters, Alexander 493
Peters, Paul 598
Peters, Ralph H. 991

Petesch, Natalie L. M.   1090
Pfaltzgraff, Robert L.   437
Pierre, Andrew J.   210
Pilarski, Jan   992
Pilat, Oliver   832
Pirie, Antoinette   69
Plate, Thomas G.   325
Platt, Alan   211, 452
Pohl, Frederik   1091
Pollak, Michael   720, 758
Polmar, Norman   70
Polyani, John C.   317
Porter, Joe Ashby   1092
Posen, Barry R.   993
Posvar, Wesley W.   212
Potter, William C.   372
Powell, John W.   723
Power, Thomas S.   213
Powers, Thomas   954
Prados, John   214
Pranger, Robert J.   215
President's Commission on the
   Accident at Three Mile Island
   903
Price, Jerome   764
Priest, Christopher   1093
Priestly, J. B.   509
Pringle, Peter   955
Pritchard, Colin   547
Prochnau, William   1094
Purcell, John   71

Quanbeck, Alton H.   216
Quester, George H.   217, 373,
   374, 401, 402

Radosh, Ronald   833
Ramberg, Bennett   676
Ramesh, Jairam   724
Ranger, Robin   453
Rapoport, Anatol   218
Rascovich, Mark   1095
Rashke, Richard   765
Rathjens, George   279
Read, Thornton   179
Reader, Mark   766
Regehr, Ernie   280
Reinhardt, George C.   219, 220
Reinig, William C.   677
Rensenbrink, John   600
Reuben, William   834
Revenal, Earl C.   281
Reynolds, Earle   539
Rhinelander, John B.   472
Richardson, Brent   531

Riker, William H.   390
Riordan, Michael   601
Ritchie, David   326
Robertson, John K.   72
Robinson, Frank M.   1100
Rochlin, Gene I.   375
Rogers, Barbara   351
Rogers, Carl R.   994
Rolph, Elizabeth S.   678
Rose, John P.   221
Rose, Mark   1096
Rosen, Ira   898
Rosenberg, Howard L.   73
Rosenblum, Simon   282
Rosenburg, David A.   283
Roshwald, Mordecai   1097
Rotblat, Joseph   74, 798
Rowen, Henry   360
Rudig, Wolfgang   776
Ruina, Jack   279
Rush, Myron   160
Russell, Bertrand   441, 540, 541, 784
Russett, Bruce   284
Russett, Bruce M.   222
Ryan, William L.   956

Saaty, Thomas L.   454
Sabato, Jorge A.   724
Sabin, Philip A. G.   995
Saffer, Thomas H.   75
Sagan, Carl   603
Sagan, Leonard A.   679
Sakharov, Andrei D.   799, 800
Salaff, Stephen   97, 403
Salkeld, Robert   327
Sanders, Benjamin   376
Sanders, Ralph   957
Schaefer, Virginia   996
Schaerf, Carlo   302
Scheer, Robert   223
Schell, Jonathan   542
Schelling, Thomas C.   455
Scherer, Frederic M.   953
Schilliger, Josef   76
Schilling, Warner R.   224
Schirmer, Peggy   890
Schlesinger, James   215
Schmidt, Fred H.   680
Schmidt, Jeffrey D.   100
Schneider, Barry R.   285, 496
Schneir, Miriam   814, 835
Schneir, Walter   814, 835
Schoenberger, Walter S.   77
Schoettle, Enid   377
Schofield, Rosalie F.   604
Schoonmaker, Mary Ellen   858
Schoonover, Lawrence   1098

Schurr, Sam H. 681
Schwarz, Urs 225
Schwebel, Milton 891
Schweitzer, Albert 543, 544
Scortia, Thomas N. 1099, 1100
Scott, Harriet F. 175
Scoville, Herbert 328, 545
"Scowcroft Commission" 238
Seaborg, Glenn T. 456, 801, 823
Seshagiri, Narasimhiah 378
Setlowe, Rick 1101
Severud, Fred N. 850
Shaker, Mohamed I. 379
Shapley, James R. 78
Sherwin, Martin J. 329
Shimizu, Sakae 892
Shiras, Wilmar H. 1102
Shrader-Frechette, K. S. 682
Shute, Nevil 1103
Sigal, Leon V. 497
Sillitoe, Alan 509
Sills, David L. 902, 904
Silver, Melinda 725
Simak, Clifford D. 1104
Simpson, George E. 1105
Sinclair, Andrew 1106
Singer, J. David 457
Singlaub, John K. 998
Skolnikoff, Eugene B. 958
Skousen, Eric N. 683
Slessor, Sir John C. 226
Slocombe, Walter 286, 458
Slusser, Robert M. 959
Smart, Ian 684
Smith, Alice K. 802
Smith, Damu 605
Smith, Dan 549
Smith, Gerard 247, 459
Smith, K. Wayne 129
Smith, Thomas V. 879
Smoke, Richard 141
Smyth, Henry DeWolf 79
Snow, C. P. 1107, 1108
Snow, Donald M. 227
Snyder, Glenn H. 228
Sokolovskii, V. D. 229
Solomon, Norman 91
Somerville, John 230
Sotrell, Robert 1109
Southwell, Samuel B. 1110
Spanier, John W. 460
Spiewalk, I. 404
Spigelman, James 955
Spinrad, Bernard 405
Spinrad, Norman 1111, 1112
Spitzer, Abe 62
Srouji, Jacque 685
Stanton, Paul 1113

Stapp, Robert 1114
Starr, Roger 719
Staudenmaier, Col. William O. 254
Steen, Peter 655
Stein, Walter 880
Steinberg, Gerald M. 960
Steinberg, Rafael 961
Steinbruner, John 499
Steinke, Rudolf 607
Stephens, Mark 905
Stern, Philip M. 803
Sternglass, Ernest 962
Stever, Donald W., Jr. 686
Stewart, Blair 287
Stewart, Hugh B. 687
Stillman, Peter G. 912
Stockholm International Peace Research
    Institute 80, 231, 380, 461, 462
Stockton, Frank R. 1115
Stone, I. F. 866
Stone, Jeremy J. 463
Strauss, Lewis L. 824
Strickland, Donald A. 804
Stuart, Don A. 1027
Summerlin, Sam 956
Swanwick, Michael 1116
Sweet, William 608, 609
Swing, Raymond 546
"Szanto" 288
Szilard, Gertrud 805
Szilard, Leo 784, 1117

Tamplin, Arthur A. 744
Taylor, Maxwell D. 232
Taylor, Richard 547
Taylor, Theodore B. 385
Taylor, William J. 515
Teller, Edward 233, 784, 851
Temple, David S. 825
Temples, James R. 726
Terman, Douglas C. 1118, 1119
Thomas, Gordon 81
Thomas, Morgan 688
Thomas, Walter 531
Thompson, E. P. 548, 549
Thompson, W. Scott 240, 245
Tobias, Sheilah 330, 1001
Tolkunov, Lev 289
Tomar, Ravindra 727
Totten, Martha W. 610, 611
Totten, Sam 610, 611
Toynbee, Arnold 439
Toynbee, Philip 509, 550
Toyoda, T. 520
Trainer, Jennifer 656
Trapnell, Edward R. 816

Trew, Anthony 1120
Trumbull, Robert 82
Tucker, Jonathan B. 290
Tucker, Robert W. 234
Tucker, Wilson 1121, 1122
Tugwell, Rexford G. 83
Turner, Gordon B. 235
Twining, Nathan P. 236
Tysoe, Maryon 1002

Uhl, Michael 84
Ullman, Richard H. 500
Union of Concerned Scientists 767
U.S.S.R. Ministry of Defense 964
U.N. Department of Political and
   Security Council Affairs 464
U.N. Secretary General 465
U.S. Arms Control & Disarma-
   ment Agency 466, 467
U.S. Atomic Energy Commission
   806
U.S. Congress Joint Committee on
   Atomic Energy 85, 86
U.S. Congress Office of Technology
   Assessment 87
U.S. Department of Defense 963
U.S. Department of State 88
U.S. Laws, statutes, etc. 89
U.S. Nuclear Regulatory Commis-
   sion 689
U.S. President's Air Policy
   Commission 237
U.S. President's Commission on
   Strategic Forces 238
U.S. Scientific Laboratory, Los
   Alamos 90
University of Michigan Survey
   Research Center 852
Useem, Bert 728

Vale, Michel 607
Van Cleave, William R. 239, 240
Von Hippel, Frank 815
Von Bredow, Wilfried 613
Vonnegut, Kurt, Jr. 1123
Voss, Earl H. 468

Wadsworth, James J. 469
Wager, Walter H. 1124
Wagoner, David 615
Wainhouse, David W. 470
Walker, Charles A. 965
Walker, William B. 381

Wallis, Jim 551
Walsh, Marilyn 355
Walters, Robert E. 241
Warburg, James P. 471
Wasilewski, Valeria 1003
Wasserman, Harvey 91, 1004
Way, Katharine 533
Weart, Spencer R. 805, 807
Webb, Richard E. 690
Webber, David J. 729
Weede, Erich 291
Weiler, Lawrence D. 452
Weingast, Barry R. 777
Weisner, Jerome B. 920
Weissman, Steve 382
Welch, Bruce L. 778
Wells, H.G. 1125
Wentz, Walter B. 383
West, Robert L. 657
Wexley, John 836
Wheeler, Harvey 1023
Wheeler, Tim 616
White, E.B. 1126
Wieseltier, Leon 242
Wigner, Eugene P. 853, 854
Wigutoff, Sharon 893
Wilcox, Fred 768
Williams, Robert C. 895
Williams, Tennessee 1127
Willrich, Mason 384, 385, 472, 966
Wilson, Deb 859
Wilson, Jane 808
Wilson, Richard 730
Winfield-Laird, Idee 913
Winter, Metta L. 894
Winters, Francis X. 134
Witts, Max M. 81
Wohlstetter, Albert 386, 387, 933
Woito, Robert 967
Wolfe, Thomas W. 473
Wolfers, Arnold 474
Wong-Fraser, Agatha S. Y. 243
Woodbury, David O. 691
Woodson, Helen 618
Woodward, E. 889
Wrong, Dennis 619
Wylie, Philip 1128-1130
Wyndham, John 1058

Yager, Joseph A. 388
Yanarella, Ernest J. 968
Yefremov, Aleksandr E. 475
Yellin, Joel 731
York, Herbert F. 331, 501, 809
Young, Nigel 620

Zagano, Phyllis 1007
Zald, Mayer N. 728
Zile, Zigurds L. 476

Zuckerman, Solly 244, 292
Zumwalt, Elmo 245